ELEMENTS OF SOCIOLOGY

A Series of Introductions

Stratification: Socioecomic and Sexual Inequality

Rae Lesser Blumberg

University of California, San Diego

WM. C. BROWN COMPANY PUBLISHERS
Dubuque, Iowa

SOCIOLOGY SERIES

Consulting Editors
Ann Lennarson Greer
University of Wisconsin-Milwaukee

Scott Greer
University of Wisconsin-Milwaukee

Printed in the United States of America
10 9 8 7 6 5

Contents

To David-Lane for the future

To the memory of my parents for the past

Preface

Typically the way the social science pie is cut up, most anthropologists study the world's "exotic" and preindustrial peoples, usually by means of intensive study of one small community; most sociologists concentrate on social behavior in the contemporary United States, often with larger samples and more attempts to quantify results; and most economists concentrate on economic behavior in present-day America, using the most math and the least observation of the three fields. It is rare for a social scientist to read the literature of neighboring disciplines. In this book I explore perhaps the most popular sociological topic of recent years, stratification. But I do so from a perspective which is cross-societal, cross-temporal and cross-disciplinary. And although I am a sociologist, the theories presented in this book are concentrated in areas not often examined by my colleagues.

Using this approach, the book deals with two kinds of stratification—socioeconomic and sexual—the strands of which are frequently intertwined in the text. These topics are interwoven here because, I propose, both types of inequality share important elements of common explanation. In both instances the degree of access of the group in question to its society's means and fruits of production constitutes a crucial explanatory variable.

In contrast, other social scientists argue that differential access to basic productive resources is more the consequence than the cause of inequality. They see socioeconomic or sexual inequality as inevitable, given "human nature," and/or the "requirements of society." Their position may seem quite plausible when viewed from the standpoint of the contemporary U.S., but is it the whole story? To what degree are the American systems of socioeconomic and sexual stratification with which we are familiar similar to what exists in all other human societies? To what extent is such inequality indelibly stamped into the biological and historical fabric of the human race? How do sexual and socioeconomic stratification differ in magnitude in the present and the past? Consideration of these questions expands the horizon of this book well beyond the contemporary U.S., across time, space and societal borders.

How well beyond present-day America the book ranges is obvious in the first four chapters where I present theories and data which cover the full panorama of our evolutionary heritage: from nonhuman primates, especially the apes; through the hunting-gathering bands in which all humans lived for some four or five million years; through the horticultural peoples which first emerged around 10,000-15,000 years ago; to the agrarian states in which occurred the maximum known levels of both socioeconomic and sexual stratification and oppression. Specifically, Chapter 1 reviews the evidence on nonhuman primates and hunting-gathering peoples and refutes the view of what I refer to as the "nasty animal school" of human nature, that men are inherently violent, territorial, dominance-seeking and superordinate to women. Having rejected this theoretical conception of the origin of human stratification, Chapter 2 deals with my speculative theory that socioeconomic inequality emerged not out of conditions of scarcity, as posited by most theorists, but rather out of conditions of abundance.

In Chapter 3, I present a proposed paradigm on sexual stratification which I have already subjected to a preliminary empirical test utilizing a pilot sample of 61 pre-industrial societies. To date, the evidence strongly supports my major assertion: women's degree of control (relative to the men of their group) over the means and fruits of production is the most important predictor of how well female status and life opportunities compare to those of the males of their group.

Returning to the mainline of human evolution, Chapter 4 takes up the story of the emergence of cultivation some 10,000-15,000 years ago, and the successive rise of horticultural (hoe-based) and agrarian (plow-based) societies. It is significant that the latter represent the maximum points of socioeconomic stratification, stultification, and general level of misery for the common people—as well as the maximum level of sexual subjugation. In contrast to hunting-gathering and horticultural societies where women usually produce the largest part of the food supply, females in agrarian societies have been edged out of production and bound to home and babies. What is most important about agrarian societies' oppressive levels of stratification is that every single one of today's industrialized societies has sprung from an agrarian base. Especially with respect to women, this seems to have had lingering consequences on female economic power, image, and status.

The second half of the book brings us up to date. Chapter 5 deals with the European emergence of capitalism, the industrial revolution, and the accelerating global transformation that has followed in their wake.

As the book approaches our own time and society, the reporting of these evolutionary and stratification trends and the framing of the picture in terms of a broader theory takes on ideological overtones. This is because in recent years it has become fashionable to divide sociological approaches to stratification (and the last few centuries of political economy) into two camps, which may be summarized as the "conflict/radical" vs. "consensus/functionalist" perspectives. In Chapter 6, I examine the quintessential opposing theories for each perspective: that of Karl Marx as the epitome of conflict theory, vs. the work of recent U.S. "functionalist" sociologists who embody the heart of the consensus approach. The consensus paradigm, which has dominated recent decades of U.S. sociology, views the existing distribution of rewards and power as generally inevitable, just, and endorsed by the majority. For much of the 1940s, '50s and '60s, the real income, social status, and international clout enjoyed by U.S. social scientists—and their country—were increasing in unprecedented manner. Accordingly, it does not seem surprising that consensus/functionalist sociology is decidedly upbeat about prospects for social mobility and continued progress and harmony under the existing system. The conflict approach, which I share, takes the opposite tack. Its recent upsurge (since the mid-1960s) also may be understood in historical context. This paradigm has grown apace with Viet Nam protests, and the burgeoning movements of blacks, women and other previously silent minorities. It is not surprising that this should be so, or that the conflict approach has gained adherents during a period in U.S. economic history, 1969-1976, when real income stagnated after almost a quarter

retardar
persistir

estanco

century of rising living standards. The concomitant tightening of the academic job market also should be recognized as a source of converts to the conflict position.

Chapter 6 concludes with the theories and statistics that back up the functionalists' benign view of why the U.S. stratification system (although its existence is admitted and its inevitability is upheld) is basically nonoppressive. I have termed this the tip of the iceberg approach, and in Chapter 7 I attempt to present data concerning the remaining ninety percent of the "iceberg of socioeconomic inequality"—those aspects of stratification that normally remain hidden. The evidence I present is drawn predominantly from government statistics, and accordingly is no better (or worse) than can be expected from those sources. But it is fair to say that the kinds of information I juxtapose on income, wealth, and tax inequality, and the extent of corporate concentration, are not among the more publicized figures concerning American life.

From socioeconomic stratification, Chapter 8 turns to sexual stratification, and examines both the visible and submerged portions of the "iceberg of sexual inequality." It contrasts the often glowing government and consensus-theorist figures concerning the visible—and allegedly rapidly melting—ten percent with the more chilling figures concerning the submerged ninety percent. This dual emphasis on both the "good news" and "bad news" views of sexual inequality is presented for the U.S. and then extended world-wide. The net balance of results is decidedly sobering, especially since in the U.S., a *growing* sexual gap is revealed in most components of socioeconomic stratification. Overall, however, the pattern seems clearly in line with the paradigm of sexual stratification presented in Chapter 3.

Finally, what remains is to examine the future in light of our exploration of the remote and recent past. If our survey is to show us anything, it is that the evidence of the past and present cannot be used as a good predictor of what socioeconomic and sexual inequality *have* to look like in the future. For one thing, the excursion through evolutionary history will show that there is nothing inherent in human nature which makes high levels of socioeconomic and sexual stratification inevitable. For another thing, we will see that for each mode of production, from communal hunting-and-gathering to capitalist vs. socialist industrialism, the level and degree of socioeconomic and sexual stratification have varied. There has not been any uninterrupted universal development toward either greater or lesser inequality, although within each epoch and productive mode the variables which are stressed in this book (concerning relative access to basic resources and fruits of production) provide considerable explanatory power. It would appear that the next chapter has yet to be written, and part of it will be written by our own efforts.

My own efforts in the creation of this book were aided substantially by the contributions of a number of other people. Chronologically, Gösta Andersen and Julie Fein were first. They served as my excellent research assistants at the University of Wisconsin-Madison during the 1973-74 academic year. Gösta Andersen is the co-author of Chapter 6 and Julie Fein helped compile the data on women and the U.S. work force in Chapter 8. Also during this period, Pauline Bart gave valuable advice and encouragement. During the hectic final preparation, I benefitted from the thorough and very helpful critiques of R. Stephen Warner, as well as those of Norbert Wiley and C. Jane Geddes, Susan Miller, Beverly Maria-Pilar Garcia. Thanks are due also to Keane, Kathleen Unger, John Gundersen, Juanita Hagan, and V. Mignon Furqueron. Series Editor Scott Greer's confidence in the final product is greatly appreciated. And very special thanks go to Bruce Harris and Sondra Buffett, without whose splendid editorial assistance there might never have been a final product!

1 | Amiable Apes and Egalitarian Ancestors: Our Homo Sapien Heritage

WHO gets what—and why? That is what stratification is all about, and this book is about two kinds of stratification: socioeconomic and sexual inequality. In fact, later in the book we shall examine the impact of *class* and *sex* in U.S. life, and see how power and privilege are distributed to people on the basis of these two criteria. One thing that is striking about contemporary America is that even after the Civil Rights Movement,[1] the War on Poverty, and the current Women's Liberation Movement much of socioeconomic and sexual inequality is like an iceberg: nine-tenths below the surface. The surface of this iceberg does not look so threatening to many of us because it has been covered over with the fabric of the American Dream: this is the land of opportunity; American workers enjoy the highest living standard, and American women the most equality. When the fabric starts to rip in places, due to factors such as hard times and an insistent women's movement, some of the facts from the hidden ninety percent start to surface. And these facts are unsettling. That by some measures Swiss, West Germans, and Swedes have higher real income than Americans, that wealth and income in the U.S. are very unequally distributed and the distribution hasn't improved in many decades, that the gap between male and female earnings has been growing steadily *larger* since 1940—these are

unpleasant facts. Moreover, they seem to fly in the face of some of our other perceptions of reality. Don't most of our fathers have better jobs and more comforts and prosperity than their fathers and grandfathers? Isn't it true that young women today have fewer restrictions on their lives and behavior than their mothers and grandmothers? As it turns out, these facts are also true, and their truth helps keep the other ninety percent of the iceberg underwater.

There is another important source of camouflage for the hidden part of the "iceberg of inequality." This is the view—still very influential in American social science—that socioeconomic and sexual inequality are not only *inevitable*, they are *necessary* for the functioning of society. Supporting this view is another equally popular one: the ultimate source of socioeconomic and sexual inequality lies in our biological heritage. Man's biological heritage, these people argue, is basically nasty, aggressive, territorial, and geared to pecking orders. Woman's biological heritage is seen as that of passive dependence on the dominant male.

These views do *not* seem to be supported by recent empirical evidence. To find out about our biological heritage and the origin

1. Racial and ethnic inequality will not be emphasized in this book, as they are treated separately in *Racial and Ethnic Relations* by Joseph S. Himes, another volume in this series.

of stratification will entail a survey of human evolution. The remainder of this chapter will be devoted to some scientific findings concerning the *generally egalitarian ways* of our ape ancestors and the simplest human societies—the hunters and gatherers.

TWO MALICIOUS MONKEYS AND THE MYTH OF THE MALEVOLENT MALE

Biologically, we are primates. The primate family tree includes monkeys, apes, and humans—in ascending evolutionary order. But much of the evidence used by the authors of the "Man the Nasty Animal—Woman the Submissive Slave" school of thought is drawn from studies of our more distant primate kin, the monkeys. And just two species of monkeys at that, the baboon and the rhesus macaque. If one is out to show an alleged heritage of aggressiveness, of a pervasive and rigid dominance hierarchy where the most desirable food and females are hogged by the top males, of female submissiveness and passivity, there are some vivid examples among baboons and rhesus monkeys. Robert Ardrey, one of the leading lights of the "Man the Malevolent" camp, even managed to find one old study each on baboons and rhesus monkeys showing they were territorial as well, fighting to acquire and defend their turf.

As we shall see, however, a number of recent studies, based on observation of non-human primates in natural, free-ranging environments, have shown that *environmental conditions* greatly influence the behavior of monkeys and apes. Even baboons proved to be the bad bullies of the stereotype only in certain high-danger habitats. And the newer studies wipe out the notion that baboons or rhesus—or our closer cousins, gorillas and chimpanzees, for that matter—are territorial. (Gorillas and chimps, in fact, are comparatively low in aggression, hierarchy and female subjugation.)

In short, the evidence seems to turn precisely upside down the contentions of the principal proponents of the "Malevolent Male" model. Though each has a slightly different ax to grind, the group includes:

1. Robert Ardrey (*African Genesis*, 1961; *The Territorial Imperative*, 1966), who claims that the human male evolved as a killer, and shares with the animals an instinct for dominance, aggression, and territory.
2. Desmond Morris (*The Naked Ape*, 1968; *The Human Zoo*, 1969), who sees the human male not only as a primate, from whence springs his dominance drive, but also as a carnivore (by adoption) from whence he gets aggression and territoriality.
3. Konrad Lorenz (*On Aggression*, 1966), who claims aggression is innate in males, and cites examples from fish and fowl, as well as the Ute Indians of Colorado.
4. Lionel Tiger (*Men in Groups*, 1969) and Tiger and Robin Fox (*The Imperial Animal*, 1972), who hold that human males are biologically programmed to hunt and to bond with each other, leading to organizational superiority over females.

All of these authors hold that much of *human* behavior is based on *biology*—our instincts and innate heritage as animals, primates, and/or long-time killer hunters. This means that the hypothesized innate behavior, such as dominance, aggressiveness, or territoriality, will be exhibited under all sorts of environmental and social conditions (although perhaps in somewhat different forms).

In contrast, the recent observational studies of the *nonhuman* primates show exactly the opposite: rather than being rigid and seemingly innate, the behavior of our monkey and ape cousins adapts flexibly to differing circumstances. In other words, an ecological niche shapes their behavior to a surprisingly great extent, both within and between species.

A lovely example of the same species behaving in very different ways in differing environmental circumstances is provided by the *baboons,* source of so much of the stereotype. Despite their common species (technically, *papio anubis*), great differences recently have been observed between those who have adapted to a predator-filled *plains* environment and other groups that live in a more congenial *forest* habitat.

The *plains* baboon of the Kenya savannah has been studied by both DeVore and K. R. L. Hall, and lives a life tailor-made for the stereotype.[2] Exposed to the frequent danger of attack on the open plains, the baboons travel in a tight, military troop. Mothers and infants are in the center, and dominant "alpha" males lead and choose the line of march. Males are considerably larger than females. Moreover, there is a linear dominance hierarchy; and the dominant alpha males are not only chosen by high-ranking females at the height of their sexual arousal cycle (estrus), but displace lower-ranking males when competing for delectable food in limited quantities. To the leaders go the best food and sex.

Compare this to the behavior of the same type of *papio anubis* baboons observed in a Uganda *forest* by Rowell.[3] First, they showed *no* evidence of a dominance hierarchy! Even though a male led the troop, old females set the direction of daily movement. And it was females, even at the height of estrus, who initiated intercourse with various (not just dominant alpha) males. Nor was this group tightly organized along military lines. In general, these less-endangered forest baboons grouped themselves more loosely than their counterparts on the open plains. And *neither* group was territorial.

From this point on, as we turn to the apes, the evidence gets even worse for the "Malevolent Male" myth. In ascending evolutionary order, these are: gibbons, orangutans, gorillas, and chimps. First, although tree-dwelling *gibbons* do show some territoriality and aggressiveness, they are the *only* apes to do so.[4] And in other ways, gibbons deviate from the stereotype. For one thing,

rather than being the big, strong protectors, males are about the same size, weight (13-16 lbs.), and appearance as females.

Next, *orangutans.* They also live in high trees, but although adult males outweigh females (160 versus 80 lbs.), the males do not hang around as their "protectors." Females and their young form stable groups; adult males travel alone and avoid each other. The male wanderers roam across the ranges of several of these female groups, and sometimes visit, accompany, or follow these groups for a while.[5]

The gentle ground-browsing *gorilla* Cook quotes Fossey's finding of less than five minutes of aggressive behavior in over 2,000 hours of observing gorillas and even this boiled down to protective action or bluff[6]) used to get a pretty bad press before Schaller studied them.[7] Perhaps this was because of their great size (up to 600 lbs. for males and about 400 for females) and nongentle appearance. The gorillas prove to be the only one of the apes whose groups are stable enough to have leaders. But these silver-backed males have not been

2. Irven DeVore, ed., *Primate Behavior: Field Studies on Monkeys and Apes.* (New York: Holt, Rinehart & Winston, 1965); K. R. L. Hall, "Distribution and Adaptation of Baboons," Symposia of the Zoological Society of London XXII (1966): 49-73.

3. Thelma E. Rowell, "Variability in the Social Organization of Primates," in *Primate Ethology,* ed. Desmond Morris (London: Weidenfeld & Nicoson, 1967); Thelma E. Rowell, *Social Behavior of Monkeys* (Baltimore: Penguin, 1972.)

4. Alexander Alland, Jr., *The Human Imperative* (New York: Columbia University Press, 1972), p. 34.

5. Lila Leibowitz, "Perspectives on the Evolution of Sex Differences," in *Toward an Anthology of Women,* ed. Rayna R. Reiter (New York: Monthly Review Press, 1975), p. 26.

6. Joan Marble Cook, *In Defense of Homo Sapiens* (New York: Farrar, Straus and Giroux, 1975), p. 81.

7. George B. Schaller, *The Mountain Gorilla: Ecology and Behavior* (Chicago: Univ. of Chicago Press, 1964).

observed to derive any advantage in terms of food or access to females in heat. In fact, gorillas have been observed to copulate less often than any other primates.[8] When they do, the female is almost always in estrus, and it is she who initiates sex. In the two instances of intercourse Schaller observed in an entire year's observation of wild gorillas, neither time was the male one of the silver-backed leaders. Unlike orangutans, adult gorilla females are always found in groups headed by a male leader or leaders. But despite this general (loose) patriarchy, Fossey discovered one matriarchal gorilla "tribe" of five males led by an old female.[9]

Chimpanzees are our closest primate relatives, and even though we keep finding new information on how many similarities there are between chimps and the simplest human societies, the hunting and gathering bands,[10] these parallels do not stress common biological instincts, but rather similarities in adaptive, *noninstinctual* behavior. Thus, even though female chimps have an estrus cycle, and copulate most frequently when they are in heat, they are known to mate throughout the sexual cycle, as humans do.[11] Even so, when a female chimp is in estrus, she is *quite* active sexually! The males wait their turns, without competitive strife.[12] Like those of human hunters and gatherers (see below), chimpanzee bands are loosely organized, and band composition is dynamic and shifting. They do tend to have a mild form of dominance hierarchy, but as among the simplest human societies to which we shall turn shortly, the dominant male is not necessarily the largest. Goodall presents evidence that intelligence can play a major part: Mike, originally a low-ranking chimpanzee, discovered that by furiously banging together two of Goodall's gasoline cans and simultaneously hooting, he could cow male and female alike. After several weeks, he emerged as the dominant male of the group.[13] Chimps' flexible social arrangements include various types of groups, how-

ever, and one involves no adult males, dominant or otherwise. This "nursery group" of mothers and children who move as separate units occurs in all environments, but especially where stocked feeding stations are present.[14] Incidentally, as among humans, size differences among male and female chimps are not great. Males average 150 lbs. and females 130, but there are some of each in the 140 lb. range. All in all, the flexibility, adaptability, friendliness, and range of behavior in chimpanzee groups does much to dispel the myth that either they

8. R. D. Nadler, "Sexual Cyclicity in Captive Lowland Gorillas," *Science* 189 (Sept. 5, 1975): 813-14.

9. Cook, *In Defense of Homo Sapiens*, p. 86.

10. Geza Teleki, "The Evolution of Primate Subsistence Patterns" (paper presented at the meetings of the American Association for the Advancement of Science, New York, 1975).

11. R. M. Yerkes and J. H. Elder, *Journal of Comparative Psychology Monographs* 13, no. 5 (1936):1-39; R. M. Yerkes, *Human Biology* 11 (1939):78-111; W. C. Young and W. D. Orbison, *Journal of Comparative Psychology* 37 (1944): 107-43.

12. Jane Goodall, "Chimpanzees of the Gombe Streat Reserve," in *Primate Behavior*, ed. De Vore. It should be noted, however, that male chimps apparently do not copulate with their mothers, possibly indicating a pre-human origin of our strongest incest taboo.

13. Jane Goodall, *In the Shadow of Man* (Boston: Houghton Mifflin, 1971.) Actually, Vernon and Frances Reynolds, "Chimpanzees in the Budongo Forest," in *Primate Behavior*, ed. Irven DeVore (New York: Holt, Rinehart & Winston, 1965), p. 415, found that "dominance interactions formed a minute fraction of the observed chimpanzee behavior. There was no evidence of a linear hierarchy of dominance among males or females . . . and there were no permanent leaders of groups." No recent observer would disagree with this, but some do write more about the little bit this, but some do write more about that level that does exist of nonsystematic dominance—submission behavior. Although there is variation, some chimps *are* more often found receiving than giving submissive behavior, and male dominance exceeds female.

14. Leibowitz, "Perspectives on the Evolution of Sex Differences," p. 27.

or we are bound by base biological instincts.

One last point before we leave the non-human primates. This one involves a study of sex role behavior among *rhesus* monkeys and shows conditions under which the stereotypically "dominant male-submissive female" relations that rhesus are well publicized for may be muted. The experimenter found that *altering prenatal hormones* modified the usually found gender patterns. But so did *altering the social environment:* in same-sex experimental groups, females proved as frequent in threatening behavior as males; and mounting and aggression were readily suppressed in males under several social environmental conditions.[15] So for both of the "malicious monkeys," the baboons and the rhesus macaques, who loom so large in the examples of the "Malevolent Male" theorists, there is evidence of social environmental adaptability.

SIMPLE HUMAN SOCIETIES: THE MISLEADING MYSTIQUE OF "MAN THE HUNTER"

Basically, the argument of the "Nasty Animal" theorists has two parts. First, much of our fixed and inequality-ridden "bad biology" stems from the animal, and is shared with some of the nonhuman primates. Second, and in addition, we picked up some further nastiness, aggressiveness, and non-egalitarian traits during the course of *human* evolution. These theorists view our human evolutionary history as the multimillion-year story of Man the Hunter, a consummate killer and carnivore. Woman is ascribed less evolutionary importance than the stone ax. Having already washed out their picture of the monkeys and apes, let us turn to their view of Man the Hunter.

Although we have found the behavior of our closest simian kin, the gorillas and chimpanzees, to be generally nonterritorial, non-aggressive, and adaptive to social and ecological variations, we must be cautious in applying our conclusions to humans. We must be equally cautious in applying the findings about surviving contemporary hunting-gathering bands to their prehistoric predecessors of the Pleistocene era. Partly this is because present-day hunting-gathering groups already have been pushed onto marginal habitats and/or already have become the victims of aggression by more technologically advanced peoples.

Even so, there are enough continuities between the archeological record of our early ancestors and the evidence on present-day preagricultural societies to once more throw cold water on the assertions of the "Nasty Animal" school. Once again, in fact, the evidence seems to be largely in the *opposite* direction to their view. As we develop our picture of hunting-gathering societies, we shall see that the importance of hunting is much less than is popularly supposed, aggression and war rare, territoriality more or less absent, and—especially in the very simplest human groups known—both stable male leadership and female subjugation minimal or absent.

Let us start with the *techno-economic base* of the simplest human societies, because this base, as modified by such *ecological* factors as climate or the availability of edible plants and animals, seems to be the most important element in shaping these simple groups. "Techno-economic base" (see Appendix) refers to the *economic* activities engaged in by people to feed themselves, and to the level and efficiency of the tools and techniques (i.e., *technology*) they bring to these economic pursuits. The techno-economic base of the simplest human bands is known as *hunting and gathering,* and the tools humans used in these pursuits ultimately became much more complex than anything ever observed among the apes (who may sometimes use a handy stick to help themselves to some tempting morsel).

15. David A. Goldfoot, "Hormonal and Social Determinants of Gender Role in Infant Rhesus Monkeys" (paper presented at the meetings of the American Association for the Advancement of Science, New York, 1975).

What else is involved in this base, and how is it uniquely human? Let us examine a series of specific characteristics of these foraging societies, which have encompassed over ninety-nine percent of human history.

(1) Even though it is traditionally referred to as "hunting and gathering," *gathering actually precedes hunting,* both (a) in importance in the diet and (b) chronologically. There can be no doubt about the importance of gathering to contemporary hunting-gathering groups. Lee and DeVore show that gathering typically provides sixty to eighty percent of the diet in such groups, except for bands in the frozen Arctic where there are no plants to be gathered during the long cold winter.[16] Lomax has identified the "African hunters" [sic] as the simplest human societies surviving on the face of the earth.[17] Today, only two "African hunter" societies are left—the Mbuti Pygmies of Zaire's dense Ituri forest, and the !Kung Bushmen of Namibia's harsh Kalahari desert. According to the data in Murdock's *Ethnographic Atlas,*[18] the !Kung diet consists of eighty percent gathered foods vs. twenty percent hunted meat; the Mbuti in the game-rich rainforest gather "only" sixty percent of their subsistence, and hunt for thirty percent of it (fishing = 10 percent).

We now know of another group that seems even simpler than these two—the cave-dwelling Tasaday who recently were discovered in the Philippines. *Hunting* was almost totally *absent* among them when a man from a more advanced indigenous group stumbled across them. Over a period of several years, he befriended them and introduced the men to the bow and arrow. The men began doing some hunting (previously there had been no sexual division of labor in subsistence activities). Several years later, he introduced the Tasaday to the Philippine ethnological authorities, who in turn introduced anthropologists, journalists, and TV crews into the lives of these gentle gatherers.

In short, the contemporary human evidence contrasts greatly with the emphasis of the "Nasty Animal" theorists that man evolved as a bloody carnivore. Moreover, the archeological evidence suggests that men have been occupationally specialized as hunters for only a limited time during their long primate history (hunting, we shall see below, is primarily a male activity among humans). During the Australopithecine era (perhaps four or five million years ago), the evidence does not indicate that our half-human kin were primarily hunters.[19] In contrast to Ardrey, who tries to paint Australopithecus man as a killer, Washburn finds the evidence suggesting the opposite, that he was much more likely to be the hunted than the hunter.[20]

As for the other primates, they all are primarily vegetarian—that is, gatherers,[21] even though occasionally some baboons[22] and chimps[23] have been observed to kill and eat a smaller animal. And humans, if available evidence is *any* guide, must be seen as omnivores, not carnivores. Only in one aspect—sharing—do we at first glance seem more like the carnivores, who share a collec-

16. Richard G. Lee and Irven DeVore, eds., *Man the Hunter* (Chicago: Aldine, 1968).

17. Alan Lomax with Norman Berkowitz, "The Evolutionary Taxonomy of Culture," *Science* 177 (July 21, 1972):228-239.

18. George P. Murdock, "Ethnographic Atlas: A Summary," *Ethnology* 7 (1967):109-236.

19. For an excellent synthesis of the recent work on the primacy of gathering in human evolution, *see* Nancy Tanner and Adrienne Zihlman, "Women in Evolution. Part I: Innovation and Selection in Human Origins," *Signs* (Spring 1976):585-608. *See also* Marvin Harris, *Culture, People, Nature* (New York: Thomas Y. Crowell, 1975), pp. 66-74.

20. Sherwood L. Washburn, ed., *Social Life of Early Man* (Chicago: Aldine, 1961).

21. Donald W. Ball, "The Biological Bases of Human Society," in *Introduction to Sociology,* ed. Jack D. Douglas (New York: Free Press, 1973) p. 129.

22. Hall, "Distribution and Adaptations of Baboons."

23. Goodall, "Chimpanzees of the Gombe Streat Reserve."

tively made kill, than the monkeys and apes, who rarely share food. (Exceptions may be seen: mothers share with infants, male chimps share tidbits with a female in heat, and adolescent chimps have been observed "begging" occasional food from their mothers. Teleki also mentions chimps sharing collectively made kills. Incidentally, Teleki considers them omnivorous rather than vegetarian.)[24] But human sharing turns out to be a whole new ball game.

(2) *Sharing*, in fact, proves to be *universal* among hunting-gathering groups. This means it is found in every one ever studied in their natural environment. Those that didn't share (if any) apparently didn't survive to be studied! (A semi-exception to this is a barely surviving society, the Ik of Uganda, discussed in Chapter 2.) As noted, carnivores share a *collective* kill. Gathering is not a collective activity: if two humans go out together to gather, it's probably either because they like each other's company or for protection. Hunting among humans may be collective or not (more often, except with large game, it's as likely *not* to be). But humans share the fruits of even *individual* hunting and gathering. Lee writes of the !Kung, among whom neither hunting nor gathering is a cooperative activity:

> Cooperation is clearly in evidence, however, in the consumption of food. Not only do families pool the day's production but the entire camp—residents and visitors alike—shares equally in the total quantity of food available. The evening meal of any one family is made up of portions of food from the supplies of each of the other families resident. Foodstuffs are distributed raw or are prepared by the collector and then distributed. There is a constant flow of nuts, berries, roots, and melons from one family fireplace to another.[25]

Lee views this uniquely human food sharing as the very foundation of social life, and of other such uniquely human traits as division of labor.

(3) *Sex division of labor* turns out to be the first form of human specialization, in fact. As noted, until the Tasaday were introduced to bows and arrows, they seemingly had no sex division of labor in their main subsistence activities. Of the other two "simplest" groups, Mbuti women participate in the great net hunts, and men do some of the gathering; in contrast, among the !Kung, hunting is almost exclusively male, although men make some contribution to gathering. In both cases, however, women are the predominant gatherers. This is true for almost all of the world's societies that have gathering as the main component of their diet. Consequently, in most hunting-gathering societies, *women are the primary producers!* Man the Hunter, meet Woman the Gatherer.

(4) Hence there is no evidence of the dependent, pregnant female, huddled in the cave awaiting her provider's return from the hunt, trading sex for food—the basis of several theories of sexual inequality, including those of Firestone and Cook.[26] *Gathering*, it seems, *is quite compatible* with woman's unique *childcare* responsibilities—especially breastfeeding. A woman can take the children with her when she gathers, for even though she may cover considerable territory, she does so slowly and at a pace dictated by her own convenience. Actually, babysitting will almost surely be available back in camp for all except the baby, which she carries. For as we shall soon see, there tends to be a surprisingly high proportion of potential babysitters in such a society: young and aged de-

24. Teleki, "The Evolution of Primate Subsistence Patterns."
25. Richard B. Lee, "!Kung Bushmen Subsistence: An Input-Output Analysis," in *Environment and Cultural Behavior,* ed. Andrew P. Vayda (Garden City: The Natural History Press, 1969), p. 58.
26. *See,* for example, Shulamith Firestone, *The Dialectic of Sex* (New York: William Morrow & Co., (1970); and Cook, *In Defense of Homo Sapiens.*

pendents—as well as productive-age adults who will be found staying around the camp rather than going out foraging or hunting on a given day. Furthermore, not just the woman in her gatherings, but the whole society, is mobile.

(5) *Band mobility:* From time to time, depending on the seasons and the local availability of game, plants, and water, the whole band wanders off to a new location. All but a very small proportion of hunting-gathering bands follow this mobile pattern. The nomadic nature of hunting-gathering societies has many important consequences for various aspects of group life, but the first one we shall explore is the impact of mobility on fertility.

(6) Surprisingly, for believers in Malthus, *family size and fertility are low, and child-spacing very wide.* Like other primate females, women have their young one at a time. But fertility among hunting-gathering groups is among the lowest in human societies. It is characterized by wide spacing between births, averaging about four years in contemporary hunting-gathering bands, and by low completed family size.[27] How did they do so before the Pill? Apparently by a variety of methods, including late weaning, low body fat (found, for example, among the well-nourished but lean !Kung women; this somehow seems to inhibit conception),[28] infanticide, and—in some groups —abortion, or plants with contraceptive properties. Incidentally, Birdsell has made similarly low family size estimates for our hunting-gathering ancestors of the Pleistocene era, although he attributes this mainly to the widespread use of infanticide as a spacing mechanism.[29] After all, the female is the mainstay of the group food supply. Anything that would interfere with her mobility and gathering—such as more than one child under age four—would also decrease food supply. In short, by not having a child every year, Woman the Gatherer avoided the bad bargain of the cave imagined by Firestone: trading sex for food.

(7) Hunting-gathering societies, because they are mobile and because they share, tend to accumulate an absolute *minimum of possessions.* In this way, duplication is reduced, and people can travel with a lighter load as they follow food and water.

(8) Mobility and scattered resources also tend to affect *group size.* Hunting-gathering bands are quite small—anthropologists and archeologists write of the "magic number" of twenty-five for the characteristic band size. And the evidence of the *Ethnographic Atlas* does show that the great majority of such groups contain less than fifty people. The most mobile of these tend to average not much more than twenty-five.

(9) The group is not only small, it is *shifting.* One of the most noticeable characteristics of the recently studied !Kung,[30] for example, is the flexibility and *ever-changing composition of the group.* (In one four-week period at a !Kung camp, Lee found that average group size "varies from 25.6 to 35.6; the actual count of personnel on hand was rarely the same two days running."[31] Individuals or whole families wander in and out, drifting from one band to another in this very "hang-loose" society. Clearly, the ultimate effect is to keep local population and resources more nearly in balance, even

27. John M. Whiting, "Pleistocene Family Planning," in *Man the Hunter,* eds. Lee and DeVore, pp. 248-249 gives estimates of spacing. Joseph B. Birdsell, "Some Predictions for the Pleistocene," in *Man the Hunter,* eds. Lee and DeVore, p. 237, gives data on completed family size. He estimates that it averages about 2.0 children.

28. *See* Gina Bari Kolata, "!Kung Hunter-gatherers: Feminism, Diet, and Birth Control," *Science* 185 (Sept 13, 1974):932-934.

29. Birdsell, "Some Predictions."

30. Good brief descriptions of !Kung life include Lorna K. Marshall, "The !Kung Bushmen of the Kalahari Desert," in *Peoples of Africa,* ed. J. Gibbs (New York: Holt, Rinehart & Winston, 1965); Richard B. Lee, "What Hunters do for a Living, or How to Make Out on Scarce Resources," in *Man the Hunter,* eds. Lee & DeVore; and Lee, "!Kung Bushmen Subsistence," pp. 30-48.

31. Lee, "!Kung Bushmen Subsistence," p. 67.

if the motivation for a move might be to get away from a family quarrel, visit a relative, or just plain wanderlust.

(10) In a sense, then, the sharing of food is paralleled by the sharing of members—and both are adaptive in a situation of highly variable and sometimes scarce resources. Lombardi has demonstrated mathematically that sharing acts to dampen fluctuations in shifting and scarce resources. Studying a poor black ghetto family in the U.S., he found that if they had not been involved in a *sharing network* of kin, they would have found themselves without food in the refrigerator and no assets to use for buying some on three successive days during the month of observation. With the sharing, they were never without.[32] Stack,[33] in fact, has found sharing networks characteristic of the poor urban blacks she studied that parallel in many ways the sharing of food and people (via shifting household composition) that typifies hunting-gathering bands. Both groups have in common little control over an environment characterized by variable and sometimes scarce resources.

(11) But just because the resource base is not always lush does not mean that hunters and gatherers spend almost all their waking hours in the food quest. Quite the contrary, they may be the *most leisured people* in the world.[34] In fact, Lee found that among the Bushmen of the Kalahari, the average workweek varied from 12 to 19 hours! Moreover, he notes, "each day's work provided food for the worker and four other people."[35] In this way, he found, sixty-five percent of the band's population were able to support themselves and thirty-five percent (children and those over 60) *who did no work at all*—and still have 3½ to 5½ days per week available for nonwork activities. Not all contemporary hunting-gathering groups are able to extract a living so easily from their environment: hard work and periodic hunger or famine is the lot of some (e.g., the Netsilik Eskimos, the Birhor of India).[36] But considering that until about 10,000 years

ago *all* humans were hunters and gatherers, and inhabited the best environments, not merely the marginal lands, as today—the short work-week and high nutritional standards of the !Kung were fairly likely to have been the norm.[37]

This completes a discussion of what Lee terms the "basic human institutions." These include the sharing of food (the most important element), the division of subsistence labor, the home base or camp to which food is carried for distribution, and the prolonged support of nonproductive young and old people. So far so good, but what of manifestations of the "Malevolent Male" malaise—what evidence is there concerning territoriality, aggression, and inequality?

(12) *Territoriality.* In this respect, hunting-gathering humans closely resemble their chimpanzee cousins in having a usually loosely defined range, the resources of which are almost never denied to visiting groups, and in having shifting group composition. In fact, evidence indicates that sharing of territory seems to *increase* with scarcity—whether we are examining Eskimos, Bush-

32. John R. Lombardi, "Exchange and Survival" (paper read at the meetings of the American Anthropological Association, New Orleans, 1973).

33. Carol B. Stack, "The Kindred of Viola Jackson: Residence and Family Organization of an Urban Black American Family," in *Afro-American Anthropology: Contemporary Perspectives,* eds. Norman E. Whitten and John F. Szwed (New York: Free Press, 1970) pp. 303-312; Carol B. Stack, *All Our Kin: Strategies for Survival in a Black Community* (New York: Harper & Row, 1974).

34. *See,* for example, Marshall D. Sahlins, "Notes on the Original Affluent Society," in *Man the Hunter,* eds. Lee & DeVore, pp. 85-88; Lee, "What Hunters Do for a Living," pp. 30-48.

35. Ibid.

36. Asen Balikci, "The Netsilik Eskimos: Adaptive Process," in *Man The Hunter,* eds. Lee & DeVore, pp. 78-82; B. J. Williams, "The Birhor of India and Some Comments on Band Organization," in *Man the Hunter,* eds. Lee & DeVore, pp. 126-131.

37. Lee & DeVore, eds., *Man the Hunter.*

men, or Australian Aboriginals.[38] Advocates of territoriality as a human universal used to be able to take comfort in one apparent case among hunters and gatherers: the Algonkians studied by Speck. He described a family hunting band claiming exclusive land ownership, and punishing trespassers, as the heart of Algonkian social organization.[39] Leacock seems to have demolished Speck's case with a new study that used both historical sources and her own field data to show that the so-called "family hunting territory" was not indigenous but had developed in response to the European-introduced fur trade. One family could not *trap* near another family's traplines for those animals whose pelts were destined to be sold. But anyone could hunt, gather, or fish on another's grounds *"as long as these products of the land were for use, not for sale."*[40]

(13) *Aggression.* Our three main examples of the very simplest human societies—the !Kung, Mbuti, and Tasaday—all have been described as gentle, peaceful people. The former two are better studied, and sources are agreed that they greatly value and try to preserve group harmony. Among the Mbuti, Turnbull found, if a dispute should arise, rather than allowing it to lead to possible violence, the parties simply part company.[41] So the shifting band composition of these societies helps keep the peace. And because of the lack of exclusive territorial rights to resources, people are *able* to circulate from one band of their group to another. At another level of aggression—war—there is evidence from a seventy-one-society comparative study that it is least frequent in hunting-gathering societies and goes up from there.[42]

(14) *Inequality.* What of hierarchy, privileged male leadership, dominance orders, and female subjugation? They are largely absent or low among hunters and gatherers, and the simpler the hunting-gathering society, the less likely we seem to find them holding sway. There are differences in *pres-*

tige among group members, although these seem to be based on personal accomplishments—skill in the food quest or oratory, valor, generosity—that the group admires. The simpler the group, the less likely that such *prestige* differences seem to be used as the basis for asserting *dominance* or special privileges. These societies have nothing we could call a formal political dimension; and although many have a "headman," he has no power to rule or coerce, and can only influence or persuade. More important, all members ·have equal access to the means of production. There are no restrictions on anyone's right to work the common resources used by the group for subsistence, and no complex tools or capital goods are required. In those societies that have a strong sex division of labor between hunting and gathering, however, Watanabe notes that women have no weapons of their own that are specially made to hunt animals. He speculates that the lack of this means of production may have helped make noncommunal large animal hunting an almost exclusively male preserve. (He notes a number of societies, however, where women hunt *small* animals or take

38. Concerning the latter group, *see* M. J. Meggitt, *Desert People, A Study of the Walbiri Aborigines of Central Australia* (Sydney: Angus & Robertson, 1962).

39. Frank G. Speck, *Family Hunting Territories and Social Life of Various Algonkian Bands of the Ottawa Valley*, Geological Survey Memoir, 70, Anthropology Series (Ottawa: Government Printing Bureau, 1915); Frank G. Speck, "Land Ownership Among Hunting Peoples in Primitive America and the World's Marginal Areas," Twenty-Second International Congress of Americanists, vol. 2 (1926).

40. Eleanor Leacock, ed., *The Origin of the Family, Private Property and the State*, by Frederick Engels (New York: International Publishers, 1972), p. 20.

41. Colin Turnbull, *The Forest People* (New York: Simon and Schuster, 1961).

42. Leo Simmons, *The Role of the Aged in Primitive Society* (New Haven: Yale University Press, 1945).

part in communal hunts—but without special weapons.)[43]

In general, rather than a hierarchical group with a privileged leadership, most hunting-gathering societies are extremely egalitarian.

Does this egalitarianism extend to the position of women? The evidence varies. The Tasaday appear to be the most egalitarian. They are alleged to have no adult hierarchy; and one report (a television documentary) referred to an *older woman* as "probably the most influential member of the group."[44] Among the Mbuti and !Kung, women are equal in terms of distribution, but there *are* clear indications of males having the edge in such nonbasic pursuits as religious affairs (seemingly more so among the !Kung than among the Mbuti).[45] Not all hunting-gathering groups are as sexually egalitarian, however. Among the Australian Aborigines, for example, despite their economic importance, women tend to be junior partners in other areas.[46] Their situation probably represents the low point for women among hunters and gatherers—a point stressed by Hobhouse, Wheeler, and Ginsberg way back in 1915.[47] Other hunter-gatherers fall between the Mbuti and the Australian Aborigines in sexual equality. As we shall see in Chapter 3, there is evidence that the high point in the status and position of *women* is *not* to be found among contemporary hunters and gatherers. Nonetheless, this mode of production is undoubtedly the high point to date of *human* egalitarianism in sharing the means and fruits of production and group decision making.

SUMMARY

We do share many things with our nonhuman primate cousins, both biologically and behaviorally. But these things are not the "bad" traits of the "Nasty Animal" theorists. Our basic adaptation, the hunting and gathering way of life we have followed through at least four million years of human cultural history, bears considerable resemblance to that of our closest nonhuman kin, the chimpanzees. In both cases, the *diet* is omnivorous with gathered foods predominating (even though most human groups rely much more on hunting than *any* thus-far observed chimp population). Also in both cases, the *band* is flexible and shifting in group membership, composed of about twenty-five to fifty individuals, and relatively egalitarian and peaceful. As more is learned about chimp kinship, similarities may emerge here as well, according to Teleki, who cites recent studies showing that the "matrifocal unit, with its special life-long ties among offspring and their mother, is a fundamental organizational feature in nonhuman primate societies."[48] But even though chimps and humans—as well as car-

43. Hitoshi Watanabe, "Subsistence and Ecology of Northern Food Gatherers with Special Reference to the Ainu," in *Man the Hunter,* ed. Lee and DeVore, pp. 74-75.

44. Quoted in Steven Goldberg, *The Inevitability of Patriarchy* (New York: William Morrow & Co., 1973-74).

45. The !Kung were in my pilot sample of 61 societies that will be discussed in Chapter 3 (concerning a theory of the position of women), and they did not come out badly on what I shall term basic "life options." For example, the women have equal initiative to men in choosing a marriage partner or terminating a marriage. Additionally, !Kung women are not supposed to be beaten, and, in fact, household authority is equal. Moreover, relations between spouses are characterized as extremely warm and amiable. But *see also* Patricia Draper, "!Kung Women: Contrasts in Sexual Egalitarianism in Foraging and Sedentary Contexts," in *Anthropology of Women,* ed. Reiter, p. 77. Discussing her field work among the nomadic !Kung, she characterizes their society as "perhaps the least sexist of any we have experienced."

46. Phyllis Kaberry, *Aboriginal Women* (London: George Routledge, 1939); Jane Goodale, *Tiwi Wives* (Seattle: Univ. of Washington Press, 1971).

47. L. T. Hobhouse, G. C. Wheeler, and M. Ginsberg, *The Material Culture and Social Institutions of the Simpler Peoples* (London: Chapman and Hall, 1915).

48. Teleki, "The Evolution of Primate Subsistence Patterns," 1975.

nivores—may share a collective kill, this seems to be where humans part company. Our uniquely *human* heritage is not based on killing. It is based on *sharing*. Hunters and gatherers share not just collectively but also *individually* acquired foods, and in most the sharing involves the whole band. The sharing also tends to involve a uniquely human sexual division of labor, where females do more of the gathering and males do more of the hunting. Gathering is typically done as an individual, rather than as a collective or cooperative activity, as is much hunting (large animals excepted). So our humanness seems based on *social* production, as asserted by Engels.[49] But the production is social not because it is collectively generated, but because it is collectively distributed and consumed.

How did all this change? What made our ancestors start down the road to material inequality on the one hand, and technological advance on the other? These problems are tackled in Chapter 2. Once again we shall see that the prevailing theories are based on a fundamentally unpleasant view of human nature, and once again we shall see that the evidence tends not to support them.

For Further Reading

Lee, Richard B., and DeVore, Irven. *Man the Hunter*. Chicago: Aldine, 1968.

A rich and still current source book on hunting-gathering societies.

Leibowitz, Lila. "Perspectives on the Evolution of Sex Differences." In *Toward an Anthropology of Women*, edited by Rayne R. Reiter. New York: Monthly Review Press, 1975.

An excellent article on sex differences and sex roles among nonhuman primates.

Marshall, Lorna K. "The !Kung Bushmen of the Kalahari Desert." In *Peoples of Africa*, edited by James Gibbs. New York: Holt, Rinehart & Winston, 1965.

Tanner, Nancy, and Zihlman, Adrienne. "Women in Evolution. Part I: Innovation and Selection in Human Origins," *Signs* (Spring, 1976):585-608.

An exciting synthesis of the newest evidence on the course of human evolution emphasizing sexual distinctions and differentiation.

Turnbull, Colin M. *The Forest People*. New York: Simon & Schuster, 1961.

————. "The Mbuti Pygmies of the Congo." In *Peoples of Africa*, edited by James L. Gibbs. New York: Holt, Rinehart & Winston,& 1965.

Turnbull writes of the Mbuti and Marshall of the !Kung. All three accounts are fascinating and authoritative.

49. Frederick Engels, *The Origin of the Family, Private Property, and the State* (New York: International Publishers, 1942).

2 | From Surplus to Socioeconomic Stratification

WHO ate the forbidden apple? In other words, what caused the basic egalitarianism of our hunting and gathering forebearers to give way to material inequality and ultimately class stratification? In this chapter we shall handle as separate questions (1) the emergence of material inequality involving differential distribution of the *fruits* of production; and (2) the emergence of class stratification involving differential access to the *means* of production as well as its fruits.

Most nonradical U.S. social science stratification theories consider this process of emerging stratification as inevitable. Implicitly, their views rest on assumptions of basic human *selfishness* and the *scarcity* of most of life's goodies. But we have just seen that scarcity in hunting-gathering groups tends to lead to greater *sharing* of resources, not greater competition for them.[1]

Actually, sharing under conditions of scarcity may not continue if the scarcity grows *so* extreme that there's no chance of enough coming in to permit all group members to survive by sharing. Beyond that point, basic survival changes the situation to one of "everyone for him/herself." A perfect example is what happened to the Ik of Uganda after they were excluded from their main hunting ground when it was declared a national park. As they slowly starved, generosity and compassion were replaced by desperation and indifference to the plight of their neighbors and even their families. Their "humanity" was lost, but some *individuals* were managing to survive.[2]

One key to the puzzle of why inequality emerges is provided by Lenski. He agrees with the notion of fundamental human selfishness. But he argues that that very selfishness causes people living in groups without consistent *surplus* accumulation to share—as a method of enhancing their survival prospects. Once surplus emerges, he proposes, so too does its unequal distribution, that is, material inequality.[3] In short, it is surplus and not scarcity that provides the *initial* impetus for unequal rewards (Marxists would agree).

But how and under what circumstances does surplus emerge? Here I part company somewhat with Lenski. Despite occasional disclaimers he tends to see surplus accumulation as being something humans strive for automatically once they get half a chance. And the amount of surplus he sees as determined primarily by the level of technology and secondarily by environmental abundance. While I do not deny that the size

1. Morton H. Fried, *The Evolution of Political Society* (New York: Random House, 1967), p. 98.
2. Colin N. Turnbull, *The Mountain People* (New York: Simon & Schuster, 1972).
3. Gerhardt E. Lenski, *Power and Privilege* (New York: McGraw-Hill, 1966); Gerhardt E. Lenski, *Human Societies* (New York: McGraw-Hill, 1970).

13

of the potential surplus accumulable by a group rises with technological level and environmental lushness, I would argue that there are few human habitats so harsh as to preclude the possibility of surplus extraction with even the rudest technology. After all, the !Kung manage to subsist on an average workweek of under twenty hours per adult producer in the heart of the parched and inhospitable Kalahari Desert. Clearly, if they worked longer and harder they could produce and accumulate surplus. But they don't. It might be objected that the !Kung's need to wander incessantly after food and water is what keeps them from the path to acquisition and accumulation. But there are other examples, at higher levels of technology and in better environments. The Kuikuru, a horticultural people of the Amazon basin, for example, also have been described as being in business for their health rather than to maximize production and surplus.[4] With their technology and environment, they could produce several times over their actual level of output. But they don't. So surplus accumulation is *not* automatic. Potential surplus may or may not be actualized by a group. Even if it is, it still is possible for it to be allocated equally among all members, as is done by the profitable but egalitarian Israeli kibbutzim (collective settlements). Yet two things cannot be denied. First, surplus accumulated and retained not by the total group but by individual members or subgroups must be seen as the first step down the road to material inequality. And second, a minority of contemporary hunting and gathering societies have taken this first step.

Who are they and how did it happen? Since these hunting-gathering groups have similar *technology* levels, let us look to their *habitats*. Here we have a fortunate example of "serendipity"—a felicitous and unanticipated finding. In two studies of the relationship of mode of subsistence and family structure, a subgroup of atypical or "deviant" hunting-gathering groups emerged, charac-

terized by large, complex family units— which happen to be relatively uncommon among hunters and gatherers.[5] In both of these studies the "deviant" groups with complex family structures were subjected to closer scrutiny. It emerged that most of them lived in *lush habitats*. Furthermore, the Blumberg and Winch analysis showed them to be atypical in other ways as well: more likely to have wealth distinctions, an inheritance system (and an unequal one at that, typically favoring *sons* over other potential heirs), and larger, less nomadic communities than hunters and gatherers having mainly small, nuclear families. The Nimkoff and Middleton data, when subjected to further analysis (by Blumberg, Winch, and Reinhardt),[6] revealed two basic patterns among the large-family hunting-gathering societies living in environmental abundance. Where there was some cooperative, large-scale activity in the group (such as collective hunting or defense) the groups largely lacked both wealth distinctions and inheritance. Conversely, in groups lacking collective hunting, gathering, or frequent war, an opposite pattern emerged where wealth distinctions were often combined with inheritance.

4. Robert L. Carneiro, "Slash-and-Burn Cultivation Among the Kuikuru and Its Implications for Cultural Development in the Amazon Basin," in *The Evolution of Horticultural Systems in Native South America, Causes and Consequences,* ed. Johannes Wilbert. Anthropology Supplement no 2. (Caracas: Sociedad de Ciencias Naturales La Salle, 1961).

5. Rae Lesser Blumberg and Robert F. Winch, "The Rise and Fall of the Complex Family: Some Implications for an Evolutionary Theory of Societal Development" (paper read at meetings of American Sociological Association, New York, 1973); and M. F. Nimkoff and Russell Middleton, "Types of Family and Types of Economy," *American Journal of Sociology* 66 (1960):215-225.

6. Rae Lesser Blumberg, Robert F. Winch, and Hazel H. Reinhardt, "Family Structure as Adaptive Strategy" (paper read at the meetings of the American Sociological Association, Montreal, 1974).

From these clues, let us construct a first speculative theory concerning the initial emergence of material inequality in human groups.

exuberante

FROM SURPLUS AND STYMIED SHARING TO THE SURFACING OF MATERIAL INEQUALITY

Diagrammatically, the proposed sequence of events would look much like figure 2.1.

In other words, certain groups living in lush environments, characterized by abundant and reliable food resources, undergo an enormously significant change. Rather than sharing most foods with a wide array of group members—the social survival insurance of people living off fluctuating and sometimes scarce resources—they consume most of it within the bounds of their own family group. At the same time, the rich environment permits them to stay longer in one place and move around less.

The lush environment, with its *ample* and (perhaps more important!) *reliable* food supply, seems to facilitate the emergence of family groups more complex than the simple nuclear family. Most frequently, this takes the form of the *extended* family, where the basic unit consists of three generations. Furthermore, the decline in group-wide sharing and the increased sedentism, I suggest, seem to facilitate the actualization and accumulation of surplus. More important, it seems to facilitate concentration of that surplus within families rather than at the level of the group as a whole. Once group sharing is no longer the mode for daily food distribution, it makes sense for family members to produce a little extra as a margin of safety against leaner days. But since the families differ in size, sex, age, and dependency ratios; and energy and competence of members, some will tend to accumulate more than others. If this differential in surplus is given social meaning by say, occasional feasts thrown by individual families or family heads in which the givers are rewarded by prestige or more concrete tokens

of esteem (e.g., wampum), the basis may be created for material inequality, as well as prestige differences, between families. In some groups there will emerge attempts to transmit acquired material and symbolic tokens to the next generation (i.e., inheritance). And so wealth differences between families—and perhaps between family members, if the inheritance is unequal among possible heirs—may become institutionalized.

In this first phase of structured inequality, there may be wealth distinctions within the group, and unequal distribution of the *surplus* produced within the group, but no one is deprived of a basic share of the fruits of subsistence. And all continue to have access to the means of production, which are either communal (e.g., land) or easily made by any individual user (e.g., gathering baskets, bows and arrows).

All this is in contrast to a second level of inequality, which involves the emergence of *class stratification*. In its simplest form, class stratification involves two groups (e.g., nobles vs. commoners) who are distinguished by their differential access to *both* the means and fruits of production. Fried argues persuasively that these two strata need *not* spring from either slavery or conquest, the most frequently cited "causes" of a two-class system.[7] I agree, and suggest that they may spring from the coalescence into two distinct in-marrying groups of the more versus less successful extended families we saw forming in Stage One. But such a system of class stratification almost never occurs among hunters and gatherers. Their level of surplus is not great enough in most cases (even when they work at accumulating it), and it seems logistically hard to restrict people's rights to go out and gain their own livelihood. Class stratification presupposes a further development of the techno-economic base: *cultivation*.

So before presenting a speculative para-

7. Fried, *The Evolution of Political Society*.

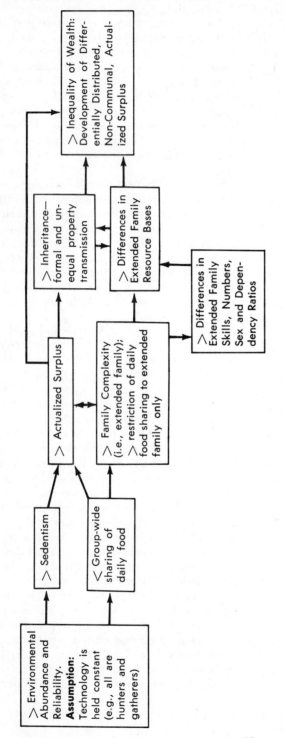

Figure 2.1 From Abundance to Inequality: One Scenario for the Origins of Stratification (Via Surplus Accumulation, a Nonautomatic Variable)

NOTE: > = Increased
< = Decreased

digm concerning the emergence of class stratification, let us tackle the prior problem of why people began *planting* as well as just harvesting (i.e., gathering) their non-animal foods.

THE EMERGENCE OF FOOD PRODUCTION

It appears that cultivation first began in the Middle East some ten thousand years ago, and developed early and apparently independently in several other areas of the world as well (e.g., Mesoamerica). Popular stereotypes—until recently also the predominant view in the social science literature—evoke pictures of the "discovery of agriculture." In this scenario, humans remained for so many millenia at the hunting and gathering level because existence was so precarious that the dawn to dusk food quest never left them the leisure to experiment with the environment and "create culture." (Not only is human cultural history as gatherers and hunters perhaps more than four million years old, but—according to Lee and DeVore (cited in Chapter 1)—we spent at least 50,000 years as modern *homo sapiens* before we began to add cultivation to our mode of subsistence.) Then one day, some forgotten genius (let's call him Og) figures it out. "Seeds sprout into plants!" he informs his incredulous friend Mog. And so the group immediately follows up on his magnificent discovery and before long are growing rather than gathering much of their food. The weight of the evidence, however, indicates that the scenario is wrong.

We already have reviewed some evidence that most hunting-gathering groups manage an adequate (and protein-rich, as it happens) diet, without the necessity of a never-ending food quest. The archeological evidence on both the Middle East and Mesoamerica[8] indicates that cultivation *evolved* over literally thousands of years, only slowly becoming an important part of group food supply. Moreover, the people helping the evolution along were almost surely *women*[9] since they were the main

gatherers, and cultivation merely adds planting to their already familiar activities of harvesting. These people spent their lives observing the growing cycles of the large number of plants found in most hunting-gathering habitats. They scheduled their movements around the seasonal availability of these resources. It does not seem likely that they remained so long ignorant of the function of seeds. According to Flannery, there is no presently known hunting-gathering group which is ignorant of the connection between plants and the seeds from which they sprout.[10]

So why did cultivation emerge so late in human history and so slowly? As it happens, cultivation involves longer and harder work (for larger yields, of course) than gathering. And the most persuasive theories to date argue that people turned to growing their food only when forced to increase their total output. *Why* should they need more food? Most likely because of local *population pressure* according to archeologists Binford and Meyers.[11] This might be because of *external* pressure, such as when a new group enters another's habitat (Binford's view), or because of *internal* pressure, as when a group in a good but spatially constricted environment that permitted a fairly sedentary life finds itself growing too nu-

8. Stuart Struever, ed., *Prehistoric Agriculture* (Garden City: National History Press, 1971).

9. V. Gordon Childe, *What Happened in History*, rev. ed., (Baltimore: Penguin Books, 1964). First pub. 1942, pp. 65-66.

10. Kent V. Flannery, "Archeological Systems Theory and Early Mesoamerica," in *Prehistoric Agriculture*, ed. Stuart Struever (Garden City, N. Y.: The Natural History Press, 1971), p. 81.

11. Lewis R. Binford, "Post-Pleistocene Adaptations," in *Prehistoric Agriculture*, ed. Struever, pp. 22-49; J. T. Meyers, "The Origin of Agriculture: An Evaluation of Three Hypotheses," in *Prehistoric Agriculture*, ed. Struever, pp. 101-121. *See also* Mark N. Cohen, "Pleistocene Population Growth and the Origins of Agriculture" (paper read at the 74th Annual Meeting of the American Anthropological Association, San Francisco, 1975).

merous to feed itself off the wild plants and animals (Meyers' view).

This brings us to a consideration of population growth patterns. Contrary to Malthusian and much popular opinion, women were not nonstop breeding machines before the invention of modern contraceptives. Human groups have always regulated population, and even in present-day Third World countries undergoing "population explosions" fertility is only about forty to sixty percent of the biological maximum.[12] Among nomadic hunting and gathering groups, where women are usually the principal producers, fertility is an even smaller percentage of the biological maximum: completed family size is low and children are widely spaced. But when these groups become more settled there is less inconvenience to a woman in somewhat more closely spaced births. Also, as cited in footnote 28 in Chapter 1, recent evidence indicates that there may be physiological changes in body fat ratios that accompany increasing sedentism among hunting-gathering women and enhance their fertility levels. In short, Meyers' theory that certain more sedentary groups began to face internal population pressure seems supported by the evidence on fertility.

If population seems the most plausible "why" of the adoption of cultivation, what is the *mechanism* for its emergence, that is, the "how"? Here, Flannery provides an answer.[13] It appears that once a group gets started down the road to cultivation, they "can't go home again." Technically, in the language of cybernetics, this means that cultivation is a "positive feedback process."[14] In such a process, an initial change that may have been small in itself sets off other, continually intensifying, escalating changes until there is little resemblance to the original state of affairs. In Flannery's view, it was genetic changes in the plants, increasing population density, the rescheduling of the group's annual food procurement cycle (e.g., letting the birds eat the purple berries because they come ripe the week you have to tend to the corn at the other end of your habitat), and the consequent impact on the ecological balance of the area over hundreds and hundreds of years that made a return to pure hunting and gathering unprofitable and perhaps impossible.

These population theories of the slow, female-nurtured, emergence of cultivation seem more in accord with the facts than the earlier "discovery of agriculture" views. Even so, the evidence is so incomplete that a final verdict is not yet possible. (It is tough even to *disprove* such theories as von Däniken's *Chariot of the Gods* view that spacemen put us on the path to progress.) Be that as it may, once cultivation emerged, the *potential* output and level of surplus of a given area rose dramatically.

At the same time, there is evidence that cultivation—which brought a relatively more settled life—was responsible for the world's first and greatest *population explosion*.[15] Not only were the women freed from the need for frequent wandering with small children, but they found that their children were useful helpers in production. Population size among such a newly sedentary food-raising group could have *doubled* every generation, with enormous consequences in a fairly short time. Population pressure on resources and scarcity would become more than a scattered rarity. Both Boserup and Harner posit population pressure as the principal cause for the intensification of food production

12. United Nations, Dept. of Economics and Social Affairs, *Demographic Yearbook,* 1969 (New York: United Nations, 1970), pp. 222-234.

13. Flannery, "Archeological Systems Theory," in *Prehistoric Agriculture,* ed. Struever, pp. 80-100.

14. M. Maruyama, "The Second Cybernetics: Deviation Amplifying Mutual Processes," *American Scientist* 51 (1963):164-179.

15. Stephen Polgar, "Population History and Population Policies from an Anthropological Perspective," *Current Anthropology* 13 (1972):203-211.

among groups that are already cultivating.[16] Each intensification of cultivation, Boserup shows, involves more and harder work while providing a larger yield from the same area. So, intensified food production is not the sort of activity people pick up on voluntarily—unless they need that larger yield.

Harner goes farther, and argues that growing scarcity and population pressure *preceded* the emergence of *class stratification.* Let us now turn to a proposed sequence concerning the origin of this higher level of inequality in human societies.

FROM SCARCITY TO STRATIFICATION

The first quantum level of structured inequality in human societies, I propose, stems from abundance. The second seems to be the child of scarcity. Diagrammatically, the proposed chain would look like figure 2.2.

Thus, the consequences of the more advanced technology of cultivation include a greater degree of sedentism, with all its consequences for population growth via closer child spacing. In addition, the advanced techniques typically concentrate that larger population on a smaller and smaller proportion of their habitat's land area. Flannery gives a dramatic example of this process in Iran.[17] During the period of exclusive hunting and gathering prior to about 7000-8000 B.C., the small, scattered population found perhaps thirty-five percent of the land to be well suited for its mode of subsistence. But once cultivation was introduced, a further constraint was added: only ten percent of the land was arable (cultivatable) by the early dry-farming techniques. Yet population increased twenty-fold and now had to be supported from one-tenth of the land surface. When irrigated farming was introduced, the situation became even more extreme, for only one percent of the total land area, at best, was suitable for irrigation. And in that one percent of the territory, population density grew further. These changes

can be seen in Flannery's graphs (figure 2.3).

As he points out, the *inverse ratio* between population growth and the percentage of total land surface to which the currently "most productive" technique can be applied helps set the stage for social stratification. Here we do find a situation of population pressure and competition for scarce resources, in which the notion of *communally controlled* means of production—especially land—is replaced by that of *subgroup owned* resources (where the subgroup may be kin groups, families, or individuals within the larger population). Once this happens, we find the sort of differential access to basic resources, including the means of production, that constitutes the essence of stratification.

How do the two classes emerge? If the more successful families of the material inequality phase are able to translate their greater wealth into greater control over the increasingly concentrated *sources* of wealth, and if they are able to consolidate their position by *intermarrying* with the other successful families (usually grown into fullfledged kin groups by this time), it shouldn't take too long for the society to start to polarize into two groups who tend not to marry across group lines. On the one hand, we find those who have consolidated their control over the scarce resources. On the other, we find the ever increasing group of those who now lack free access to the means of livelihood, because the land is controlled by someone else. In order to gain access to the land, in one way or another they will

16. Ester Boserup, *The Conditions of Agricultural Growth: The Economics of Agrarian Change Under Population Pressure* (Chicago: Aldine, 1965); Michael J. Harner, "Population Pressure and the Social Evolution of Agriculturalists," *Southwestern Journal of Anthropology* 26 (1970):67-86.
17. Kent V. Flannery, "Origin and Ecological Effects of Early Domestication in Iran and the Near East," in *Prehistoric Agriculture,* ed. Struever, pp. 50-79.

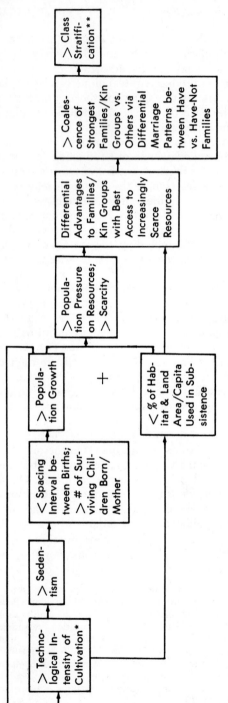

Figure 2.2 From Scarcity to Social Class: One Scenario for the Rise of Class Stratification

*Figure 2.2 assumes the outcomes of figure 1.1: Surplus actualization at a sub-community level already occurs; and wealth differences between families, transmitted by inheritance, already exists.

**In other words, the strongest kin groups coalesce to form an upper stratum with differentially favored access to the scarcest production resource (usually land or water). This occurs as the growing group must feed itself on the decreased proportion of the original habitat suitable to the more intensive subsistence technology its very increase in numbers has militated its adopting.

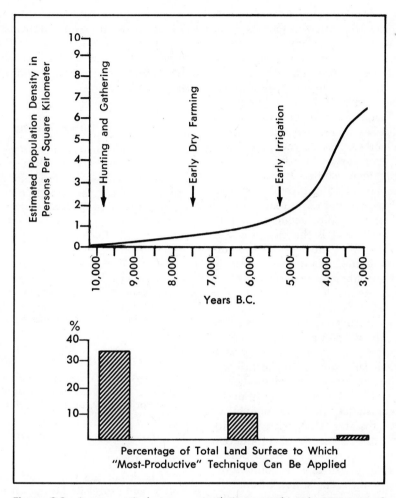

Figure 2.3 Inverse ratio between population growth and percentage of total land surface to which "most productive" technique (hunting and gathering, dry farming, early irrigation) could be applied at various stages of Iranian prehistory. Stuart Struever, ed., **Prehistoric Agriculture** (Garden City, N. Y.: The Natural History Press, 1971), p. 76. Reprinted by permission of the author.

have to give up a part of what they produce. Accordingly, they will have to produce more than they might have if only their family consumption needs were involved. Surplus, scarcity, and stratification now tend to rise together.

One last point. Is there scarcity with re-spect to the means of production *before* the emergence of population pressure on land? Harner argues that there is, in a recent anthropological restatement of the "dog eat dog" world view. In evidence, he cites the Jivaro tribe he studied in South America (they are the warlike bunch who are famed for shrinking heads).[18] They live in a "free land" situation in the Amazon jungles, have some cultivation but have not yet found it necessary to intensify it, and have all the territory they need for their hunting and gathering as well. Nevertheless, he argues, there is a basic scarcity in their group—female labor. Females are the cultivators, and the man who has more than one wife can appropriate her surplus output and throw more and bigger parties to bring him prestige and "big man" status. Raids to steal women from neighboring groups are common. Clearly, this group is already on the road to deliberate surplus accumulation by individuals. Since that is the case, there is a motivation for the controllers of the surplus to increase their share by increasing their productive labor force and their overall production. An artificial scarcity of labor has been created as a spin-off of this deliberate quest for surplus. There is every indication that the women produce enough to feed the group, so this is not a scarcity with respect to basic subsistence. In short, I propose, prior to the emergence of deliberate surplus acquisition, it would be only under unusual circumstances of environmental or demographic disaster that basic scarcity with respect to the means of production might emerge. Once people start to pursue the brass ring of surplus accumulation, however, it's a different story. Ultimately, surplus for the few comes to mean scarcity (even in basic subsistence needs) for the many.

We shall return to a quick ride on the evolutionary elevator of rising surplus, scarcity, and stratification in Chapter 4. First, however, we must pick up the story of sexual equality. And here too, we shall see, degree of control over the means and fruits of production soon emerges as the most important predictor of the relative status of the women of a group in comparison with their menfolk.

For Further Reading

Fried, Morton H. *The Evolution of Political Society.* New York: Random House, 1967.

A well-written and generally plausible reconstruction of the passage from egalitarian rank to stratified (class) societies.

Harner, Michael J. "Population Pressure and the Social Evolution of Agriculturalists." *Southwestern Journal of Anthropology* 26 (1970):67-86.

Ingenious use of Ethnographic Atlas data, which support his hypotheses on population pressure leading to social hierarchy—if you accept his index as a measure of population pressure.

Lenski, Gerhard E. *Power and Privilege.* New York: McGraw-Hill, 1966.

Even when I disagree with some of his theory, I continue to applaud the scholarship, originality, and scope of this first-rate work.

Struever, Stuart, ed. *Prehistoric Agriculture.* Garden City, N. Y.: The Natural History Press, 1971.

Check out the articles by Binford, Flannery, and especially Meyers on the origin of cultivation.

18. Michael J. Harner, "Scarcity, the Factors of Production, and Social Evolution," in *Population, Ecology, and Social Evolution,* ed. Steven Polgar (The Hague, Netherlands: Mouton, 1975).

3 | Sexual Stratification: A Paradigm of Female Productivity, Power, and Position

WITH the possible exception of the Tasaday, there is no known society of recent date in which women seem to be completely equal with men.[1] Among other societies that come close, the actual patterns are very different. Two examples should suffice: (1) The cooperative, communal Mbuti Pygmies of the African rain forest, whose women participate in the group net hunts and share collective control of the means of production, and (2) the warring, political Iroquois of Colonial-era North America, whose women raised most of the food by hoe horticulture and controlled the means and fruits of production. Iroquois chiefs and council elders were men, but the senior matrons had the power to nominate them, and influence in other political and war decisions as well.

Elsewhere, the position of women varies enormously. U.S. and U.S.S.R. women fall short of the near-equality of the Mbuti and Iroquois, but live in a different universe than say, Saudi Arabia's veiled, voteless, and vigilantly restricted women.

What causes these huge differences in the relative equality of women among the world's peoples? In this chapter, I shall present a synopsis of my own work in which I propose a paradigm to account for the position of women.[2]

In pursuing the question of the relative equality of the sexes cross-culturally, we will look at two aspects of the position of women: (a) the degree of female *power,* relative to the males of her class or group. (In simple, preclass societies, we can compare the women to the men of the total group, but for class societies we have to examine the position of women separately for each class, for it may vary greatly by stratum.) And (b) the extent to which females approach equal treatment and *opportunities* with the males of their class or group.

Concerning power, Lenski has identified three principal sources relevant for a society's inequality system: (1) power of property; (2) power of position (i.e., in the group's political or other major hierarchies); and (3) power of force.[3] Empirically, there is only one of these three power sources in which women's position has been found to

---

1. In this book, although we shall be examining the degree of relative equality of men and women in a given group, we shall make no assumptions about potential *upper limits* on sexual equality, including whether hormonal differences militate against it as alleged by Steven Goldberg in his book, *The Inevitability of Patriarchy* (New York: William Morrow, 1973-74).

2. The basic theory is contained in Rae Lesser Blumberg, "Structural Factors Affecting Women's Status: A Cross-Societal Paradigm" (paper read at the meetings of the International Sociological Association, Toronto, 1974).

3. Gerhard E. Lenski, *Power and Privilege* (New York: McGraw-Hill, 1966), pp. 57-58.

run the gamut from low to high: the power of property, or economic power.

Concerning economic power, there are societies where women have virtually *no* control over the means and fruits of production, relative to their menfolk of the same class or group (e.g., the Rwala Bedouin of the North African desert). Conversely, there are other societies where women have the *major* control in these areas, leaving men with very little economic power (e.g., the Iroquois). In fact, there are ethnographic accounts of a fair number of widely scattered preindustrial societies (in most of which the women are hoe horticulturalists and/or market traders) where women have the upper hand economically.

But men monopolize power in the other two arenas. There are no known societies where women have more than a small amount of the "power of position" in the political, administrative, or religious hierarchies. The women of the Soviet Union, despite their highly placed distribution in the labor force, are as infrequent in high governmental posts as are women in the U.S.[4] And though the older Iroquois women might select the chief, he had to be a male.[5]

Women fare even worse with respect to the power of force: women almost *never* exercise it and are often on the receiving end: wifebeating, for example, is distributed widely around the world. Collins has hypothesized that it is the greater male size and sexual aggressiveness (i.e., brute force) that is at the heart of sexual inequality.[6] The problem with this argument is that there are many human and primate societies where the males do not brutalize the females. Recent studies of nonhuman primates[7] do not show any consistent relationship between the extent of "sexual dimorphism" (males' greater size and strength) and stereotyped sex role behavior. Furthermore, many of the simplest human hunting and gathering societies do not show female subjugation to be based on the power of force. For example,

Tasaday and !Kung women (who are full economic partners) apparently are not subject to male threats of physical or sexual force. Even though women universally fare worse than men with respect to their powers of position and force, female economic power seems to act as a *check* on male use of physical force: in my sixty-one-society pilot sample (to be discussed below), I have found that where women's economic control is high, male resort to wifebeating tends to be low.

In short, for empirical as well as theoretical reasons, I propose that women's *relative economic power* is the main determinant of the *relative equality* of the sexes in a given group.

How do women get economic power? First, let us define power in the manner of Max Weber as "the probability of persons or groups carrying out their will even when opposed by others."[8] Next, let us define female economic power as women's degree of control, relative to the males of their class or group, of the means of production and allocation of surplus. The means of production include, of course, land, capital, and labor. For women to gain control of a sizeable proportion of the first two, I suggest, they must have begun with a strategic contribution to the third. So we must look first to the extent to which women are economically

4. Marilyn Power Goldberg, "Women in the Soviet Economy," *The Review of Radical Political Economics*, 4, 3 (July 1972).

5. Karen Sacks, "Social Bases for Sexual Inequality: A Comparative View," in *Sisterhood is Powerful*, ed. Robin Morgan (New York: Vintage, 1970).

6. Randall Collins, "A Conflict Theory of Sexual Stratification," *Social Problems* 19 (1970):3-21.

7. Summarized in Lila Leibowitz, "Perspectives on the Evolution of Sex Differences," in *Toward an Anthropology of Women*, ed. Rayna R. Reiter (New York: Monthly Review Press, 1975) pp. 20-35.

8. Hans Gerth and C. Wright Mills, *From Max Weber: Essays in Sociology* (Fairlawn, N. Y.: Oxford University Press, 1946), p. 180.

productive—that is, their role in "bringing home the bacon."

Actually, a large number of theorists view female contribution to the economy as the first building block to equal status.[9] Recently, Sanday examined a small sample of twelve preindustrial societies and found that where women's contribution to production was very low, so was their status.[10] Conversely, however, mere work does not guarantee either power or privilege. After all, slaves work too . . . Moreover, Sanday found groups where women did *most* of the productive labor and were treated little better than slaves (e.g., the Azande of Africa). In short, helping to "bring home the bacon" seems a *precondition* for equality—it is apparently necessary, but insufficient by itself.

FEMALE PARTICIPATION IN PRODUCTION

Consequently, my paradigm begins by predicting the conditions under which women will participate in the main productive activities of their society. Before turning to this topic, let us clear up a common and ethnocentric myth about women and work.

According to this myth, for most of human history, women have been economic parasites, who contributed little (beyond domestic and childcare chores, which are not seen as economically productive) to their family's subsistence. The husband is seen as the main provider, "whereas the wife is primarily the giver of love. . . ."[11]

How much more than love do women contribute? On a worldwide basis, we can provide an answer, thanks to the life work of George Peter Murdock, an anthropologist who has compiled data on many hundreds of mainly preindustrial societies in his *Ethnographic Atlas*.[12] Using it, Aronoff and Crano calculate that women contribute *forty-four percent of the food supply* as a worldwide average.[13] Women are not parasites.

Nevertheless, the range of variation of women's work is quite great. In my own calculations using the computer version of the *Ethnographic Atlas* (which contains data on 1,170 societies), I found that in about two percent of all societies women contributed virtually nothing to the food supply; in a similar proportion, women contributed two-thirds or more. What causes this variation in women's participation in their society's main productive activities? Specifically, I suggest, two principal factors are involved: (1) the extent to which the economic activity in question is compatible with a woman's childcare responsibilities,

9. The list includes Kay M. Martin and Barbara Voorhies, *Female of the Species* (New York: Columbia University Press, 1975); Regina E. Oboler, "Economics and the Status of Women" (paper presented at the meetings of the American Anthropological Association, New Orleans, 1973); Eleanor Leacock, "Introduction" to *The Origin of the Family, Private Property and the State,* by Frederick Engels (New York: International Publishers, 1972); Karen Sacks, "Social Bases for Sexual Equality"; and Margaret Benston, "The Political Economy of Women's Liberation," *Monthly Review* 21 (1969): 13-27.

10. Peggy Sanday, "Toward a Theory of the Status of Women," *American Anthropology* 75 (1973):1682-1700.

11. Talcott Parsons and Robert Bales, *Family, Socialization and Interaction Process* (Glencoe, Ill.: Free Press, 1955), p. 151.

12. George P. Murdock, "Ethnographic Atlas: A Summary," *Ethnology* 7 (1967):109-236. *See also* George P. Murdock, *World Ethnographic Atlas* (Pittsburgh: University of Pittsburgh Press, 1967). The *Ethnographic Atlas* presents data on scores of variables which anthropologists consider most important in societies. Scattered among its codes on some 1200 societies are undoubtedly a number of errors, and even its most faithful advocates admit it has methodological shortcomings. But its economically-linked variables have proven the most trustworthy, and the EA has shown its worth in dozens of studies whose findings have stood up to other data sources. It remains the unimpeached largest scale data source for macro-societal comparative research.

13. Joel Aronoff and William D. Crano, "A Re-Examination of the Cross-Cultural Principles of Task Segregation and Sex-Role Differentiation in the Family," *American Sociological Review* 40 (1975):12-20.

especially breastfeeding; and (2) the state of available male labor supply relative to demand.

1. Compatibility with childcare, especially breastfeeding. Ethnographic data show that in most human societies, children are not weaned until around two years of age. (The baby bottle is a nineteenth-century invention, and even today, a great majority of the world's women breastfeed their babies.) Thus, most women (and until recently, virtually all women) experience a biological constraint on their labor during a number of their prime working years: they have to be in proximity to their youngest child several times during the day. What kinds of tasks are conveniently compatible with such childcare obligations? In general, tasks which (1) are done close to home or do not require hard, fast travel; (2) are not dangerous to any small children in the vicinity; and (3) may be easily picked up, interrupted, and then restarted.[14] That strength is less of a factor is argued persuasively by Brown. Two compatible activities by these criteria are gathering and hoe horticulture. And both these activities have predominantly female labor forces. Conversely, incompatible activities such as hunting or herding large animals have an overwhelmingly male labor force (calculated from Murdock, *Ethnographic Atlas*).

But compatibility is not the whole story. Even in preindustrial societies, where women must breastfeed each child, there are cases of women in modally male activities and vice versa.[15] Moreover, if only compatibility were involved, we could not explain female employment in industrial societies, both capitalist and socialist. After all, most modern sector jobs today involve work outside the home in places to which mothers cannot bring young children—yet women are found in large and increasing numbers in these "incompatible" industrial-economy jobs, even when they have small children. Why is this so? Compatibility of an activity with childcare responsibilities may be a fa-

cilitating factor and its converse an inhibiting factor for female participation, but perhaps even more important is the relationship between male labor supply and demand.

2. Male labor supply versus demand. For the short run, the number of live human bodies needed by a society to produce a given level of output at its then current level of technology is more or less fixed. But sometimes there are too many or too few males relative to the level of labor demand. When this happens, "compatibility" is often thrown out the window.

In periods of male labor *glut,* when many men are un- or under-employed, they may invade "traditionally" female fields and squeeze the women out, especially in societies where men are considered principal breadwinners. In India, a desperately job-short country, men even work as domestic servants. And in the U.S., during economic recession and hard times, men may increase their representation in elementary school teaching, social work, and other "women's preserves." The early 1970s affirmative action decision against the telephone company opened the way for both male operators and female "linepersons." Not too many of the latter were hired, but during the ensuing recession years, more and more often one could hear a male voice answer a dial for "information."

Conversely, if an activity is important to the economy and the available male labor force is *insufficient,* women will be urged into the vacant slots, even if the task is con-

14. Judith K. Brown, "A Note on the Division of Labor by Sex," *American Anthropologist* 72 (1970):1074-1078; Beatrice Whiting, "Work and the Family: Cross-cultural Perspectives" (paper read at the Conference on Women: Resource for a Changing World, Cambridge, 1972); Rae Lesser Blumberg, "Structural Factors Affecting Women's Status," 1974.

15. George P. Murdock and Caterina Provost, "Factors in the Division of Labor by Sex: A Cross-cultural Analysis," *Ethnology* 12 (1973):203-225.

sidered drastically inappropriate for women. Plow agriculture is considerably less childcare-compatible than hoe horticulture, and this fact is reflected in worldwide statistics showing scant female participation in the former and heavy involvement in the latter. Yet, Goldberg has shown that in the U.S.S.R. up to seventy-three percent of the heaviest, nonmechanized farm labor in dry plow agriculture is done by women.[16] And they are middle-aged women at that. Clearly Russia's horrendous World War II male deaths are an important factor in this state of affairs. An even stronger example of what women may be called upon to do when their country runs desperately short of males is provided by Israel. There, women fought in combat in its 1948 war, but not in the 1956, 1967, and 1973 wars when the military and manpower situations were more favorable.

Actually, the shortage of males in an activity may result from several different types of situations. First, it might stem from factors that *reduce* the number of *males,* such as war and sex-selective migration that leave the rest of the population relatively unaffected. Second, it might stem from factors that *reduce* the number of *people,* such as invasion, disease, and large-scale emigration. And third, it may come from situations that *increase* the general *need for labor,* such as changes in productive base or technology, or economic expansion per se. As we shall see in Chapter 6, this last reason—rising demand—has been the key reason for the rising rate of female participation in the U.S labor force since 1900.

FROM WORK TO ECONOMIC POWER

Most of the theories linking woman's fate to economic factors postulate that even though females must be economically productive, that alone is not enough. The road to equality is reached only when women have gained control over their production— that is, have a strong and autonomous position vis-à-vis control of economic resources. But under what circumstances can women's labor be translated to autonomous economic control?

To begin with, *the strategic importance and indispensability* of the female producers and/or their products are important in this regard. What makes for such a strategic impact? First, the *women's economic activities* should be important to the group—providing a significant proportion of total output and/or having high "short-run substitution costs." This means that replacing the activity on short notice would be a difficult and costly process. Second, the *women producers themselves* must be valuable to the group— such that, replacing them on short notice would be a tough and expensive matter. It should be stressed that mere "substitutability at the margin" is enough to weaken women's position. It appears that if even five to fifteen percent of a group can be easily substituted, then this is enough to undermine the group's bargaining position regardless of the importance to the society of its produce.

As justification for my position, I invoke Lenski's assertion that in traditional agrarian (plow-agriculture based) societies, five to fifteen percent of the population was composed of a class he terms the "expendables."[17] These were the excess sons and daughters of the peasantry that the governing elite was unwilling to see supported on the land, even at bare subsistence. Typically, they migrated to the cities where their life conditions as coolies, prostitutes, beggars, petty thieves, and the like were usually so miserable that they rarely reproduced themselves. But each generation was replaced by more migrants from the land. I suggest that it is precisely the existence of this class of expendables that causes peasants almost everywhere to have so little economic power in comparison with their economic contribution. The existence of the expendables

16. Goldberg, "Women in the Soviet Economy."
17. Lenski, *Power and Privilege,* pp. 281-284.

means "substitutability at the margin"—that is, that any individual peasant is replaceable, and by people who had been trained to become peasants prior to their being pushed off the land. So too with women, I propose. Where replacements can be brought in at low cost for even a part of the female productive labor force—whether by trading, slaving, raiding, or polygyny in pre-industrial societies, or by tapping into a reserve army of housewives in the case of capitalist industrial nations—the possibilities for women's economic power are eclipsed.

A third group of "strategic indispensability" factors involves the other side of the coin. If women control the technical expertise of what they are doing, their strategic importance should be enhanced.[18] In general, such a situation is most likely when women work autonomously from direct male supervision.[19] Competing demand for the women's products and/or the women themselves is also more favorable than being stuck in "the only game in town." Finally, where women producers can organize in their own behalf, they are more likely to be able to influence control over production.

In addition to the "strategic indispensability" factors, two other elements—the society's kinship system and its social relations of production—must also be considered. With respect to the *kinship system,* women tend to be in a better position to exercise economic power where maternal kin ties are emphasized. In preindustrial societies, the average position of women is better in matri-centered groups than in those emphasizing paternal kin.[20] In particular, when the wife can continue to live with or near *her* relatives while the husband is separated from his kin, her degree of autonomous control over the family or group's productive resources is facilitated. In short, kinship patterns of descent, residence, and inheritance can facilitate or hinder women's path to economic power.

This brings us to the society's *social rela-*

tions of production, that is, who controls its means of production, and allocates its surplus production. In simple hunting-gathering societies that produce little or no surplus and distribute it communally when a windfall hits, the means of production are available to all members of the group. Similarly, in the socialist Israeli kibbutz, members own everything collectively. But sometimes even communal resources are in fact controlled by a group not representative of the total community—especially with respect to sex composition. This has happened in the kibbutz, where women have gradually been edged out of the important agricultural production jobs and into the low-esteemed kitchens and laundries from which they had supposedly been liberated—and where there has been a parallel decline in their voice in the kibbutz's economic committees that run much of the show with respect to kibbutz political economy.[21]

18. *See* Arthur L. Stinchcombe, "Agricultural Enterprise and Rural Class Relations," in *Political Development and Social Change*, eds. J. L. Finkle and R. W. Gable (New York: Wiley, 1966) for a parallel argument concerning peasants sharecropping for absentee landlords.

19. Oboler, "Economics and the Status of Women."

20. Ruby R. Leavitt, "Women in Other Cultures" in *Women in a Sexist Society*, eds. V. Gornick and B. K. Moran (New York: Basic Books, 1971) pp. 393-427; Kathleen Gough, "The Origin of the Family," *Journal of Marriage and the Family* 33, 4 (1971):760-771.

21. Rae Lesser Blumberg, "From Liberation to Laundry: A Structural Interpretation of the Retreat from Sexual Equality in the Israeli Kibbutz," (paper read at the meetings of the American Political Science Association, Chicago, 1974); Rae Lesser Blumberg, "Kibbutz Women: From the Fields of Revolution to the Laundries of Discontent," in *Women in the World*: *A Comparative Study*, eds. Lynne B. Iglitzen and Ruth Ross (Santa Barbara: ABC CLIO, 1976), pp. 319-344; Rae Lesser Blumberg, "The Erosion of Sexual Equality in the Kibbutz: Structural Factors Affecting the Status of Women," in *Beyond Intellectual Sexism*: *A New Woman, A New Reality*, ed. Joan I. Roberts (New York: McKay Publishing, 1976), pp. 320-339. *See also* Chapter 8, pp. 112-116.

Sex differences in economic control, which may pop up in classless communal societies, tend to be even more pronounced in societies with class stratification. In such societies, a woman's economic control is influenced by: (a) the nature of the larger stratification system and her place in it; as well as (b) her productivity and strategic indispensability vis-à-vis the men of her own class. The society may be set up in a very inegalitarian manner, so that the economically dominant class restricts access to production and takes the lion's share of the wealth, leaving very little for the remaining class or classes. For example, the women may belong to a class comprising fifty percent of the population that controls only five percent of the wealth, but this fact does not tell us how that five percent is allocated between males and females of the class. Here, the position of a woman (with respect to the men of her class) may be expected to vary according to the power points accruing to her from her productivity, strategic indispensability, and kinship connections.

THE POKER CHIPS OF POWER

As we shall see in Chapter 6, sociology is divided by the debate as to whether (as asserted by Marx) the most important determinant of people's power and life chances is their economic position, that is, their relative control over the society's means of production. (Marx also sees a society's economic arrangements as being the most important influence on its other institutions, such as the political, legal, familial, and ideological systems.) Other sociologists disagree, and argue for the equal or greater importance of noneconomic variables. Whatever the resolution of this debate with respect to a *society's* system of resources and rewards, there seems to be less doubt with respect to *women*. For them, economic power is both the biggest and most achievable of what we may term the "poker chips" of power they have been able to command. Continuing with the card game metaphor, what else can be seen as poker chips of power affecting the outcome of sexual equality? Political position and force, the other two dimensions asserted by Lenski, clearly are important. As noted, however, these are invariably male-dominated, and can be used to oppress and restrict women. But, where women have economic clout, they can use it to counter such male use of power. Ultimately, economically powerful women may gain *some* share in political power, and win physical and normative immunity from males' direct use of force against them.

Two other factors often have been mentioned in the literature as influences on women's status. These are (1) the ideology of general male superiority, and (2) men's participation in childrearing and domestic tasks. An ideology of male supremacy is alleged to correlate with low women's status; and male participation in babytending and household activities is asserted as being conducive to sexual egalitarianism.[22] These factors may *correlate* with women's status, I suggest, but that is not the same thing as *determining* it. Rather, these factors may *intervene* between the main poker chips of power and woman's fate, but they are in themselves shaped by woman's position with respect to the principal chips.

Cashing in the Poker Chips: Status and Life Options

How can we measure the position of women in meaningful terms? There are so many different aspects of woman's fate that have been mentioned in the literature, and often

22. *See* Michelle Zimbalist Rosaldo and Louise Lamphere, eds., *Woman, Culture and Society* (Stanford: Stanford University Press, 1974) concerning this latter point.

they don't correlate very well with each other. *Deference,* for example. The Victorian lady had the door opened for her getting in a carriage, but had it slammed in her face when she sought the vote or the right to control her own property after marriage. Conversely, in certain African groups where women grow and control the food supply, and trade in the market on their own account, they still maintain deference customs to their husbands involving mealtime etiquette.[23] Most measures of status, honor, or prestige are not straight-line translations of "poker chip power" (e.g., Mafia bosses have more power than prestige; with impoverished aristocrats it's the other way around). Nor do measures of status, deference, and prestige necessarily correlate with what might be chafing restrictions on freedom or autonomy of action. Clearly, we cannot measure women's power by the degree of honor, deference, status, or prestige they may have. But then, how can we measure it?

One approach is available that avoids all these controversies, and seems to offer an acceptable currency for cashing in power poker chips as well. This involves examining a series of life events and opportunities that occur in all known human societies, and then assessing the equality of women relative to the men of their class or group concerning each of these. I have referred to these events and opportunities as *life options* and view them as a realistic way of measuring the position of women in a group.

Life Options   There are a number of life options that potentially exist for humans of both sexes in all societies, and what is important here is not just the absolute level of female freedom with respect to these options, but how that freedom measures up *relative to the males* of her class or group. A partial list of life options might include the woman's relative freedom to: (1) decide whether, when, and whom to marry; (2) terminate a marriage; (3) engage in premarital sex; (4) engage in extramarital sex; (5) regulate reproduction to the extent

biologically possible (including family size, spacing, sex ratio, and the means of achieving same, such as contraception, abortion, infanticide, abstinence, etc.); (6) move about spatially without restriction; (7) exercise household authority; and (8) take advantage of educational opportunities.[24]

I have avoided mentioning any life options tied in with jobs or political rights, lest these be considered tautological (e.g., woman's economic power gives her greater freedom to take advantage of occupational opportunities).

THE PARADIGM

I have proposed a paradigm to account for the position of women relative to men of their group. This theory is intended to test the following assertions: (1) a woman's position is most affected by her relative control over the means of production and the surplus available to her group; (2) a precondition for such economic power is not just productivity, but strategic indispensability as a producer; (3) economic power also may be facilitated by kinship arrangements that take females into account in descent, marital residence, and inheritance arrangements; (4) women are more likely to be oppressed physically and politically where they do not have any appre-

23. *See* Remi Clignet, *Many Wives, Many Powers* (Evanston, Ill.: Northwestern University Press, 1970), p. 168, concerning the Abouré of the Ivory Coast.

24. Two other approaches to women's status involving the notion of life alternatives or options, and including some of the variables in this list, may be found in Constantina Safilios-Rothschild, "A Cross-Cultural Examination of Women's Marital, Educational and Occupational Options," *Acta Sociologica* 14 (1971):96-113; and Elise Boulding, "Women as Role Models in Industrializing Societies: A Macro-System Model of Socialization for Civic Competence," in *Cross-National Family Research*, eds. Marvin B. Sussman and Betty E. Cogswell (The Netherlands: E. J. Brill, 1972), pp. 11-34.

ciable economic power; and (5) women can translate power into greater control over their lives, that is, greater equality relative to the males of their group with respect to basic life options. That's the paradigm we have been discussing in this chapter—now, does it work?

A Pilot Test of the Paradigm

Recently, I have been able to test parts of this theory with data from sixty-one pre-industrial societies (ranging from the !Kung to the Koreans). Using the *Human Relations Area Files*, where ethnographic information on several hundred societies is filed, it was possible to categorize these sixty-one societies in terms of most of the variables discussed above.[25] The coding is incomplete at the time of this writing. (For example, I have information on women's economic power but little indication as to how they managed to get it in the first place. This is because I have not yet measured the "strategic indispensability factors" hypothesized as major influences of women's degree of economic power.) Be that as it may, *female economic control* was measured as discussed above—the proportion of means of production controlled by women; the proportion of surplus (if any) allocated by them; and, in addition, the extent to which women could accumulate wealth without restriction, and share in inheritance.

Force was measured by the circumstances under which men beat their wives—ranging from apparently never to "at will."

The dependent variable,[26] *life options*, was measured by a combination of four options—women's relative freedom with respect to (1) initiating marriage, (2) initiating divorce, (3) premarital virginity, and (4) the degree to which women exercised household authority.

Other variables measured were: sexual division of labor in the main productive activities, system of marital residence, ideology of male supremacy, and male participation in childcare and domestic tasks.

Some Preliminary Results

As predicted, the main determinant of variations in the position and privileges of women was their degree of economic control over the group's productive resources and surplus. Merely working made no difference on life options—even when women were the main labor force in the most important productive activity. This is in line with the previous discussion. In a variety of statistical operations, which social scientists call "multivariate analysis," three things came clear: (1) the independent variables (economic power, force, marital residence, ideology of male supremacy, etc.) were able to account for *most* of the variation in the dependent variable, life options; (2) *economic power was overwhelmingly the most important predictor of women's life options;* (3) only force, of the remaining factors, had any significant net impact on life options over and beyond that produced by women's economic power.

These results are only preliminary, and come from a study of a fairly small pilot sample. Not even all the variables in the

25. Full details on the theory, the sample, the coding, and the results will be available in a forthcoming paper. Incidentally, the *Human Relations Area Files* (available at some larger university libraries) also were developed by Murdock, and file data about a society under 888(!) separate categories. The *HRAF* has many, but apparently nonsystematic, errors, and shares many of the methodological pitfalls of the *Ethnographic Atlas*, Murdock's later creation. But like the *EA*, the *HRAF* has stood up fairly well to the tests of time and many studies. And despite its flaws, it remains the richest multisociety data source for comparative research. Also like the EA, its techno-economic data (on which I concentrate) tend to be its most reliable.

26. An *independent variable* is one believed to cause, or produce an effect in, some other phenomenon. A *dependent variable* is the one which the independent variable affects. Thus "matches produce fires" is a statement in which "match" is an independent variable, and "fire" the dependent variable.

paradigm have been measured yet, let alone other factors that might also enter into the net balance of women's position. So it is not possible to state that the matter of woman's fate has been resolved for all places and all times. But there seems to be significant and clear-cut support for the paradigm, and so it shall be taken into account in subsequent chapters.

For Further Reading

Collins, Randall. "A Conflict Theory of Sexual Stratification." *Social Problems* 19 (1971): 3-21; and Sanday, Peggy. "Toward a Theory of the Status of Women." *American Anthropologist* 75 (1973):1682-1700.

The articles cited above provide two different approaches to a theory of sexual inequality than the one I have given in this book.

Friedl, Ernestine. *Women and Man: An Anthropologist's View.* New York: Holt, Rinehart and Winston, 1975.

Friedl's basic propositions differ somewhat from my paradigm, but she uses them well to integrate much of the material on the position of women in hunting-gathering and horticultural societies.

Leacock, Eleanor. "Introduction" to *The Origin of the Family, Private Property and the State*, by Frederick Engels. New York: International Publishers, 1972.

A scholarly, provocative argument in an updated but still classically Marx/Engels vein.

Martin, Kay M., and Voorhies, Barbara. *Female of the Species.* New York: Columbia University Press, 1975.

A good overview of women through evolutionary history.

Reiter, Rayna R. *Toward an Anthropology of Women.* New York: Monthly Review Press, 1975.

Gough's article in this book is excellent and many other chapters can be rated good to outstanding.

4 | Horticultural and Agrarian Societies: Egalitarianism Falls as the Evolutionary Elevator Rises

IN this chapter, we shall take a ride up the evolutionary elevator, and see what happened to surplus, socioeconomic stratification, and the position of women in the sorts of societies that exist between today's two evolutionary extremes: hunting-gathering bands on the one hand, and industrial societies on the other.

In social science analyses with an evolutionary approach, societies often are characterized in terms of the complexity level of their means of livelihood. This is what we have been referring to as techno-economic base, although some authors use other terms such as mode of subsistence.

What is surprising is how *few* major techno-economic bases there have been in human evolutionary history. In ascending order from hunting and gathering, the main line of the evolutionary tree would read: horticultural, agrarian, and then industrial. Lenski has subdivided both horticultural and agrarian societies into simple and advanced subgroups on technological criteria. In addition, he recognizes hybrid societies, and characterizes three other types of societies as being off the main evolutionary path: fishing, herding, and maritime groups.[1] Capsule descriptions of these offshoots should suffice.

Fishing societies tend to be groups at a preagricultural technological level living in an unusually abundant ecological niche with resources so concentrated and generally reliable as to free them from having to move around a lot. Often they have larger communities and are more stratified than their less fish-endowed hunting and gathering counterparts. But they tend to be not much more complex politically.

Herding societies represent the other side of the environmental coin. Typically, these are groups who have knowledge of cultivation, but whose ecological conditions are too poor or arid to permit a life as settled, reasonably sedentary cultivators. (Some herding societies are the arid country offshoots of horticultural groups; others of agrarian societies.) The roaming pastoral life they adopt makes for smaller community size than that of their sedentary farming neighbors, but they tend to be as stratified and politically complex. Often the pastoralists— if on horse—periodically came swooping down to raid and plunder their cultivating cousins. In no other type of society are we as apt to find patrilineal descent groups so prevalent (fully 83 percent of herders have them, according to my calculations from the *Ethnographic Atlas*). Moreover, in these largely patriarchal groups the position of

1. *See* Gerhard E. Lenski, *Power and Privilege* (New York: McGraw-Hill, 1966); and Gerhard E. Lenski, *Human Societies* (New York: McGraw-Hill, 1970), especially pp. 124 and 290-304.

women tends to be low, and worse on the average than in fishing societies.

Maritime societies, such as the Phoenicians and the Venetians, are an even rarer human adaptation and none have survived to the present day.

Returning to the *mainline societies,* we find that every single one of today's *industrial* societies—capitalist or socialist, in Europe or Japan—emerged from an *agrarian heritage.* This has affected both socioeconomic and sexual stratification, for agrarian societies as a group represent the lowpoint both for human equality and for the position of women. This also points up that another way of looking at these societies would be from the standpoint of their *social relations of production*—who controls the means of production and allocates surplus. This is the approach taken by Marxists, who characterize modes of production in terms of their social relations (e.g., communal, feudal, capitalist, socialist). But *both* the techno-economic base and the social relations of production are components of the overall *mode of production* as this has been defined in the Appendix. Agrarian societies often may be organized feudally, but the agrarian Israeli kibbutz is organized in terms of socialism. Industrial societies today are split into those known as capitalist versus those known as socialist (although neither camp is "pure"). In short, the same social relations of production may be found with more than one techno-economic base, and the same techno-economic base may be organized on the basis of more than one type of social relations of production. On the whole, however, there is a fair-sized correlation between techno-economic base and social relations of production. In this chapter, we shall discuss societies in terms of their techno-economic base and also examine variations in their social relations of production—including sexual relations of production.

HORTICULTURAL SOCIETIES

Several times, I have referred to hoe horticulture to distinguish it from plow agriculture, but the simplest form of horticultural cultivation involves merely a digging stick. This is the form in which it first evolved perhaps some 10,000 years ago in the Middle East, with women as chief cultivators (if contemporary horticultural groups are *any* guide). Horticulture may have developed independently in several places, and all the evidence points to its slow evolution from scratch in Mesoamerica,[2] although at a somewhat later date than in the Middle East (no more than 7,000 years ago). It did not spread like wildfire. In fact, it took something like 3,000 years for the new technology to cover the 5,000 miles from the Middle East to China; about 2,200 years were required for New World horticultural societies to spread the 2,000 miles from their origin near Mexico City to the headwaters of the Ohio River (near modern Pittsburgh)—about a mile or so a year.[3] What may have been spreading were horticulturalists, rather than their technology—as their growing numbers caused them to move in on the less populous hunting and gathering groups. This does not mean that early horticultural societies were warlike. Quite the contrary, the archeological record shows a long initial period of peaceful settlements.[4] Only later (after the start of deliberate surplus accumulation, I suggest) did a pattern of intercommunity frays, fortifications, and the habit of burying males with weapons of war emerge.

In comparison with hunting-gathering so-

2. Kent V. Flannery, "Archeological Systems Theory and Early Mesoamerica," in *Prehistoric Agriculture,* ed. Stuart Struever (Garden City, New York: Natural History Press, 1971), pp. 80-100. J. Thomas Meyers, "The Origin of Agriculture: An Evaluation of Three Hypotheses," in *Prehistoric Agriculture,* ed. Streuver, pp. 101-121.

3. Lenski, *Human Societies,* pp. 198, 209.

4. Ibid., pp. 197-8.

cieties, in almost every instance we find that the horticultural groups: (1) were larger; (2) had more sedentary settlements; (3) grew at a higher rate; (4) were able to amass more and bulkier possessions; and (5) had a higher upper limit on surplus accumulation. The first four characteristics are interrelated. Presumably, it was population pressure that had helped push the group into relying on cultivation in the first place. Once they did so, the size of yield that could be grown on their tiny garden-size plots meant that a larger population could be fed. In fact, once they became cultivators, they initially found themselves in a situation of "free land." This is because only a small proportion of their hunting-gathering habitat need be used for all the garden plots the group could or would want to tend. But with the tiny garden plots came less of a need to roam. With less roaming, people were able to make and keep bulky possessions—such as heavy pottery, stone cups, stools, etc.—for the first time. Also, they no longer had to avoid any unnecessary duplication. With less roaming, the women found it less necessary to maintain such a long spacing interval between children, and population could be allowed to grow. After all, the land could support larger numbers with its increased yields.

This brings us to the fifth point. The yield per unit of ground was much higher with even primitive digging stick cultivation (where the same plot is cultivated for several years and then abandoned when its yield begins to decline). But would the group use the higher-per-unit yield as a springboard to increase *total* group output? In other words, would they follow the route to surplus accumulation and, ultimately, stratification?

The answer, it seems, depends on which path they followed once they began cultivating. There are at least four, and each path seems to lead to a different outcome with respect to the group's inequality system.

The first path involves a minimal journey along the road to surplus accumulation—or population growth. Groups taking this route (such as the Kuikuru of the Amazon jungles, noted in Chapter 2) have kept their lives simple, their production low, and their numbers well below the carrying capacity of their technology. The other paths involve more creation and accumulation of surplus, but vary as to who controls the surplus, and with what result. In other words, these paths differ with respect to the social relations of production.

The second path, followed by other horticultural villages, is to produce a moderate amount of surplus, but to retain and distribute it communally. Often redistribution comes about in periodic festivals and feasts; after all, horticulturalists can afford more ceremonies than most hunting-gathering groups. An important variation of this pattern occurs when the surplus goes first to the center (e.g., the headman). Then the leader, acting as trustee of the people, redistributes the surplus at the ceremonies (which sometimes involve other villages). Under these circumstances, the headman is able to gain prestige for himself in the process. If religion, or a status competition with neighboring villages, should provide motivation to the villagers to further increase their surplus, the leader may be able to retain a cut while still redistributing the majority of the take. Since the first surplus consists of *consumer* rather than *capital* goods (i.e., things one eats or wears, rather than things that one uses to make more things) the village and the headman are forced to *give away* anything that cannot conveniently be stored. Sometimes villages on this second path manage to retain the principle of communal control of resources, including surplus. At other times, the ethnographic record shows, the leader enhances his position from that of a mere conduit to that of a "Big Man" discussed on pp. 37-39 below, who wins prestige and followers by means of his generosity.

The third and fourth paths involve the accumulation and retention of surplus at a level less inclusive than the total community —that of the family or even the individual. In the third path, *women*, who are the chief cultivators, emerge as equal or better partners in the control of group resources and surplus. According to Chapter 3, the kinship system and the extent to which the women are strategically indispensable to group well-being should influence the likelihood of this outcome. Moreover, it appears that of horticultural societies producing noncommunal surplus, those in which women have a near-equal or better degree of economic power tend to go in for *lower* levels of surplus accumulation than those traveling the fourth path. Schlegal shows empirically that among matrilineal societies, those in which the position of women is highest also tend to be least likely to have social stratification—or societal complexity, as measured by intensive trade or craft specialization.[5]

The fourth path emerges when men use women's labor in cultivation in order to deliberately produce surplus—and prestige— for their own benefit. Typically, the chief beneficiary is the man for whom the woman labors, in most cases, her husband. (Her father may be the beneficiary when she is young; also, in some matrilineal societies, the person controlling her labor and surplus may be her mother's brother.) In this way, the surplus of one group is appropriated for the benefit of another—the hallmark of class stratification.

Moreover, *scarcity* is created with respect to one of the three major means of production—labor. But this is a very special kind of scarcity. The scarcity is of women's labor, since they are the chief cultivators and their labor is scarce *only* with respect to the production of *surplus*. In such a society, everyone still retains full rights to a basic share of group output, and there is enough for everyone to have a similar and adequate standard of living. But with respect to surplus, female labor comes to be manipulated as a scarce good, something to be competed for. The form of manipulation that tends to emerge in groups following the fourth path is *general polygyny*—a situation where a substantial number of males have more than one wife.

A basic paradox is at work. Women produce food and perhaps ceremonial objects. These are not capital goods—they can only be consumed. How much extra food or fancy feather masks can one man use? In many groups following this fourth path, his reason for acquiring the extra wives to produce the extra goods is, paradoxically, to *give away the surplus*. In this way, he can trade excess consumer goods for prestige and influence. But wives are another matter. They are producers—and since he controls the bulk of their surplus production (although rarely their basic output)—the wives can be considered as *capital goods* that *create* rather than consume value. You won't find men voluntarily giving away their wives at a feast (sexual dalliances are, of course, another matter, and in many of these societies a man is much less jealous of his wife's sexual favors than of her production).

Since the sex ratio at birth in most human groups varies narrowly and is close to fifty-fifty, so long as one group of men have more than one wife each, another group of men have to do without. And what they do without is not just a wife and a helpmate, but also the means of accumulating surplus to be translated into prestige. Sometimes polygyny is handled by delaying the age of first marriage of men and pushing down that of women—so that men old enough to be married have their pick of a wider age span, and hence larger group, of women. At other times, the men actively seek wives outside the group—often by raiding. This in-

5. Alice Schlegal, *Male Dominance and Female Autonomy: Domestic Authority in Matrilineal Societies* (New Haven, Conn.: HRAF Press, 1972), p. 78.

creases the supply of women available to the men, decreases the pool of men needing extra wives because of the casualties that this method entails, and increases the substitutability at the margin of women producers so as to undermine their economic autonomy and bargaining power still further. A neat arrangement for the men who come out on top! Anthropologists call them "Big Men" and note their paradoxical generosity, which sometimes makes them less wealthy in material goods than their followers.[6]

In fact, we seem to have found an interesting syndrome among preclass societies in our exploration of the fourth path. The syndrome involves the artificially created shortage of female labor among people not suffering from any natural dearth of the basic means of production (e.g., land shortage resulting from continued population growth). Accordingly, general polygyny may emerge, although there may not yet be corporate descent groups, since these have been shown to *follow* the onset of population pressure in preclass societies practicing cultivation.[7] Under such circumstances, the type of family that seems most likely to emerge is that of one male head trying to accumulate the greatest number of hard-working wives. Technically, this is called "independent family system with general polygyny." (Blumberg, Winch, and Reinhardt[8] have predicted and empirically analyzed the factors that seem to account for the emergence of "independent familism with general polygyny," and found female labor to play a prominent role.)

Two other consequences seem to follow: marital residence is likely to be with the *husband's* male relatives (general polygyny, in fact, almost never emerges when women continue to reside with their own kin after marriage); and considerable fighting about women takes place—much of it *within* the group as men quarrel over attempted wife-stealing precipitated by adultery. Anthropologists are currently in heated debate as to whether warfare patterns determine residence patterns or vice versa.[9] All are agreed, however, that where residence is with the *bride's* close family, there is less polygyny and feuding (internal war) within the group, whereas the converse is true for residence with husband's kin.

One effect that may accompany residence with husband's kin is a further undermining of women's economic autonomy. They are now on the man's home turf, and he is likely to have instituted other measures that militate against female producers forming an alliance to increase their bargaining power (e.g., co-wives working scattered garden plots as individuals rather than working together; each co-wife retaining *individual* rights to her output—after the husband has skimmed off his cut of the surplus—so as to be put into a competitive rather than cooperative situation; co-wives being given separate residences).[10]

It is perhaps for these reasons that we

6. *See*, for example, Morton H. Fried, *The Evolution of Political Society* (New York: Random House, 1967), p. 118.

7. Michael J. Harner, "Population Pressure and the Social Evolution of Agriculturalists," *Southwestern Journal of Anthropology* 26 (1970):67-86.

8. Rae Lesser Blumberg, Robert F. Winch, and Hazel H. Reinhardt, "Family Structure as Adaptive Strategy" (paper read at the meetings of the American Sociological Association, Montreal, 1974).

9. Carol Ember, "An Evaluation of Alternate Theories of Matrilocal vs. Patrilocal Residence" (paper read at the meetings of the American Anthropological Association, New Orleans, 1973); Melvin Ember and Carol Ember, "The Conditions Favoring Matrilocal versus Patrilocal Residence," *American Anthropologist* 73 (1971):571-594; William T. Divale, "An Explanation for Primitive Warfare: Population Control and the Significance of Primitive Sex Ratios," *The New Scholar* 2 (1970): 173-192.

10. The relationships among separate co-wife residence, female labor and residence with husband's kin are both predicted and established empirically in Rae Lesser Blumberg with Maria-Pilar Garcia, "The Political Economy of the Mother-Child Family: A Cross Societal View," in *Beyond the Nuclear Family Model*, ed. Luis Leñero-Otero (London: Sage Publications, 1977), pp. 99-164.

find among groups characterized by "Big Man" redistribution patterns not just polygyny and male battles for prestige and political influence being waged with women's expropriated surplus but also what may be the highest levels of warfare and female subjugation found among simple preclass horticultural societies.[11]

For some simple horticulturalists, the path they have chosen leads no further in an evolutionary sense. Whether by warfare, infanticide, primitive birth control, or whatever, numbers are kept in harmony with resources.[12] In other groups, growing numbers, however, mean that the days of "free land" are soon over. Population pressure and/or deliberate attempts to increase surplus lead to more intensive reliance on cultivation[13]— and further competition. Harner has developed an ingenious way of measuring this competitive pressure on resources.[14] The greater the population/resource pressure on groups that already are cultivating, he posits, the more they turn away from hunting and gathering to more intensive and reliable methods of food production (more cultivation, fishing, or herding). Using the *Ethnographic Atlas*, he predicts and shows that his measure of population/resource pressure seems to precede first the development of complex corporate descent groups in preclass societies, and then the development of class stratification and political complexity themselves. Still, I propose, the descent groups and the class stratification emerge not out of bitter competition over *basic* subsistence, but rather over competition for deliberately accumulated *surplus*. Thus the scarcity is with respect to the cream, not the milk of life itself. And not all groups produce or compete for cream.

Lenski takes a somewhat different approach. He differentiates horticultural societies into "simple" and advanced," using technological criteria, because to him technological innovation is the driving engine of social evolution, and surplus accumulation is more or less automatic. "Advanced" hor-

ticultural societies are those that have metallurgy, according to his most recent classification scheme.[15] I suggest that another principle for dividing horticultural groups into simple and advanced might be degree of deliberate surplus accumulation. Use of a surplus criterion might have solved one problem that emerges from Lenski's scheme with respect to African horticultural groups. Because of diffusion from the Middle East and North Africa, *all* African cultivators have long had metal (namely, iron) tools. But in terms of socioeconomic and political complexity, African "advanced" horticulturalists are split into two quite different groups empirically. About one-third of them have preclass, politically autonomous village-societies; the remainder have more elaborate and inegalitarian stratification and political systems. In short, even though "advanced" horticulturalists as a group tend to be more complex than "simple" cultivators on a worldwide basis, a single technological criterion cannot distinguish between two sub-

11. Highland New Guinea seems to take the prize for this. (*See*, for example M. J. Meggitt, "Male-Female Relationships in the Highlands of New Guinea," *Cultures of the Pacific*, eds. T. Harding and B. Wallace, New York: Free Press, 1970.) However, some South American groups such as the Achuara and the Jivaro are not far behind. *See* e.g., Michael J. Harner's "A Test Among the Achuara of Engels' Model for Husband-Wife Equality in Primitive Society" (paper read at the meetings of the American Anthropological Association, New Orleans, 1973); and his "Scarcity, the Factors of Production, and Social Evolution," in *Population, Ecology and Social Evolution*, ed. Steven Polgar (The Hague: Moutin, 1975), pp. 123-138.

12. Andrew P. Vayda, ed., *Environment and Cultural Behavior* (Garden City, New York: The Natural History Press, 1969), p. 204; William Divale, "An Explanation for Primitive Warfare."

13. Ester Boserup, *The Conditions of Agricultural Growth: The Economics of Agrarian Change Under Population Pressure* (Chicago: Aldine, 1965).

14. Harner, "Population Pressure."

15. Lenski, *Human Societies*, p. 125.

groups of "advanced" horticulturalists in Africa.

Nevertheless, Lenski's classification (which correlates highly with degree of deliberate surplus accumulation, I propose) offers some valuable insights on the development of (a) class stratification; (b) political complexity; (c) warfare; and (d) marriage as an economic transaction. Let us review each of these in turn.

(a) *Class stratification* takes a big leap forward among the groups classified as advanced horticulturalists. Lenski's calculations from the *Ethnographic Atlas* show that eighty-three percent of simple horticultural groups lack classes (as do ninety-eight percent of hunting-gathering societies, for that matter). In contrast, only forty-six percent of advanced horticulturalists lack a class system, that is, the *majority* have unequal access to both means and fruits of production. Most often the class system is of the nobles-vs.-commoners sort, although some advanced horticultural societies are oriented enough to warfare and have absorbed enough ethnically diverse peoples to have a ruling class of warrior nobility that is distinct in ethnic as well as stratification terms from the rest of the people. In such cases it is no longer a situation of the most successful kin groups of the same population coalescing into an elite that starts to intermarry. With a dual class system, redistribution to the lower class tends to be less ("Big Men" now may have soldiers and tax collectors and are no longer less well off than their average followers). Certainly the flow of goods to the dominant class is heavier. In situations of conquest, wealth differences may begin to grow at *both* ends —some grow ever richer on surplus extraction while for the first time others are no longer left with enough to constitute the basic standard of living. In other words, here we may find the beginning of *relative poverty* as well as relative wealth. Previously, barring episodes of natural catastrophe, sharing assured everyone of a full

ration of what was needed to satisfy basic needs; only surplus was competed for. Now, with the growth of their power, the ruling-nobles class can skim their take off the top. Some of the people under their control are no longer "their" people, and they may not bother to leave them enough for a decent life.

(b) *Political complexity* seems to be the next step up in this progression of inequality. Here, my position differs from Lenski, who in his 1966 *Power and Privilege* explicitly considers the development of political complexity to be a *forerunner* of greater material inequality in the distribution of surplus. But some recent evidence seems to point in the other direction. Haas has coded all of the 277 North American Indian societies delineated by Murdock, and found that level of political organization had almost no influence on material inequality (both, however, were greatly affected by degree of surplus accumulation, which *preceded* them in Haas' statistical model). In fact, his findings indicate that in the more frequent sequence, stratification inequalities precede the development of central political rule. Moreover, he notes, "there are more than twice as many cases where wealth inequalities are greater than political inequalities than vice versa."[16] In other words, the *origin* of stratification inequality does not require prior political inequality.[17]

Nonetheless, advanced horticulture marks a huge flip-flop in human political autonomy. Until this level, the overwhelming number of human groups were composed of *politically autonomous* villages or bands. They might have had village political leaders, but their village was a sovereign unit politically, beholden or paying tribute to no higher level of political authority. Spe-

16. Ain Haas, "The Origin of Inequality among North American Indians" (University of Wisconsin-Madison, 1973), p. 31.

17. Fried, *The Evolution of Political Society,* makes a similar argument.

cifically, Lenski's calculations reveal that in *seventy-nine percent* of simple horticultural societies, the villages *are autonomous*. But with advanced horticulture, his figures show that *seventy-one percent* of the villages *are not*. There has been a complete reversal.

As a result of the combining of previously autonomous villages into one political entity (required to contribute surplus and political loyalty to the center), the size of the average *society* is much larger in advanced (vs. simple) horticulture. Thus, "on the average, advanced horticultural societies are 60 times the size of simple horticultural and 140 times the size of hunting and gathering societies."[18] At the same time, average *community* size has not grown nearly as much: it's three times larger than in simple horticulture groups and seven times larger than among hunting-gathering bands.

(c) *Warfare* becomes much more frequent and more oriented to conquest among advanced horticulturalists, although there is no evidence that it precedes either stratification or political complexity. (Haas, for example, found almost no direct effect of external threat on political development, using a statistical technique called a "path analysis.") Concerning *frequency* of fighting, Lenski has reanalyzed data coded by Simmons on seventy-one societies[19] and shown that warfare is frequent among only eight percent of hunting and gathering societies and forty-four percent of simple horticultural ones—compared to eighty-two percent of advanced horticultural groups.[20] Moreover, the nature of warfare is different. Advanced horticulturalists are characterized by metal use. One of the first uses of metal is in weapons, and the emergence of these costlier, scarcer, and more efficient instruments of death signifies that the means of war are no longer more or less equally distributed among all male adults within and between groups. For some, conquering one's fellow humans may become more profitable than conquering nature.

Also, the greater efficiency in warfare of the few (those with control of the metal weapons) means that they can raise armies from the many, with which to further expand the area from which they draw tribute. With sufficient numbers, military might, and not unduly long lines of supply (transportation is still primitive at this level of societal complexity and if you can't get there in time, you can't prevent a newly conquered people from reasserting their autonomy), warfare now rivals or exceeds local production as a source of surplus. For the aim of war is not usually *lebensraum* (living space for one's own people) but the extraction of surplus from the conquered ones by plundering, taking captives, exacting tribute and/or taxes. Some of the plunder can be redistributed to the rank and file of the militarist society without precluding its ruling class from increasing its share of the surplus both absolutely and relatively. But to see just how much surplus a ruling class is capable of extracting from the masses, we must turn to agrarian societies—the next step on the march to "civilization" and inequality. Before we can do that, however, there are still several remaining topics to be covered with respect to horticultural societies, and all of them seem to touch on women's role as producer in these groups.

(d) *Marriage* becomes almost invariably an *economic* transaction among advanced horticulturalists, which is not surprising in light of women's continuing importance as cultivators coupled with the increased emphasis on surplus production at this level. Lenski and Lenski show, with *Ethnographic Atlas* data, that the percentage of advanced horticultural societies requiring an economic transaction to formalize a marriage rises to ninety-seven percent (!)—up from sixty-one

18. Gerhard E. Lenski and Jean Lenski, *Human Societies*, 2nd ed. (New York: McGraw-Hill, 1974), pp. 198-199.
19. Leo Simmons, *The Role of the Aged in Primitive Society* (New Haven: Yale University Press, 1945).
20. Lenski, *Human Societies*, 1970, p. 138.

percent among simple horticulturalists and forty-nine percent among hunters and gatherers.[21] The form of the economic transaction is most often "bride price," but may also be bride service, or some other form of exchange that must be tendered to the woman's parents or kin group. Bride price and other economic marriage transactions that stress the economic value of women decline among agrarian societies. In fact, among these societies, where women tend to take a back seat as far as economic productivity is concerned, we find instances of the opposite custom—*dowry*. Dowry is a payment the bride's parents have to make to the groom's parents in order to get rid of her. Several studies show that bride price/ bride service is correlated with high female contribution to subsistence, and dowry with low female productivity.[22] In industrial societies, neither bride price nor dowry is given. In short, the relationship between economic transfer to the bride's parents and societal complexity is more or less *curvilinear*. This means that such a payment is most likely in the middle reaches of societal complexity represented by horticulture, and least likely among the simplest hunting-gathering societies and the most technologically advanced industrial nations.

As it turns out, four other family system variables are also curvilinearly related to societal complexity, and all hit their peak at the level of horticultural societies. These are: (a) general polygyny, (b) familial complexity, (c) corporate unilineal descent groups, and (d) matri-centered residence and descent.

(a) *General polygyny* is most frequent at the horticultural societal level because two preconditions are fulfilled: (1) deliberate accumulation of surplus occurs at a level less inclusive than the total group (i.e., individually or familially); and (2) women are important producers. In societies less complex than horticultural ones, deliberate pursuit of noncommunal surplus is not common; in societies more complex, the role of

women in production nosedives (a point we shall explore below).

(b) *Family complexity* is greatest here because it seems fostered by (1) deliberate accumulation of surplus at a level less inclusive than the total group (i.e., same as condition 1 for general polygyny); and (2) absence of a complex class stratification system backed up by the power of the State, which tends to rob families of many of their prerogatives and functions. Blumberg and Winch considered "high complexity" family systems to be either those practicing general polygyny or those having some form of the extended family.[23] Then, using both *Ethnographic Atlas* data for preindustrial societies and contemporary nation-state data for industrializing and industrialized societies, we were able to demonstrate empirically the curvilinear relationship between societal complexity and family complexity.

(c) *Unilineal descent groups* are those in which either one's maternal or paternal relatives are forgotten in the reckoning of kinship and inheritance, depending on whether the system is patrilineal or matrilineal. I suggest that these groups are fostered by basically the same two preconditions that underlie familial complexity, plus one other: the intensification of the population/resource pressure Harner has measured.[24] The curvilinear relationship between unilineal descent and societal complexity long has been posited by anthropologists. This relationship has been shown empirically by Blumberg, Winch, and Reinhardt in whose

21. Lenski and Lenski, *Human Societies,* 1974, p. 200.
22. For example, D. B. Heath, "Sexual Division of Labor and Cross-cultural Research," *Social Forces* 37 (1958):77-79, and my own calculations from the *Ethnographic Atlas* computer tape.
23. Rae Lesser Blumberg and Robert F. Winch, "Societal Complexity and Familial Complexity: Evidence for the Curvilinear Hypothesis," *American Journal of Sociology* 77 (1972):898-920, and 78 (1973): 1522.
24. Harner, "Population Pressure."

Ethnographic Atlas calculations the peak is reached among horticultural groups. These calculations also indicate that descent groups seem to develop more slowly than family complexity.[25] Specifically, among preagricultural societies, descent groups are relatively less frequent than high complexity family systems. Apparently, descent groups emerge when several high complexity extended or polygynous families become bound together so as to better assure that surplus is brought into and kept "all in the family." The "glue" seems to be descent from a common ancestor and inheritance restricted to descent group members.

(d) *Matri-centered family systems* also reach their peak among horticultural groups. Specifically, here we find the highest incidence of three practices, known to anthropologists as: (1) "matrilocal residence," (2) "matrilineal descent," and (3) "matrilineal inheritance." Matrilocal residence means that a young couple goes to live with or near the *bride's* close relatives (i.e., the female doesn't have to leave her home village when she marries). Matrilineal descent means that a child belongs to the kin group of his/her *mother*, and relatives are reckoned to be those to which one is related through the female side. Matrilineal inheritance means that property passes through the *female* side, so that a child never inherits from his/her own father. But even though these practices reach their peak among horticultural groups, still the *majority* of such societies reckon descent, inheritance, and residence on the father's, not the mother's, side.

Nevertheless, because only a small proportion of the world's societies have matri-centered family systems, a brief glance at where the *maximum* concentrations occur seems justified.

Matrilocal residence In my calculations from the *Ethnographic Atlas*, I found that it was societies in the early stages of horticulture that were most likely to have marital residence with the wife's kin. In these so-cieties, the men may still do a fair amount of hunting or fishing, but the women's contribution to horticultural production overwhelmingly makes them the main food-getters in their society. In these "incipient horticultural" groups (Murdock's 1967 classification), I found that forty-and-one-half percent have residence with the wife's kin. But in general, these societies were not far enough along on the path to surplus accumulation to have actual matrilineal descent groups. Rather (as discussed below), it appears that the peak of matrilineal descent occurs among the most dedicatedly horticultural peoples, not societies practicing merely "incipient" horticulture.

As implied earlier in the chapter, there is a controversy in the literature as to what determines matrilocal residence. Worldwide, there is no correlation between female importance in subsistence production and matrilocal residence. But there is such a relationship among North American Indian societies[26] and among hunters and gatherers.[27] Moreover, both Ember and Divale have shown that groups that fight only external wars against other societies are more likely to have matrilocal residence.[28] One day they'll get it all sorted out. Meanwhile, we can say that no matter how it happens, residence with women's close kin *does* favor the female. My own pilot study showed women more likely to gain economic power in societies where they have the option of residing with their own rela-

25. Blumberg, Winch, and Reinhardt, "Family Structure as Adaptive Strategy."

26. Harold E. Driver and William C. Massey, *Comparative Studies of North American Indians*, (Philadelphia: American Philosophical Society, 1957).

27. Carol R. Ember, "Residential Variation Among Hunter-Gatherers" (paper read at meetings of the American Anthropological Association, Toronto, 1972).

28. Divale, "An Explanation for Primitive Warfare," pp. 173-192; Ember and Ember, "Matrilocal versus Patrilocal Residence," pp. 571-594; Ember, "Residential Variation."

tives. Moreover, Schlegal studied a sample of sixty-six matrilineal societies, and found that women are not *necessarily* free and equal in such groups. More often than not, they are under the domination of their husbands (45 percent of the time), or their brothers (33 percent). Thus, in only twenty-two percent of the cases (14 out of 64 societies) was a woman not dominated by a male. Significantly, however, in not a single one of those cases did the wife lack some (or total) control of family property, and in seventy-one percent of those cases, the woman resided with her *own* close kin.[29] In short, Schlegal's findings back up my own. Matrilocal residence is associated with greater female equality because it helps women gain control over property.

Matrilineal descent Also using the *Ethnographic Atlas*, Lenski found that the maximum incidence of matrilineality occurs among societies *most* dependent on horticulture—specifically, those that depend on supplementary hunting and/or herding for less than fifteen percent of their diet. Among such societies, thirty-nine percent are matrilineal.[30]

To put the above figures in perspective, the worldwide *Ethnographic Atlas* data show that matrilocality occurs in only sixteen percent of societies, and matrilineality in a mere fourteen percent. And in general, as we have noted, matri-centered kin institutions tend to be more favorable for women's position.

Before going on to the potentially depressing topic of traditional agrarian societies (depressing if you are in favor of human liberty and sexual equality), we should note one last thing about horticultural societies: their *fertility patterns*. With the increased sedentism permitted by horticulture, population began to grow by leaps and bounds, at least initially. It became less inconvenient for a woman to do her work with more than one child under age four. At the same time, it often became more convenient for both sexes to have more children: wom-

en could use their offspring, especially their daughters, to help them in the garden plots; men could use their sons for political allies, and their daughters to bring in a bride price and perhaps more political allies. So family size was definitely up over that of hunters and gatherers. But horticulturalists were still compelled to make sure that large family size did not so debilitate and hinder women that their production (and their surplus production) would be adversely affected. The solution adopted by such groups practicing general polygyny tended—and tends—to be long taboos on sexual intercourse after the birth of a child, combined with prolonged nursing, apparently assuring a fairly long spacing between children (approximately three years, although the evidence is not exact). Recent findings indicate that polygynously married women tend to have fewer, more widely spaced children than their monogamously married counterparts in agricultural societies.[31] In short, women in horticultural groups tend to be valued as producers of material goods as well as for their role as baby machines.

AGRARIAN SOCIETIES

If you believe in reincarnation, hope that you will never come back as a peasant in a traditional agrarian society—worse yet, as a woman in such a group!

Technically, agrarian societies make use of the *plow* rather than the hoe or digging stick. The Latin origin of the two words "horticulture" and "agriculture" provides a big clue to one essential difference between them.[32] *Horti* means garden; *agri* means field. Horticulture is done on small-scale

29. Schlegal, *Male Dominance and Female Autonomy.*

30. Lenski, *Human Societies,* 1970, p. 221.

31. American Association for the Advancement of Science, *Culture and Population Change* (Washington, D. C.: American Association for the Advancement of Science, 1974), p. 32.

32. Lenski and Lenski, *Human Societies,* p. 207.

garden plots whereas agriculture requires larger fields; it is "land-extensive." Relative to horticulture, agriculture requires less labor per unit of land; however, agarian societies have many more people. So even though agrarianism can produce a higher total yield and support many more people, fewer of them are needed to work a unit of cultivated land. This is a classic situation for both the intensification of stratification and the creation of a class of *surplus* laborers, and both occur among many agrarian groups.

Of course, the march to "civilization" continues. Agrarian societies are not only able to free more people from direct production of their food, they also are more likely to have urban centers, writing, and a "High Culture"—in which only a tiny fraction of the population participates. Although only a few agrarian societies grew so mighty, the ancient empires of Egypt, Persia, Rome, and China were all agrarian-based. Agrarian societies are overwhelmingly characterized by a small ruling class (less than one percent of the population, on the average) that usually believes in squeezing the last drop out of its peasantry, and by men who usually believe in squeezing the last child out of their women. After all, given the surplus population, both worn out peasants and wives can be replaced.

Let us attack these topics in turn: the concentration of surplus and political power in the hands of the tiny ruling class, and the concentration of relative sexual power in the hands of the males.

Childe has characterized the emergence of plow agrarian societies as the second great social revolution of the human race (the first was the emergence of horticultural societies).[33] From the archeological record, it appears that plow agriculture emerged between 5,000 and 6,000 years ago in the Middle East and spread slowly. By the end of the fifteenth century A.D., according to Lenski, agrarian societies had become established in most of Europe, North Africa, the

Middle East, and South and East Asia.[34] And it was an agrarian system that the Europeans brought to the New World.

Under agrarianism, because both total output and the pace of surplus extraction average much higher than under horticulture, sizeable cities in which the people do not produce their own food become possible. In traditional agrarian societies, the ruler and governing class tended to reside in the cities,[35] along with the servants, soldiers, artisans, and priests who function as retainers to the elite. (Urban population averaged under ten percent of the total in classic agrarian societies, and men outnumbered women about two to one because of sex-selective migration. Moreover, the cities of traditional agrarian societies were notoriously unhealthy places that had much higher death rates than rural areas.) The masses continued to live on the land and produce food for themselves and everyone else. But they had been converted to *peasants*.

One of the components of a definition of "peasant" is that he/she (usually he, as we shall see) pays what the economists call "rent."[36] What this means is rip-off. According to Wolf, peasants have four claims against what they produce: (1) basic sustenance; (2) replacement fund (what they need in seeds, fertilizer, and new equipment to plant another crop the following year); (3) ceremonial fund (feasts, funerals, weddings, religious rites, etc.); and (4) "rent" — the proportion of the crop that is taken by those to whom the peasant is in thrall. The last two are surplus. If the peasant doesn't put aside enough for basic sustenance and replacement fund needs, hardship and even starvation can follow in short order. Unfortu-

33. Gordon V. Childe, *Man Makes Himself* (London: Watts, 1936).

34. Lenski, *Power and Privilege*, p. 189.

35. Gideon Sjoberg, *The Pre-industrial City* (New York: Free Press, 1960).

36. *See* Eric Wolf, *Peasants* (Englewood Cliffs, N. J.: Prentice-Hall, 1966), pp. 9-10.

nately, even though the peasant's priority of needs goes from (1) down to (4), it is (4)—"rent" typically amounting to one-half the crop—that is subtracted from his output first. And it comes off the top. But the ruling class couldn't care less, by and large, if the peasants are squeezed. Except for brief periods after wars, disasters, and plagues (agrarian societies are marked by higher rates of all of these than preceding systems), peasants are always in oversupply. And the ruling class has developed what Lenski terms the "proprietary theory of the state," one of whose tenets is that peasants are not quite human anyway.[37] Lenski documents that in medieval England the word for a peasant's children was *sequela*, meaning "litter" or "brood;" the word for human offspring was *familia*. Furthermore, estate records in Europe, Asia, and post-conquest America often listed the peasants with the livestock.[38]

Lenski traces back the proprietary theory of the state—"in which the state is a piece of property which its owners may use, within rather broad and ill-defined limits, for their personal advantage"[39] to the practice that emerged among horticultural societies of turning over at least part of surplus production to the leader. The leader made use of the surplus as trustee of the group—throwing feasts to which neighboring groups would be invited in good times, redistributing it to group members in periods of hardship. The leader won prestige and greater political influence for his generosity, but had no real power so long as the surplus was not very large. Once, however, it was large enough to free himself and a staff of dependent retainers from productive work while they functioned as "middlemen," the situation began to change. For the leader could use his staff to enforce *his* wishes, and also to drum up a larger amount of surplus. Some of the surplus ended up in the leader's hands, to be used to serve *his* ends. Thus was born the proprietary

theory of the state that was greatly expanded on by later rulers.

It is estimated that the ruler and the ruling class—generally around one percent of the population—received *at least half* (and sometimes up to two-thirds) of the *total income* in the average traditional agrarian group.[40] Their main assets were (1) land; and (2) political office, which was used strictly for personal gain. Of the two, land was economically the more important.

Even today, enormous concentrations of land are to be found in the hands of the top one or two percent in currently underdeveloped societies with an agrarian base. In Chile, prior to the land reforms of the Christian Democratic Frei and Marxist Allende governments, 1.4 percent of the population owned sixty-three percent of the arable land. In South Viet Nam, as U.S. involvement to "save the people from Communism" began to grow (1965), 2.5 percent owned fifty percent of the arable land. Similarly, in Lebanon, a microscopic 0.2 percent of the population owns one-half the cultivable land.[41] In most cases, the largest part of the remaining arable land is not controlled by the peasants either, but is under de jure (legal) or de facto (might as well be legal) control of a small group of landlords and wealthy peasants.

Squeezed from all sides, how did—and do —peasants react? It would appear that, in both traditional and contemporary societies with an agrarian base, peasants often view only one possible solution to the problem of their poverty: having enough sons to try to get ahead of the squeeze. In other words, of the three main factors of production— land, capital, and labor—the peasant tends to have more control over the latter, and then only by growing his own labor force

37. Lenski, *Power and Privilege*, pp. 214-219.
38. Lenski, *Human Societies*, 1970, pp. 270-271.
39. Lenski, *Power and Privilege*, p. 214.
40. Ibid., p. 228.
41. All figures cited from Lenski, *Human Societies*, 1970, p. 266.

so as to cut labor costs. (In several places, Lenski recognizes that peasants need large families because of the children's labor, but he still writes: "barring an effective method of controlling fertility, which no agrarian society ever discovered," there is no way of avoiding a class of surplus labor.[42] I propose that it wasn't ignorance of contraception, but need for children to survive the greed of the governing class, that produced the large families. And it was the greed of the governing class that drove a portion of peasant children into what Lenski terms the "expendables" class each generation.[43]) As we shall examine below, the predominant labor force in plow agrarian societies is male, so it is sons who are wanted. With hard-working sons (and peasant children can start to earn more than their keep as early as age six; childhood is short among the oppressed), a peasant might be able to cultivate more land, or raise a larger crop. With a few good years, he might be able to acquire additional land, so that his extra sons would not face a bleak and landless future when he died. In short, in Mamdani's words, peasants "are not poor because they have large families. Quite the contrary, they have large families because they are poor."[44] We should be aware, however, that even though having a large family is rational from the standpoint of the *individual* peasant, it clearly does harm to the position of peasants as a *class*. The excess peasants undermine *all* peasants' bargaining power.

Since women tend not to be productive in the main tasks of agrarian production, they can be used—and used up—as virtually nonstop breeding machines (high infant mortality, sometimes half of all live births, makes this even more necessary if high family size is to be achieved). So in agrarian groups, the spacing interval is short, averaging perhaps two years.[45] Polygyny is all but nonexistent among the poor cultivators (in some agrarian societies, the wealthy might maintain more than one wife for the status

and sexual pleasure of it); rather, female infanticide and male-oriented child nutrition and health care are not uncommon. Life tends to be so hard for the masses in most agrarian societies, however, that the death rate—especially the infant death rate among these poorly nourished people—usually approaches the higher birth rate.

Historically, until the mixed blessings of the world market economy and Western death control (mainly of infant mortality) hit them, traditional agrarian societies grew rather slowly. In fact, today's "population explosion" stems in part from the fact that the social structure of most of the world's agrarian societies has not changed much—it's often as oppressive as ever. Many people remain motivated to have large families in order to survive. But to their countries, enmeshed in a world economy—and usually on very unfavorable terms—each new mouth means more expenditure than return.[46]

---

42. Lenski, *Power and Privilege*, p. 295.
43. Ibid., pp. 281-284. As mentioned on p. 27, he estimates this class (e.g., beggars, thieves, whores, coolies) as five to fifteen percent of the population. Their conditions were so miserable they rarely reproduced enough to replace themselves. But every generation, their numbers were replenished by excess sons and daughters of the peasants—those whom the dominant classes precluded from becoming peasants themselves lest elite strove to extract.
44. Mahmood Mamdani, *The Myth of Population Control: Family, Caste, and Class in an Indian Village* (New York: Monthly Review Press, 1972), p. 14.
45. Steven Polgar, "Population History and Population Policies from an Anthropological Perspective," *Current Anthropology* 13 (1972):203-211.
46. Stephen Enke, "The Gains to India from Population Control: Some Money Measures and Incentive Schemes," *Review of Economics and Statistics* 42, 3 (May 1960):175-180, was the first to show the draining effect of children on poor Third World countries. But for evidence that fertility decline is substantially related to greater equality in income distribution in these countries *see* William Rich, *Smaller Families Through Social*

Before going into the generally sorry condition of women under agrarianism, let us gain an overview of what has happened to the stratification, political complexity, warfare, and kinship systems of agrarian societies in comparison with horticultural societies. In brief, the first three are up, and the last is starting to decline.

Stratification Here the big news is the emergence of complex systems of class stratification in which, rather than merely a dual system of commoners and a noble ruling class, we now find *three or more* social classes among the nonslave population. In the 1170-society computer version of the *Ethnographic Atlas*, less than two percent of the pre-plow cultivating societies have a stratification system with three or more classes. In contrast, over twenty-eight percent of the agrarian societies have developed such a complex class system. What are these classes? Lenski identifies the following groups (which he considers classes) in the larger traditional agrarian societies: governing class (of which the ruler was sometimes so rich and powerful as to practically constitute a class apart); retainers (officials, soldiers, servants) and priests; merchants; artisans; peasants; "unclean" or degraded classes; and the "expendables." The overwhelming majority, of course, are peasants. In the discussion of these classes below, I rely heavily on Lenski's[47] cogent arguments and insights, although with somewhat different emphases and objectives.

In most agrarian societies, there was a continual seesaw of power within the *governing class*—between the ruler and the nobles. Lenski considers this a continuum that ranged from autocracy on one end (the ruler governs as a total despot) to feudalism on the other[48] (where the nobles hold sway, often fighting among themselves, and the ruler is lucky to be considered "first among equals"). Success in wars, the administration of state irrigation works, eliminating rivals to the throne—these were factors that strengthened the hand of the ruler. The factors that enhanced the grip of the feudal nobility included poor transportation and communication, an inheritance rule that favored the first-born son and thus prevented the break-up of large estates, and the habit of fighting its own wars rather than hiring mercenaries. But, as Lenski concludes, "the outcomes of all the countless struggles between rulers and their governing classes had almost no effect on the living conditions of the common people, except as these struggles sometimes led to violence and destroyed their very livelihood" (emphasis deleted).[49] Peasants rarely lived to see their crops burned two years in a row.

47. Lenski, *Power and Privilege,* pp. 189-266.

48. Historically and geographically these two processes tended to reach their extremes in two different parts of the world. The despotism end of the scale is usually associated with Asia—especially with the irrigated agrarian states, beginning with Mesopotamia (after 3,000 B.C.) and continuing through traditional India, China, and Southeast Asia. Opposing theses regarding the importance of state-aided irrigation works in promoting this "oriental despotism" are to be found in the works of Karl Wittfogel, *Oriental Despotism, A Comparative Study of Total Power* (New Haven: Yale Univ. Press, 1964), who expands Marx's argument that irrigation was a major determinant of autocracy, versus Robert M. Adams, *The Evolution of Urban Society: Early Mesopotamia to Prehispanic Mexico* (Chicago: Aldine, 1966), who discounts irrigation as determinative. The feudalism end of the scale reached its height centuries later in Europe and Japan, precisely the countries where industrialism first flowered. Because of the Eurocentric bias of so much of what we learn as "world history," most of us are more familiar with feudalism. The definitive work on European feudalism is that of Marc Bloch, *Feudal Society,* translated by L. A. Manyon (Chicago: Univ. of Chicago Press, 1962).

49. Lenski, *Power and Privilege,* p. 241.

and Economic Progress (Washington, D. C.: Overseas Development Council, 1973) Monograph no. 7; James E. Kocher, *Rural Development, Income Distribution and Fertility Decline* (New York: The Population Council, 1973); and World Bank Staff, *Population Policies and Economic Development* (Baltimore: Johns Hopkins Press, 1974).

The main thing of interest about the *retainer class* is the basis of their rewards. The more difficult it was to replace them, the higher their rewards. Thus, those with more ability, rare talent, or extensive training received more. As we shall see in the next chapter, this is the alleged basis for the distribution of rewards as posited by the "functionalist" theorists. But the "functionalists" claim that individuals are rewarded for service to "society." What these retainers were rewarded for was service to the *elite*.[50] And what was good for the elite often spelled trouble for the masses.

Merchants were a new and rising class in agrarian society. In most of these societies the ruling class deliberately tried to keep them near the bottom of the *prestige* system as part of their not-always-successful efforts to control them. But they needed their economic services. As Lenski points out, even though merchants remained subject to the *political* authority of the governing class, when it came to the economic sphere, the relationship between merchants and elite was a *market* relationship, not an authority one.[51] The ruling classes of different agrarian societies had varying degrees of success in curbing the rising power of the merchants without killing the goose that had begun laying such nice golden eggs. Merchants had special expertise; and too much confiscation, trade regulation, or naked coercion could wipe out the merchant class—and then who would replace them? Merchants also were useful because through the taxes the ruling class placed on their goods, part of the responsibility—and *blame*—for extracting surplus from the common people was shifted away from the governing class onto the merchant's more vulnerable shoulders. In fact, merchants were often from minority ethnic groups (e.g., Jews), making them even more convenient as scapegoats.[52] In Asia (e.g., agrarian Japan, China, India) merchants were less successful in their struggles against the ruling class than in Europe, where in the rising towns and cities they were eventually able to *become* the ruling class.

Artisans, "unclean" classes, and the "expendables" (the latter's plight we have already reviewed on p. 27 and in note 43, p. 46) often share one thing in agrarian societies: initial recruitment from the excess landless and non-inheriting peasants. The artisans were the best off of the lot, but not very much so. And because of the hard living conditions, and high death rates in the towns, many of their ranks were opened each generation to newly sluffed-off members of the peasantry. For the bottom two groups, the "unclean" and the "expendables," life was often what Hobbes had incorrectly imagined as the "state of nature"—solitary, poor, nasty, brutish, and short.

In fact, for *all* classes in traditional agrarian societies, there was considerably more *downward mobility* than the upward variety usually studied by many U.S. sociologists. These societies expanded slowly, and were in a condition Lenski terms "technostasis." In other words, inventions and technological advances came very slowly. One reason for that, of course, is that expertise and incentive had been divorced. What good is it for a peasant to build a better plow or an artisan to build a better mousetrap if all they achieve is a higher level of rip-off to compensate for their higher level of productivity? And the ruling class had no knowledge whatsoever about things so mundane as plows and mousetraps. Since children provided a great deal of positive benefits for *all* classes (labor, old age security in a system without welfare, political alliances, etc.), they proceeded to produce more offspring than there were status vacancies. Hence the net downward flow ending in the "expendables"—and starvation.

Political complexity Here the important development was the emergence of the full-

50. Ibid., p. 247.
51. Ibid., p. 250.
52. Ibid., pp. 252, 256.

fledged state. In the state, we find three or even four layers of jurisdictional hierarchy beyond the village (e.g., parish, district, province, national state). Only around five percent of recent horticultural societies have reached this level of political development; in contrast, it occurs in approximately twenty-eight percent of the cases among recent agrarian societies.[53] Even so, however, among the type of society representing the highest level of inequality in human evolutionary history, there are bright spots. For example, nearly a quarter of the agrarian societies in the full *Ethnographic Atlas* still have autonomous villages—that is, *no* political complexity. And more than a quarter still have a *total* absence of stratification —that is, not even wealth distinctions. So there are many roads to progress, and not all of them lead to the complex, class-stratified state. Undoubtedly, many of these "unusually egalitarian" agrarian societies are living in less than lush habitats (e.g., the Pitcairn Islanders, descendents of the famed "Mutiny on the *Bounty*," who struggle to raise potatoes and a few other crops from the harsh soil of their domain; they have remained egalitarian). In other cases, perhaps it is a matter of the people *not striving* to maximize *noncommunal* surplus—the road to inequality.[54]

Warfare In most traditional agrarian societies, especially the larger, state-organized ones, warfare was endemic; peace was rare. For example, Sorokin's massive survey of hundreds of years of history among eleven European agrarian countries in their preindustrial days[55] reveals that the general average was to be involved in a war nearly *every second year*. In addition to external wars, agrarian societies were frequently wracked by two types of *internal* conflict: (1) uprisings among members of the *governing class* (e.g., between contending nobles, or attempts to depose the current ruler—a very profitable business since the ruler's income sometimes exceeded that of the remainder of the governing class combined);[56] and (2)

frequent rebellions among the *peasants*. The latter type of conflict is less well known, since our medieval history stems from sources left by the ruling class, and depicts the peasantry as a stolid, peaceful sort. Lenski summarizes the situation nicely:

> Because of a tendency to romanticize the past, many people today are unaware of the frequency of both internal and external conflict in the great agrarian empires. In Rome, for example, 31 of the 79 emperors from Augustus to Romulus Augustulus were murdered, six were driven to suicide, four were forcibly deposed, and several more met unknown fates at the hands of internal enemies. . . . Peasant risings were another source of internal stress. One expert states that "there were peasant rebellions almost every year in China," and an authority on Russia reports that in the short period from 1801 to 1861 there were no less than 1,467 peasant risings in various parts of that country. Though most of these risings remained local actions, it was only because authorities acted swiftly and ruthlessly. Had they not, many would have spread as widely as the famous English Revolt of 1381 or the German Peasants' War of 1524-1525.[57]

Paradoxically, *if* the ruling class frequently had to call peasants to arms, and *if* the peasants' basic equipment and military skills were not notably inferior to that of the professional soldiers, then peasants

53. Calculations in this section are based on my computations from the 1170-society computer version of the *Ethnographic Atlas*.

54. *See also* Wolf, *Peasants*, pp. 6-10.

55. Pitirim A. Sorokin, *Social and Cultural Dynamics* (New York: Bedminster Press, 1962). First published 1937.

56. Lenski, in *Power and Privilege*, p. 212, notes that the average yearly income of the English kings by the end of the 14th century amounted to "85 percent of the combined incomes of the nearly 2,200 members of the nobility and squirearchy"— and that English kings' incomes were small potatoes compared to rulers of greater states (e.g., early Persia, Turkey, and India).

57. Lenski, *Human Societies*, 1970, pp. 257-258.

were likely to be less exploited politically and economically.[58] Otherwise, only sudden depopulations by plague and war, and the "abundant land vs. scarce labor" conditions of a frontier offered short-lived improvement in the lives of the common peasants.

Kinship Concomitant with the rise of complex class stratification and the large state, the prerogatives of the corporate kinship groups tended to be usurped. People might still uphold the ideal of the close-knit extended family and the clan, but the scope of their economic and political powers became increasingly constricted. Part of this has to do with the greater *individuation of property rights*—no longer was the corporate family holding the admission ticket to "the only game in town."

At any rate, for the *common people*, poverty, small landholdings, and the demographic consequences of high rates of disease and low life expectancy, all combined to make *residence* within an extended family household rare. Among the poor peasants, most households were nuclear.[59] Furthermore, since they had so little property to protect corporately or otherwise, the clans or descent groups among the poor were not very powerful in their lives either—especially in comparison to the elite.

And for the society in general, it becomes somewhat less likely to find a *system* of extended familism, or corporate unilineal descent, among agrarian societies than among horticultural ones. In fact, these results are much clearer if we divide agrarian societies into two groups: those who rely on *dry* plow agriculture, often in combination with large animal husbandry, and those who practice a system of *permanent irrigation*. Among the latter, the classic example is wet or paddy rice. We then see that the irrigationist agrarian groups (which, incidentally, are the most likely to have the full-fledged State) have even lower rates of extended familism and corporate unilineal descent than the dry agrarian-based societies.[60] Moreover, this distinction into dry and wet

agrarian societies proves very useful in our next topic, women's reduced position in production and all aspects of power and status.

The Fate of Women in Agrarian Societies

As shown in Michaelson and Goldschmidt's study of forty-six peasant societies, female subjugation proved invariably high.[61] Moreover, in comparison with previous modes of subsistence, women are conspicuous by their lack of importance in agrarian production. Their role in production declined, I suggest, for two major reasons. First, as noted previously, *agri*culture means field cultivation whereas *horti*culture involves garden plots. Moreover, agriculture, as practiced, is much more likely to be combined with large animal husbandry. Often, in fact, large draft animals are used to pull the heavy plows. So in terms of compatibility with simultaneous childcare responsibilities, the main activities of agrarian society provide definite problems for women. Specifically, fields may be farther away from hearth and home, the large animals are mobile, the plows do benefit from heavier muscles, and the larger-scale nature of agricultural production means that work schedules and conditions are less easily arranged so as to be able to bring the baby, or interrupt the work to care for the child once one is in the fields.

Second, and more important, I propose, are the changes related to the emergence of

58. Lenski, *Power and Privilege*, p. 275.

59. Rae Lesser Blumberg and Robert F. Winch, "The Rise and Fall of the Complex Family: Some Implications for an Evolutionary Theory of Societal Development," (paper read at the meetings of the American Sociological Association, New York, 1973).

60. Blumberg and Winch, "Societal Complexity and Familial Complexity," 1972.

61. Evalyn Jacobson Michaelson and Walter Goldschmidt, "Female Roles and Male Dominance Among Peasants," *Southwestern Journal of Anthropology* 27 (1971):330-352.

a surplus labor force. In the first place, dry agrarian production is less labor-intensive per unit of area than horticulture, and it must support many more mouths. So there is likely to be a shortage of jobs—one of the reasons already proposed as a factor in squeezing women out of production. With more hungry men competing for work, woman's lower compatibility would count against her. To get agricultural employment, she would have to accept a lower and lower fraction of the returns given to men. In fact, Sullerot reports findings concerning women's shrinking agricultural earnings in agrarian Europe: in the twelfth century, female remuneration was approximately eighty percent that of males; by the fifteenth century, no more than half; by the sixteenth, only about forty percent the male rate.[62] And since in agrarian societies most people work not as individuals but as members of families, family heads would be acting queerly if they sent out a female member for scarce work when a male member could be better rewarded.

The surplus labor population emerged, it has been proposed, because of the peasants' attempts to cash in on their children's labor so as to try to get ahead of the rip-off demanded by a rapacious ruling class. And since women, of course, would have to be producing those extra children, their mobility and ability as agrarian producers would be further reduced. It's tough enough getting back and forth to the fields with only one tot, let alone two or even three under five or six years of age.

This does not mean that peasant girls and women are idle. Far from it. They are needed in the agricultural peak seasons of planting and harvesting—along with most other able-bodied people in the neighborhood. For dry agrarian production tends to be highly seasonal in its labor needs. And it is very convenient for those who profit from it to have a surplus labor force of underemployed bodies who can be pressed into service during peak production periods, and

then forgotten about during the rest of the year. Many male landless and noninheriting peasants fall into this unenviable category, too. In addition, the women are needed for a host of *processing* tasks connected with subsistence—preparing food, clothing, certain equipment—as well as the greatly expanded childcare responsibilities occasioned by higher fertility and closer spacing. Probably for these reasons, peasant women in agrarian societies have long been noted to be relatively less oppressed by their menfolk than more idle women in more favored economic circumstances within the same society.

Furthermore, if the basis of the economy is wet rice, there is a very good chance that the role of women in production will be higher. This is because of the enormous labor demands involved in growing rice by the paddy method. The transplanting of seedlings by hand, for example, is a tremendously time-consuming and labor-intensive operation that frequently falls to women in wet rice areas. The position of women tends to be generally better under wet rice systems than under dry plow agriculture, presumably at least in part because of their greater role in production.[63] In some wet rice societies (e.g., Indonesia, Philippines, Burma), women have managed to follow the same route as their sisters in West African horticultural societies and become very important in market trade. Thus, they dispose of surplus production, often on their own account. Where that happens, their position may be quite strong—as indeed it is in the three societies mentioned. Indonesia is particularly interesting because it has had two especially patriarchal religions over the last few hundred years. A long-established Hindu religious system was supplanted by

62. Evelyne Sullerot, *Woman, Society and Change* (London: World University Library, 1971), p. 35.
63. Ester Boserup, *The Role of Women in Economic Development* (New York: St. Martin's, 1970).

centuries of Islam. But in those regions where women have long been active in rice cultivation and trade, neither religion was able to reduce the status of Indonesian women to the average level found in the dry agrarian regions that make up the heartlands of both Hinduism and Islam.[64]

Despite such bright spots, however, agrarian societies tend to oppress women sexually, economically, legally, politically, and religiously. And as Lomax et al. ingeniously demonstrate, the women are oppressed even musically: in contrast to females' clear, relaxed, harmonious singing in societies where their productivity and status are high, these unproductive, male-dominated women sing in a nasal, narrow voice.[65] Sexually, virginity is typically required and the negative sanctions for nonmarital sex of any kind can be horrendous for the woman. She is breeding children for a male-dominated family group, and any suspicions concerning paternity would be very awkward where there was property to be transmitted. For this reason, sexual mores among the poorer peasants tend to be somewhat freer in such societies. Economically, even where women help out in production, their labor and its product are rarely under their control in the dry agrarian regions. Legally, they tend to be treated as *minors*, and handed over from the jurisdiction of their fathers to that of their husbands. Politically, they almost invariably have no role, except in certain cases among royal families where there is no male heir and keeping power in the family overrides mores on sexual roles. Religiously, agrarian societies are the cradles of the world's great—and patriarchal—religions. Islam, and to a lesser extent Hinduism, have come in for special attention in this regard. It has often been alleged that a sexually oppressive religion plays an independent role in explaining women's low status in the Middle East, India, Pakistan, and thereabouts.[66] To date, however, no one has attempted to sort out the influence of type of techno-economic base (e.g., dry vs. wet agrarian)

from that of religion. The Indonesian example makes it clear that this must be done before any conclusions about religion, per se, can be advanced.

One final topic: since agrarian societies are for the most part *class* societies—specifically, seventy-one percent of them, according to Lenski's calculations from the *Ethnographic Atlas*[67]—we must examine the position of women in the various classes. As we go up the social scale from the peasantry, we find that women have even less of an economic role, and it is here, among the nonrural, nonpoor women of agrarian societies that we find the world's strictest and most bizarre practices of *female seclusion*. Veils, foot-binding, *purdah* (where a woman is not allowed out of the house, by and large), *suttee,* involving widows flinging themselves atop their husbands' funeral pyres (partly because their subsequent life with his kin would be even worse)—all these abound among classes in agrarian societies just well off enough to be able to conspicuously do without the labor of their women. Consequently, as we go up the class system we find a greater and greater gap between the position of women and the men of their class. A woman in the urban elite may outrank all peasants of either sex, and possibly even have the power to have a hapless peasant or servant summarily executed should he displease her—but still spend her life as a caged bird. At this level, too, men could afford more than one wife, whether legally as in Islam or informally as in the widespread system of concubinage and mis-

64. Cora Vreede-de Stuers, "Indonesia," in *Women in the Modern World*, ed. Raphael Patai (New York: Free Press, 1967).

65. Alan Lomax et al., *Folk Song Style and Culture* (Washington, D. C.: American Association for the Advancement of Science, 1968), pp. 164-169, 194-198.

66. This has been suggested even by Roserup, *The Role of Women*, 1970, despite her generally materialist orientation.

67. Lenski, *Human Societies*, p. 137.

tresses. So sometimes for women even to hold onto the crumbs they received by virtue of their *class* (not sexual!) position, they had to engage in harem politics or other behind-the-scenes attempts to wield influence by the classic ploys of the powerless, from flattery to bitchiness. Additionally, an elite woman, if she bore many sons, might see them rise, and her position improve as a result. So it was to her advantage to have many children. They were her best route to immediate prestige and possible future status.

It is probably significant for the understanding of the prevalent ideology about women and the position of women in today's industrial societies, to remember that all such societies sprang from an agrarian base. The rise of these societies is the topic of Chapter 5.

For Further Reading

Boserup, Ester. *The Conditions of Agricultural Growth: The Economics of Agrarian Change Under Population Pressure.* Chicago: Aldine, 1965.

An important work arguing the role of population pressure in causing each rise in the intensity of cultivation.

Lenski, Gerhard E., and Lenski, Jean. *Human Societies.* 2nd ed. New York: McGraw-Hill, 1974.

The only major sociology text that takes an evolutionary materialist (but non-Marxian) approach. The authors present a broad, empirically documented panorama of human history.

Michaelson, Evalyn J., and Goldschmidt, Walter. "Female Roles and Male Dominance Among Peasants." *Southwestern Journal of Anthropolgy* 27 (1971):330-352.

All the empirical documentation you would ever want to make you thankful that you are not a peasant woman.

Vayda, Andrew, ed. *Environment and Cultural Behavior.* Garden City, N. Y.: The Natural History Press, 1969.

A good collection of articles emphasizing the role of environment in which horticultural groups are frequently featured.

Wolf, Eric. *Peasants.* Englewood Cliffs, N. J.: Prentice-Hall, 1966.

A short, but classic, work on peasants.

5 From Exploration to Exploitation: The Rise of Capitalism, Industrial Development, and Underdevelopment

THUS far, I have spoken of agrarian societies as the low point of inequality, hard work, poor nutrition, and general misery for the masses (not to speak of the debased position of the women of all classes). This might imply that the rest of our story is going to be all about increasing liberty, well-being, and the pursuit of happiness as we explore the beginnings of industrial society. After all, we would not be sitting in a college or university, striving for or already possessing a white collar job ticket to some modest corner of the American Dream, if this were an agrarian society still. (The odds against this would be better than 95 to 5, based on the ratio of have-nots to haves in traditional preindustrial societies.)

But there is a whole new gulf of human suffering to be crossed, as we trace the origins first of capitalism (for that arose before the Industrial Revolution) and then of industrialism. Under agrarianism, people, so long as they remained serfs or small peasant farmers under a feudal system, were more or less bound to the land. They may not have owned it, but so long as they paid their dues in required labor days to the lord, or share of the crop to the landlord or tax-collector, they had some assurance of a certain place (humble though it may be) in the sun.

Under capitalist industrialism, however, both *land* and *labor* were turned into *com-*

modities. Actually, it took several hundred years for this transformation,[1] which began around 1500, but during that time: (1) *land* was turned into a commodity that could be freely bought or sold (this was much more difficult in agrarian societies, and often it was easier to conquer land than buy it); (2) *labor* was turned into a commodity also. People no longer had "rights" to try to earn a living off some little tract of land because they had always "belonged" to the place. During the course of the rise of capitalism in England, for example, *most* of the peasantry were uprooted and pushed off the land into the towns. The constant trickle of "expendables" from the land to the urban settlements that had characterized agrarian society became a flood in the early days of capitalism in *all* the affected countries. In the towns and cities, the labor restrictions of the medieval guilds were crumbling also. Lacking land, capital, or valuable tools, the only thing the peasant had left to sell was his or her own body—that is, his or her *laborpower*—for the best price that could be gotten. That price is called a wage, and the wage bargain is characterized as voluntary on both sides. The employer took on no long-term obligation to look after the person in times of hardship or sickness (not

1. *See,* e.g., Karl Polanyi, *The Great Transformation* (New York: Rinehart, 1944.)

that much of that had been done by agrarian lords), and the laborer was theoretically free to sell that laborpower elsewhere—if a buyer could be found.

Since there were many more laborers looking for work (and having to accept *some* sort of job, or starve) than potential employers, guess who came out on top in that "voluntary" exchange? In England, home of the world's first Industrial Revolution, things got so bad that those actually able to find a job worked twelve- or fourteen-hour days for barely enough to sustain life, and sent even their small children (often starting as young as six) into the dangerous and deadening toil of the factories and mines.[2] In fact, this story has been repeated many times as other countries industrialized. The Industrial Revolution emerged, in part, off the common people's backs. But it emerged from other changes in commercial relations, colonization, and technology as well, and that is the side you more often read about in history books. Just what were the main factors leading to the birth of this new mode of production? A brief survey is in order.

First, we should note that the Industrial Revolution was the first major breakthrough to originate in northwest Europe, rather than the Middle East. For the most part, as Lenski also argues, Europe could be classed as a backwater of human progress until about the beginning of the sixteenth century. By that time, *trade* was becoming a lively enterprise. A rising class of *merchants and manufacturers* reversed the medieval division of labor between different corporate guilds by introducing division of labor into a single workshop and fabricating finished products such as textiles virtually from scratch. And they began to expand their trade even into foreign areas in response to rising demand. Additionally, the often anarchic political system of feudalism was giving way to rising centralized power—*nations* were being born. The centralized governments sought to encourage trade and the revenues it generated, but in a regulated, state-directed way that is termed *mercantilism*. (Under mercantilism, the state grants monopolies and intervenes in all possible phases of commercial activity.) The period of mercantilism extended from the sixteenth through the eighteenth centuries, peaking in the seventeenth. The aims of the mercantilist states were two: profit and power.[3] These goals produced exploration, rivalry over control of sea lanes and profitable trading areas—and chronic warfare, piracy, and plundering. Leadership passed quickly from

2. The full story is told, in poignant but scholarly tones, by E. P. Thompson in his classic, *The Making of the English Working Class* (New York: Random House, 1964). A vicious cycle was created: the surplus of "free" labor drove down wages so that the employed worked longer for less, thus further reducing the number of jobs ("100,000 weavers doing the work of 150,000" is how Thompson [p. 280] characterizes the crux of the problem). Employers further reduced the cost of "free" labor by displacing adult males with lower-paid women and children wherever possible. In the 1830s, Thompson documents (pp. 308-309), the labor force in English textile factories—the core industry of the early Industrial Revolution—was over half women and children. Conservative economic historians have played down such facts and have tried to make a case that living standards rose for the masses during the formative years of the Industrial Revolution. Thompson's exhaustive and brilliant research (pp. 189-447) forces him to reject this upbeat view. His own more harsh conclusion is that the Industrial Revolution was indeed "cataclysmic" for the populace. In short, "between 1780 and 1840 the people of Britain suffered an experience of immiseration, even if it is possible to show a small statistical improvement in material conditions" (pp. 444-445).

3. Douglas F. Dowd, *The Twisted Dream: Capitalist Development in the United States since 1776* (Cambridge, Mass.: Winthrop, 1974), p. 7. Wallerstein has a different view of mercantilism. He sees it as a strategy of semi-withdrawal from the emerging capitalist world market that was pursued most vigorously by the not-quite-leading nations as a method of catching up with the then-current front-running power—*See* Immanuel Wallerstein, "The Rise and Future Demise of the World Capitalist System: Concepts for Comparative Analysis," *Comparative Studies in Society and History* 16 (1974):387-415.

the Spanish to the Dutch (in the seventeenth century); then Britain and France took over the center stage as full-fledged colonial powers. The Age of Exploration tended to be financed by mercantilist governments (e.g., Portugal) that initially were more interested in trade than territory. Large and profitable trading operations were set up in the East Indies (e.g., the spice trade) and West Africa—where human beings were the commodity that were captured, bought, and sold. But by 1533, the biggest prize in European history had been won: the New World had been conquered, with the collapse of its two largest and richest empires, the Aztecs and the Incas.

Gold and silver (at first stolen from the Indians, and then sweated out from mines in Bolivia, Peru, and Mexico) began to flood the European continent. The impact was enormous: this gold and silver "increased Europe's supply of precious metals sevenfold and raised prices two- or three-fold between 1540 and 1640."[4] In other words, all that gold and silver brought a century of raging *inflation*. The consequences of the inflation were no less profound than that of all the silver and gold that had caused it.

Inflation raised prices, hurting two major social groups and showering riches on a third. First, *landlords*, the still-entrenched ruling class, "suffered because money rents failed to rise as rapidly as the cost of living. The more aggressive landlords raised rents and introduced capitalistic practices into agriculture." In England, some of the landlords were driven to an even more extreme course of action—the notorious Enclosure Movement, which we shall examine below. Second, *laborers* suffered because wages rose more slowly than prices. But on the other hand, "high prices and low wages resulted in profit inflation," so that the real "beneficiaries of this century-long inflation were capitalists, including merchants [and] manufacturers."[5] They were able to accumulate more capital. Meanwhile, their profit inflation coupled with worker wage deflation

created a more unequal distribution of income favoring the emerging capitalist class.

The capitalists used their bonanza in a unique way in comparison with all prior modes of production—they used their *accumulated wealth to produce more wealth*. Capitalism is unique in making goods multiply. In fact, it appears that it has to, in order to exist: all its internal dynamic militates toward more and more production, and an ever-expanding search for markets. As Dowd puts it: "However much they disagree on other matters, all economists who have studied capitalism—from Smith through Marx, Marshall and Keynes—agree on the necessity of expansion."[6]

In order to become full-fledged capitalists, the merchants and manufacturers had to free themselves from two constraining groups—the lords of the old ruling class, and the medieval guilds. Both of these groups restricted the capitalists in their commerce and their production. Slowly, they got out from under. But in order to have a system in which wealth would be free to multiply, capitalists needed one more element: a free labor force—that is, one they could hire and fire in accordance with the vicissitudes of their business needs.[7] Here too they were

---

4. Dudley Dillard, "Capitalism," in *The Political Economy of Development and Underdevelopment*, ed. Charles K. Wilber (New York: Random House, 1973), p. 63.

5. Quotes in this paragraph are from Dillard, "Capitalism," in *The Political Economy . . .* , p. 63.

6. Dowd, *The Twisted Dream*, p. 78.

7. Wallerstein's treatment of the rise of capitalism involves rather different emphases. First of all, he sees *agricultural* capitalism as having preceded the rise of capitalism via the merchants and manufacturers. Second, since he considers the most important defining characteristic of capitalism to be *production for a market for maximum profit*, he is less concerned about whether or not a "free" labor force emerged in each and every instance of capitalist development. "Free" labor developed in the "capitalist core" countries of Northwest Europe, but in the New World, he argues, Caribbean island planters and Latin American large landowners produced for a capitalist world market with

helped by the inflation, as peasants who were unable to pay higher rents and who were no longer tied down by feudalism were pushed into the urban areas and—bereft of all means of production save their bodies—were now forced into being this "free" labor force.

In England, the capitalists had another enormous aid in the creation of a free wage-labor force, again thanks in good part to the inflation: the Enclosure Movement.

Although serfdom had pretty well disappeared from England by the end of the fourteenth century, both the peasants and the fairly small class of agricultural laborers still enjoyed the use of the common land. There, they could pasture their cow or other animals, cut firewood, and cultivate subsistence plots. For the poorer peasants and laborers especially, their rights to use the common land spelled the difference between getting along or going under.

During the Enclosure Movement, these commons were taken over, largely for sheep pastures, by the larger landlords, and their use denied to the peasants. Moreover, peasants were evicted—often wholesale—so that the landlords could convert to sheep runs. Sheep were profitable because the price of wool kept rising during the whole inflationary period, whereas the traditional arrangements with peasants produced a declining return for the landlords. So, as Barrington Moore puts it, "sheep ate men. The peasants were driven off the land; ploughed strips and commons alike were turned into pastures. A single shepherd could manage flocks grazing over land that once had fed many humans."[8] The Enclosure Movement began on a small scale in the sixteenth century with the inflation,[9] and

grew to a statistical avalanche by the mid-eighteenth century.

The initially slow pace of the Enclosure Movement is partly due to the fact that before the British Civil War (which began in 1640 and has been termed a "bourgeois [capitalist] revolution"), the power of the Crown was sometimes used on the peasants' behalf, to thwart Enclosure proceedings initiated by the nobility. This was a by-product of the struggle for power between the nobility and the monarchy. But the Civil War broke the power of the king. Finally, with the Stuart Restoration (1688), the last barriers to the powers of the enclosing landlords were broken. England was now ruled by what Barrington Moore calls a "committee of landlords"—eighteenth-century Parliament. During the eighteenth century, Enclosures became a tidal wave, leaving substantial areas of the countryside depopulated in its wake. The rising capitalist class had gotten its "free" labor force that had to work for wages or starve.

Two points of interest are first, that the family connections between the enclosing landlords and the rising big capitalist bourgeoisie were "close and intimate to the point where it is often difficult to decide where the one begins and the other leaves off."[10] And second, that it was rarely the biggest landlords, the titled nobility, who were the innovators in introducing capitalist practices and agricultural innovations on the enclosed sheep-and-grain estates. Rather, the aristo-

black slaves and Indians who were virtually serfs. Still, even without "free" labor, he proposes, these New World countries were drawn into the developing "capitalist world system," albeit as part of its "periphery" (Wallerstein's terminology is discussed on p. 59 below). *See* Wallerstein, "World Capitalist System," p. 399-400.

8. Barrington Moore, Jr., *Social Origins of Dictatorship and Democracy* (Boston: Beacon Press, 1966), p. 12.

9. According to Marx (in *Capital*, vol. I, Chapters 27-31) the Reformation also played a role in England, because the lands of the Church were expropriated, given to royal favorites or sold cheap to speculators who drove out the hereditary peasant subtenants and combined their holdings into one. The Church had provided the religious bulwark of traditional feudal land tenure and its fall hastened the conversion of land to capitalist use and tenure.

10. Moore, *Social Origins*, p. 19.

cratic landlord merely *arranged* the "legalities" of the enclosure; the large tenant farmers who took over the enclosed estates on his behalf were the ones much more likely to pursue improved methods of cultivation.[11] Thus, technologically innovative rural capitalism was born, able to produce much more food as well as wool, with a vastly reduced labor force. The net results?

"By 1820 or so, almost all the agricultural land in England had been enclosed; by the close of the 19th century a few thousand families owned almost all of it."[12] The younger, stronger displaced peasants went to the cities to make their often miserable wage bargain; the older, feebler ones eked out some work making enclosure hedges and/or went on the even more miserable standard of "poor relief"—the fate of more than half of one Midlands village documented by Moore.[13] Even though all this took place over a long period of time, and mainly under the umbrella of "law and order," this "must not blind us to the fact that it was massive violence exercised by the upper classes against the lower."[14]

Meanwhile, the capitalists had not been idle. As demand rose, so did the pace of technological innovation, and with it the *factory system* was born.

Technology created the factories, which required a specially constructed building and an inanimate power source such as a steam engine or waterfall. Many scholars have sought to blame the ills of the early Industrial Revolution on technology per se (e.g., the image of the rise of the inhuman, smoke-belching mills). I suggest it was capitalism, not technology that led these factories to be run as quasi-prisons, as many of them were. "Work discipline" included fines and floggings for minor infractions of rules prohibiting everything from tardiness to "whistling on the job or leaving a lamp lit a few minutes too long after sunrise."[15] The emerging capitalist industrial system involved free market competition (once the mercantilist restrictions had been swept away) by fairly small-scale capitalists who had to make a profit in order to survive. This they could do only by trying to stay ahead in terms of technological innovation and sweating their workers. They had to. The losers were gobbled up by the more successful capitalists, and in those days there was constant price competition as the pace of technological innovation among these still-small firms grew. Thus, the new system of industrial capitalism was born with the twin needs to expand and exploit. As we shall note in Chapter 7, there is a whole school of social science that claims that these needs of *capitalism*, as divorced from *industrialism*, continue unabated (although in different forms) to this day. But other social scientists disagree. After all, did not industrial capitalism produce the greatest outpouring of goods—and the greatest increase in the standard of living of the people—in world history? For the moment, we shall leave the issue up in the air. But even capitalism's severest critics, Karl Marx and Frederic Engels, in their *Communist Manifesto* written in 1848,

11. Ibid., pp. 19, 24-25.
12. Dowd, *The Twisted Dream*, p. 40.
13. Moore, *Social Origins*, p. 28.
14. Ibid., p. 29.
15. Gerhard E. Lenski and Jean Lenski, *Human Societies*, 2nd ed. (New York: McGraw-Hill, 1974), p. 299. Thompson presents a cogent argument that although some aspects of work discipline and the imposition of strict time schedules on workers were influenced by the technical requirements of large-scale machine production, it was not industrialism but rather industrial *capitalism* that underlay British employers' generations-long struggle to remold the work habits and time sense of their work-force according to the capitalist dictate: "time is money." *See* E. P. Thompson, "Time, Work-Discipline, and Industrial Capitalism," *Past and Present* 38 (1967):55-97. In America, successive waves of factory-bound immigrants bringing the older, free-wheeling work rhythms and norms meant that here too the "Protestant" work ethic was imposed at high cost, not uniformly, and over a span of generations. *See* Herbert C. Gutman, "Work, Culture, and Society in Industrializing America 1815-1919," *American Historical Review* 78 (1973): 531-88.

agreed about the great outpouring of productivity the system unleashed:

> The bourgeoisie [capitalists], during its rule of scarce one hundred years, has created more massive and more colossal productive forces than all preceding generations together. Subjection of nature's forces to man, machinery, application of chemistry to industry and agriculture, steam-navigation, railways, electric telegraphs, clearing of whole continents for cultivation, canalization of rivers, whole populations conjured out of the ground—what earlier century had even a presentiment that such productive forces slumbered in the lap of social labor?

At this point, however, let us examine another controversial thesis[16] that is finding increased empirical support of late: that the process that created *development* in England and the rest of northwest Europe and then spread to the United States, Japan, and a few other favored lands, simultaneously created *underdevelopment* in much of the rest of the globe.

This thesis is argued, for example, by Griffin who asserts: "the history of the underdeveloped countries in the last five centuries is, in large part, the history of the consequences of European expansion."[17]

Immanuel Wallerstein puts this thesis into still broader perspective. He argues that capitalism and a "world economy" developed together as two sides of the same coin. By 1640, he asserts, the outlines of our present "world system" had stabilized into three tiers. The top layer consists of the "core" capitalist countries, and the bottom consists of a "periphery" of nations involved in the world economy primarily as raw-material-producing areas. In between, stabilizing the system because they are simultaneously exploiter and exploited, are the "semi-periphery" countries, struggling to achieve "core" status.

When the process got started, in the 1500s, Europe encountered a vast, rich New World, which it conquered. But it also encountered wealthy nations in the Orient, which had many desirable manufactures, luxury goods, and commodities such as spices. The problem was that, at the start, Europe had almost nothing to offer in return that was desired in Asia. This problem was resolved, according to Griffin, by two European technological breakthroughs: large ocean-going sailing vessels and powerful naval cannons.

The history of Java in Indonesia provides a vivid but not unique example. At the beginning of the 1500s it was a prosperous region, and its port of Malacca was number one in international commerce, clearing the most shipping per year. By 1641, the Dutch had a trade monopoly. In the nineteenth century, they required forced cultivation of certain legally stipulated crops, under the so-called Culture System.[18] The peas-

16. In contrast, I mention only in passing the still-controversial role of religion in the rise of capitalism. Max Weber in his *The Protestant Ethic and the Spirit of Capitalism* (New York: Charles Scribner and Sons, 1958) has written the classic work on the side of those who claim that the emergence of the ascetic, individualistic Protestantism of the Reformation was a major cause of subsequent capitalism. The other side is admirably presented by R. H. Tawney in *Religion and the Rise of Capitalism* (New York: Mentor, 1950), who notes that the new commercial classes were early and enthusiastic supporters of Protestantism, and helped mold *it* in their business-oriented image. I favor Tawney, in keeping with my theoretical orientation which emphasizes material factors as more determinative than values in precipitating social change. To be fair, Max Weber in *The City* (New York: Collier Books, 1962) has taken a somewhat more multi-causal approach less insistent on the primacy of religious values.

17. Keith Griffin, "Underdevelopment in History," in *The Political Economy of Development and Underdevelopment*, ed. Wilber, p. 69. The concept, "development of underdevelopment," was originated by Andre Gunder Frank. *See* his "The Development of Underdevelopment" chapter in his *Latin America: Underdevelopment or Revolution* (New York: Monthly Review Press, 1969).

18. *See also* Clifford Geertz, *Agricultural Involution: The Processes of Ecological Change in Indonesia* (Berkeley: University of California Press, 1963).

ants were left so little time and land for food crops that famines emerged by the 1840s. "The fertile island had been transformed into a vast Dutch plantation, or, from the point of view of the people, a forced labour camp."[19] Meanwhile, the Dutch "utterly destroyed" Java's indigenous commerce and industry—shipbuilding, ironworking, brass and iron founding, and the merchant marine all but disappeared. Chinese merchants were brought in as middlemen and the local merchants turned to piracy.[20] After the 1840s, data are available on Javanese rice consumption per capita: they show a steady decline from 114.0 kg. in 1856-70 to 89.0 kg. in 1936-40. After independence, the situation did not immediately improve—in 1960 consumption was down to 81.4 kg.[21] By that time, Java was one of the most densely populated places in the world, as peasants produced extra children in an often unsuccessful attempt to stay one step ahead of hunger.[22] This is rational for the individual *peasants* in terms of the labor-intensity of wet rice cultivation, their main crop, but causes grave problems for their *country* since expenditures on services for the extra mouths sap the capital that might have gone to attempts to develop (or in part *re*develop) the economy.

The list of places where indigenous commerce and industry were deliberately destroyed definitely includes India, according to some sources. Griffin writes that India was more advanced economically than Europe as late as the early seventeenth century, but that once the British moved in, they acted to remold India to their own economic benefit. As a result: "[i]ndustrial decay was complete by the 1880s."[23] During the whole nineteenth century, the proportion of the population dependent on agriculture *increased*, that is, "development" decreased. Population explosion followed. Using 1900-1901 as a base of 100, per capita food production plunged to a near-famine level of 58 by 1950.[24]

The story goes on an on. Large-scale slave trading, begun by the Portuguese in the sixteenth century in *West Africa*, soon disrupted the region from Guinea to Angola, and devastated the indigenous city-states and empires which seemingly were comparable to European levels of development at the outset. In *Algeria*, colonized by the French, food consumption "was between five and six times higher in 1863 than it was in 1954."[25] In the islands of the *Caribbean* and *Polynesia*, depopulation occurred as diseases to which the indigenous people had no immunity were inadvertantly introduced. In fact, the Indians of the Caribbean islands were almost wholly exterminated. Those in the rest of *North, Central,* and *South America* were vastly reduced in numbers. Often they were forced into a form of serfdom (as in Peru, Bolivia, Guatemala, etc.) or pushed into remote jungles (in the Amazon and Orinoco basins) or herded into impoverished reservations (in the U.S.). In Central and South America, even the new nations that emerged from Spanish colonialism were trapped into underdevelopment as they became suppliers of raw materials and agricultural products—on very negative terms of trade—for the developed industrial countries.[26]

19. *See* M. Caldwell, *Indonesia* (New York: Oxford University Press, 1968), p. 47; and quoted in Griffin, "Underdevelopment in History," p. 73.
20. Griffin, "Underdevelopment in History," p. 73.
21. Caldwell, *Indonesia*, p. 21.
22. Geertz, *Agricultural Involution*, 1963.
23. Griffin, "Underdevelopment in History," p. 73. Barrington Moore, in his *Social Origins*, p. 348, gives a different view: what the British destroyed was not *manufacturing* but rather the *handicrafts* of a still overwhelmingly agrarian society.
24. *See* K. Mukerji, *Levels of Economic Activity and Public Expenditures in India* (New York: Asia Publishing House, 1965); and Griffin, "Underdevelopment in History," p. 74.
25. Ibid., p. 76.

In short, these Third World nations *cannot* replicate the path to development followed by the original members of the "Industrial Club" because these nations developed partly at the *expense* of much of the present-day Third World. Which countries can today's underdeveloped states use as their "New World"—now that all nations are increasingly tied together in a world economy in which they are at the low end of the totem pole, and the gap between rich and poor nations *widens* rather than narrows?

In sum, the rise of capitalism, followed by the Industrial Revolution, together have irrevocably changed the face of the globe (which has shrunk under the speed of modern transport, for one thing). Lenski and Lenski have come up with a list of long-term consequences of industrialization. Some are rather obvious (e.g., the division of labor has become enormously more complex). But their first six items offer an interesting statistical summary:

1. World population has multiplied five times just since 1750, a rate of growth at least seven times higher than the rate during the agrarian era.
2. The rural-urban balance in advanced industrial societies has been completely reversed: agrarian societies were 90 percent rural; advanced industrial are 90 percent urban.
3. The largest communities of the industrial era are already ten times the size of the largest of the agrarian era.
4. Women in industrial societies have only a third to a half as many children as women in [agrarian] societies.
5. Life expectancy at birth has almost tripled in advanced industrial societies.
6. The per capita production and consumption of goods and services in advanced industrial societies is at least ten times greater than in traditional agrarian societies.[27]

To this we should note that the increased life expectancy *at birth* is largely because of great reductions in *infant* mortality. People who survive infancy don't actually live three times as long; they don't even live twice as long.

Also, we should add that women in industrial societies are back in the economic mainstream—comprising a third to a half of the labor force in most of the advanced industrial nations, with highest rates of participation in the socialist industrial countries. The combination of lower fertility and higher labor force participation (which are interrelated, of course) has resulted in far-reaching changes in the lives of women, and has been one of the undeniable advances of the Industrial Revolution in increasing human potential, in comparison with the preceding agrarian era. Still, women in industrial countries have not yet been able to use their laborpower to gain a significant share in control of the means and fruits of production, as we shall see in Chapter 8.

Summary

In the 1500s and early 1600s, a new economic system, capitalism, arose in northwest Europe; soon it impacted on much of the rest of the globe. Some nations were enriched; other areas became dependent suppliers of raw materials. Capitalism involves production for a market, with the owners of

26. *See,* for example, Frank, "The Development of Underdevelopment"; Theotonio Dos Santos, "The Structure of Dependence," in *The Political Economy of Development and Underdevelopment,* ed. Wilber, pp. 109-117; Celso Furtado, "The Concept of External Dependence in the Study of Underdevelopment," in *The Political Economy of Development and Underdevelopment,* ed. Wilber, pp. 118-123; and, for an earlier statement concerning these negative terms of trade, *see* Hans Singer, "The Distribution of Gains Between Investing and Borrowing Countries," in *Economic Development and Social Change,* ed. George Dalton (Garden City, N. Y.: The Natural History Press, 1971), pp. 336-351 (originally published 1950).
27. Lenski and Lenski, *Human Societies,* 1974, pp. 300-301.

the means of production striving for high levels of profit. These owners, the early capitalists, did not consume their profits in the manner of previous elites. Rather, they reinvested them, so that their capital grew and multiplied itself. Under capitalism, the sluggish stream of social change of the agrarian era became a rushing torrent. Whole new social classes were created, as land and eventually labor became commodities to be bought and sold on the market. New patterns of sexual stratification began to emerge as work became separated from the home and employers began hiring women and children at lower wages than men for a growing range of tasks. Many of these tasks involved the new machines that proliferated as the pace of invention speeded up in the late 1700s and early 1800s. By then, capitalism had given birth to the Industrial Revolution. But under the changing social relations of production that emerged as capitalism displaced agrarian feudalism, peasants were pushed off the land and traditional occupations made obsolete at a faster rate than the new machines created new jobs. Material goods did multiply, but for the common people, the Industrial Revolution—as it emerged under capitalism—involved massive dislocations and widespread immiseration far outweighing any small increase in consumer items.

Other scholars have laid the ideology of capitalism to a new religion (Protestantism), and they have attributed the suffering accompanying the Industrial Revolution to a runaway technology (e.g., machine-filled factories) that neither employer nor employee had had time to assimilate. Implicitly or explicitly, this chapter has rejected both positions. The ideology of capitalism suited the interests of the capitalists; and the "evils of the smoke-belching factories" involved the manner in which capitalists utilized labor to run the machines, not something inherent in the industrial technology that created the machines. And because capitalism engendered its own world economic system as it rose, today it is difficult to pinpoint phenomena that are intrinsic to industrialism, as opposed to capitalism, even in those industrial countries (such as the Soviet Union) calling themselves socialist.

For Further Reading

Geertz, Clifford. *Agricultural Involution: The Processes of Ecological Change in Indonesia.* Berkeley: University of California Press, 1963.

   Tells how the Javanese were forced into an ecological trap by Holland's centuries of milking the world's most profitable colony.

Moore, Barrington, Jr. *Social Origins of Dictatorship and Democracy.* Boston: Beacon Press, 1966.

   A fascinating and classic work comparing the differing historical routes to modern industrialism that were followed by England, France, the United States, China, Japan, and India.

Rhodes, Robert I., ed. *Imperialism and Underdevelopment.* New York: Monthly Review Press, 1970.

   A good reader on obstacles to development, including a slightly higher proportion of radical analyses than Wilber (see below).

Thompson, E. P. *The Making of the English Working Class.* New York: Random House, 1964.

   A readable and classic study of what the Industrial Revolution meant for the lives of the English "common people."

Wallerstein, Immanuel. "The Rise and Future Demise of the World Capitalist System: Concepts for Comparative Analysis." *Comparative Studies in Society and History* 16 (1974): 387-415.

   In one brief article one can get the flavor and many major points of his distinguished major work, *The Modern World-System: Capitalist Agriculture and the Origins of the European World-Economy in the Sixteenth Century.* New York: Academic Press, 1974.

Wilber, Charles K. *The Political Economy of Development and Underdevelopment.* New York: Random House, 1973.

   Contains many of the articles cited in this chapter in a well-conceived reader.

6 | Two Views of Class in Industrial Capitalist Society: Marx vs. the United States Functionalists

Rae Lesser Blumberg
and Gösta Andersen

NINETEENTH Century European social theorists tried to make sense of the bewilderingly rapid array of benefits and evils that poured forth from the copiously productive new industrial capitalist system. The dislocations and evils were perhaps more evident in Europe, which did not have the vast natural resources, the open frontier, and sense of manifest destiny of Britain's ex-colony in North America. In the industrializing Old World, the wretched sufferings of the common people being forged into a modern wage-labor working class were much more visible.[1]

But meanwhile, in the U.S., conditions looked more hopeful for native white American males: jobs were available—in fact, the U.S. was chronically short of labor until the great flood of immigration from the 1880s to the 1920s—the frontier had not yet closed, and, for the enterprising, most businesses were still small enough in scale to offer hope of starting one and prospering, even without large initial capital. By the 1880s, the U.S. had assumed industrial leadership of the world, producing more industrial output than the next two manufacturing nations, England and Germany, combined. Moreover, in both Europe and the United States, political democracy was being expanded. The vote was successively extended to more and more nonpropertied males. Even a few social welfare measures were being introduced here and there to help alleviate the insecurities of wage labor (e.g., some relief for the injured, aged, and infirm), despite the still-laissez-faire tone of the capitalist national governments.[2] And for more and more people, education and the standard of living both were rising. In fact, Lenski is led to the optimistic conclusion that the industrial mode of production, once past its birth pangs, produced a definite (though not enormous) *reversal* in the basic trend toward inequality that had marked the progression from hunting and gathering to horticultural to agrarian societies.[3]

That the average industrial society has a lower level of inequality (and a higher stan-

1. E. P. Thompson provides a brilliant description of *The Making of the English Working Class,* (New York: Random House, 1964).
2. Following Adam Smith's enormously influential 1776 book, *The Wealth of Nations,* in which he argued that a free market and noninterfering government were the pathways to prosperity and well-being for all, the remaining mercantilist trade restrictions were gradually dismantled. Thus began the nineteenth-century heyday of laissez-faire capitalism, during which time the government's hands-off attitude toward capital and labor aided the former enormously while failing to protect the latter from exploitation, or penury should they become unable to work.
3. Gerhard E. Lenski, *Power and Privilege* (New York: McGraw-Hill, 1966), p. 308.

dard of living for the common people) than the average agrarian society would be hard to deny for most social scientists who have studied the problem. But whether there is a *continuing* trend toward *decreasing* inequality in industrial capitalist societies would seem to split the social theorists of the nineteenth and twentieth centuries into two camps corresponding roughly to what has been called the great dichotomy in stratification theories: the conservative vision based on *consensus*, and the notion that the system of rewards is basically just, versus the often radical approach involving *conflict*, and the notion that the system is basically unjust.[4] Those who have espoused the notion that modern society is becoming ever more egalitarian than its predecessors have come from the ranks of the consensus theorists (often called functionalists), although not all scholars using the consensus approach share this view.

In this chapter, we shall examine the theories of the two polar extremes of the conflict versus consensus approach to inequality. The classic conflict theory is that of Karl Marx. The classic consensus theory is that of U.S. sociology's functionalists (e.g., Talcott Parsons, Kingsley Davis, and Wilbert Moore). Marx formulated his approach in mid-nineteenth-century Europe, as he viewed what he saw as the wretchedness, as well as the technological marvels, wrought by the rising capitalist industrial system. Parsons and Davis and Moore formulated their approach in mid-twentieth-century America, as they viewed what they saw as the relative abundance, opportunity, and equality wrought by the U.S.'s mature capitalist industrial system. The U.S. functionalist approach to stratification has produced a flood of empirical research since the 1940s, and it is this research that we have characterized as concentrating on the tip of the "iceberg of inequality." Accordingly, both functionalist stratification theory and the research it helped generate will be presented in the second part of this chapter.

THE THEORY OF KARL MARX (1818-1883)

Marx was a German social philosopher, economist, sociologist, and political scientist. Due to his critical attitudes towards those in power, he had to spend the last part of his life in exile in England. Perhaps most people associate his name with communism, turbulence, and violent revolution. Certainly, Marx was a revolutionary—he tried to work actively to alleviate the plight of the poor masses of his time. And his activist disciples have brought approximately half the world's population under governments that consider themselves socialist followers of his doctrines. However, he was also—and mainly—a social scientist and scholar. His work has been tremendously important in shaping the thinking, issues, and theoretical controversies of both modern sociology and economics. In a sense, the dominant paradigms of both U.S. sociology (functionalist) and economics (neoclassicist) may be seen as reactions to his views. *The Communist Manifesto,*[5] which he and Frederick Engels wrote in 1848 as a popularized version of some of his basic ideas, is his best-known work, both among opponents and supporters. But his main scholarly contribution is his *Das Kapital (Capital)*, a three-volume work on the capitalist system which was left unfinished at his death.[6] In fact, the manuscript tantalizingly breaks off just as he begins to formally define *social class*. However, his previous writings make his usage of social class clear, even without a formal definition. People form a social class, whether they are aware of it or not, when they share a common economic rela-

4. S. Ossowski, *Class Structure in the Social Consciousness* (New York: Free Press, 1963), p. 170.

5. Karl Marx, *The Communist Manifesto* (New York: International Publishers, 1948). First pub. 1848.

6. Karl Marx, *Capital (Das Kapital)* (New York: International Publishers, 1947). First pub. 1867.

tionship to *production* and its control.[7] For example, under agrarian feudalism, land was the most important of the factors of production, and the principal (and opposing) classes were the large *landlords* who controlled the land, and the exploited and subjugated *serfs* or *peasants* who worked it. To Marx, the exploitation consisted in the fact that the landlords extracted surplus from the peasants in the form of *rent* (in labor days owed to the lord and/or in portion of the crop).

To Marx, the history of humanity and society is seen as a succession of different "social formations," or distinct phases, each with its own *mode of production.* Essentially, mode of production refers to the ways in which production is carried out—and the people get fed—in a given society. This includes two basic components:

1. *The forces of production* are all the tools, machines, skills, buildings and equipment, as well as the level of technology, organization and science used in carrying out production of goods. As we have seen before (and as discussed in the Appendix), Marx's notion of the forces of production subsumes what is treated in this book under techno-economic base, division of labor, and organizational complexity.

2. *The relations of production* refer to the ways in which people who participate in production relate not only to each other but also to the surplus that is produced. As we have seen, with the development of the techno-economic base (or in the more general Marxian sense, the advance in the forces of production), the potential surplus greatly increases. In other words, the *social relations of production* are precisely the relationships between those who actually *produce* the surplus (the peasants, the workers) and those who *appropriate* or *control* it (the landlords, the capitalists).

To Marx, the mode of production is the key to understanding the rest of the institutions of a given society, because it tends to shape them. As he puts it in one of his better-known passages:

> The mode of production in material life conditions the general character of the social, political and spiritual processes of life. It is not the consciousness of men that determines their existence, but, on the contrary, their social existence that determines their consciousness.[8]

This passage is often cited to show that Marx was an *economic determinist.* Actually, this is a distortion of his position. The above statement is not one of economic determinism, but rather one that stresses the importance of something more social—the *mode of production.* Recall that the mode of production consists of both the technological base of production and the social relations that organize production. To Marx, it is not technology alone, nor economics alone, but the overarching mode of production, which is the distinctive element of a *social* formation. Moreover, in his more historical writings (e.g., *The Eighteenth Brumaire of Louis Bonaparte*),[9] he shows that he is greatly sensitive to the nuances of other, noneconomic factors. His writings make it clear that the connections between the economic base and the remainder of the social institutions—the kinship and familial system, religion, ideology, customs, political and governmental forms, and so on—are not those of simple, unidirectional causation. Each of these other institutions has a certain history and life of its own in a society, and to some extent can shape the mode of production

7. To Marx, social classes exist objectively, independent of whether people perceive them or not. *See* T. B. Bottmore, *Classes in Modern Society* (New York: Allen & Unwin, 1965).

8. This and subsequent quotes by Marx in this section are excerpted from the Preface to *A Contribution to the Critique of Political Economy* (New York: International Publishers, 1968), pp. 181-185.

9. Karl Marx, "The Eighteenth Brumaire of Louis Bonaparte," in *Karl Marx and Frederick Engels: Selected Works* (New York: International Publishers, 1968), pp. 95-180. First pub. 1852.

in addition to being shaped by it. Over the long run, though, it is the forces of production that constitute the dynamic or leading element in social change. In other words, the forces of production (especially advances in technology) cause more—and more important—changes in the other spheres of society than vice versa. (On this one point, Marx and Lenski are in perfect agreement.)

In fact, it is advances in the forces of production that cause the basic *conflict* that eventually moves societies from one social formation and one mode of production to another. Marx goes on to present his theory of social change:

> At a certain stage of their development, the material forces of production in society come in conflict with the existing relations of production, or—what is but a legal expression for the same thing—with the property relations within which they had been at work before. From forms of development of the forces of production these relations turn into their fetters. Then comes the period of social revolution. With the change of the economic foundation the entire immense superstructure is more or less rapidly transformed.

In other words, the development of new technology and economic organization sooner or later results in a "lack of fit" between the innovation in the productive forces and the existing social relations of production. This "lack of fit" between forces and relations of production Marx termed a *contradiction*. And, Marx asserts, contradiction between the forces and social relations of production eventually leads to *conflict*. As an example of this process let us look at the factory. Its development as a new form of economic organization that centralized the new machines and the new nonhuman energy sources clearly marked it as an "advance in the forces of production." But in order to staff and run it successfully, the labor restrictions of feudalism and the production restrictions of the guilds had to be wiped out. Thus, the interests of the rising capitalist class were placed in *direct conflict* with those of the landed aristocracy and the guild masters. Out of this kind of conflict, new social formations and new modes of production emerge. How and when? Marx continues:

> No social order ever disappears before all the productive forces for which there is room in it have developed, and new, higher relations of production never appear before the material conditions of their existence have matured in the womb of the old society.

From this famous passage we can better see how Marx views the process of social change. Every hitherto existing social formation can develop its productive forces only so far before they *come into contradiction with the social order that gave them birth*.

If techo-economic advance sets up the driving force of the contradiction, and the contradiction leads to conflict, what kind of conflict acts as the vehicle of social change? To Marx, the conflicts created, once there is sufficient surplus, are *class* conflicts. Major social change occurs when a rising new class overthrows or supplants the established dominant class. Thus, the *bourgeoisie* (capitalists) slowly rose out of the feudal order, and these entrepreneurs, merchants, and financiers increasingly chafed at the restrictions imposed by the existing feudal order on their surge to accumulate capital. This new class eventually broke the yoke of feudalism and freed the serfs and peasants to become wage-laborers, the new underclass of the new social formation, capitalism. Marx termed this new underclass the *proletariat*.

In contrast to the earlier feudal system where the serfs and peasants were exploited through rent, the capitalist system, to Marx, is characterized by a class relationship in which the capitalist owner of the means of production (machines, tools, factories) exploits the labor of the proletariat producers, not through rent but through "surplus-value." Surplus-value arises when workers are able to produce goods worth more on the market than it cost the workers to clothe, feed, and shelter themselves at some reasonable standard. To Marx, this fact is the basis of exploitation under capitalism because it is the capitalist, not the producer, who manages to benefit from this greater worker productivity. Let us trace the process: The proletarian, who "owns" only his/her own laborpower "sells" this to the capitalist. The capitalist, whose concern is to produce a profit, "exploits" the laborer by paying a wage which is *smaller than the value of what the laborer produces*. The difference is the surplus-value which the capitalist extracts from the worker.[10] To Marx, this is the crucial essence of the class relationship in capitalist society.

To reiterate, the two major social classes of the capitalist system are the capitalists, whose defining characteristic is their ownership and control over the means of production, including the (purchased) laborpower of the worker; and the proletariat, or wage-laborers, whose defining characteristic is that they sell their laborpower to the capitalists for a wage, in order to survive and reproduce.

Marx's basic criterion of social class, in short, is not a person's prestige or status, but a person's position as a controller or a non-controller of the means of production. To him, all the other manifestations of inequality and stratification—status differences, inequality in political power, differences in accorded privileges—are subordinated to the above, and only can be completely understood in terms of the relationship to the means of production. So too with politics and ideology. Given that the capitalist class is economically dominant, to Marx it follows that it also will be *politically* dominant. In other words, the capitalist class will control, indirectly or directly, the major share of political power and the state. Simultaneously it will shape and control the *dominant values* and ideologies of society; that is, the

ruling values and ideologies of capitalist society reflect the values of the ruling capitalist class.

Nevertheless, capitalists' control over the values and symbol systems of the society is less than total. Moreover, they cannot prevent competing values from arising out of the proletariat's conflicting interests, especially over the long run.

In the *short run*, the wage-laborers and the capitalists will be in conflict over such things as wages, job security, fringe benefits, hours, conditions of work, etc. The workers will try to maximize their wages and benefits; the capitalists will try to minimize them in order to enhance profits (labor costs are, after all, the major cost of production in most industries).

In the *long run*, however, Marx foresaw that as the forces of production developed further, this conflict would escalate until ultimately the proletariat's interest could be served only by overthrowing the domination of the capitalist class. He predicted that the workers would take over the factories, mines, offices and the state and establish themselves as the ruling class. This, to Marx, would signal the advent of *socialist* society, in which class conflict would ultimately dissolve, and the state itself finally wither away. As Marx phrased it, at the end of the passage we have been citing, the capitalist "social formation constitutes, therefore, the closing chapter of the prehistoric stage of human society."

Critics of Marx—and there are many—have focused their criticisms heavily on these

---

10. Let's say the worker produces $50 worth of output a day and receives $25/day as a wage. The owner is the beneficiary of $25/day in surplus-value. Marx uses the polemic term "exploitation" for the capitalist's pocketing of the worker's surplus value. One may argue that capitalists "deserve" their profits because they supply the capital, raw materials, organizational expertise and take the risks. Marx would disagree: he considers the extraction of workers' surplus-value as "exploitation" in both the technical and value judgment sense.

long-term predictions. They generally have argued that, first, even if one can distinguish a proletariat and a capitalist class (which few sociologists wish to do), the experiences of most Western capitalist countries do not point to any increase in conflicts among these classes; and, second, there does not seem to be any sign of the proletariat taking over the means of production. Rather, what has happened, they argue, has been the phenomenal rise of the middle class—mainly wage-labor to be sure, but comfortably situated—that has *reduced* class polarization, and the prospects for class conflict. Accordingly, socialist revolutions have *not* occurred first in the most industrialized nations as predicted by Marx, but in relatively less developed ones (Russia, China) with a smaller "cushioning" middle class. And when socialist revolutions *have* occurred, they have brought bureaucratic centralized power and often totalitarian controls—not the classless, stateless, liberation predicted by Marx.

Actually, however, Marx's primary emphasis was on the way in which the capitalist system would develop—prior to any final uprising of the proletariat. Of course, he also held that the logic of capitalist development *would eventually* lead to the birth of a new, higher social formation which he called socialism (and no country has yet developed a system corresponding to what he had in mind). But let us put aside the controversy of the rise of a *post*-capitalist social formation, and take a closer look at the kind of developments in the *capitalist* class structure that Marx envisaged.

First, in the early stages of capitalism in eighteenth-century England, for example, the class structure was not clear-cut along the lines of a proletariat and a bourgeois capitalist class. There still were strong vestigial elements from the feudal order. A class of landlords persisted, although increasingly weakened. More important, a large heterogeneous class of *independent small producers* (petty-commodity producers) such as craftsmen, peasants, artisans, and *independent small tradespeople* (petty-bourgeois) existed alongside the modern bourgeoisie and working classes.

However, Marx believed that the *logic* of capitalist development eventually would do away with the "remnant classes of the past." This would occur because under capitalism, there is an inexorable tendency toward the gradual accumulation and concentration of wealth and property among fewer and fewer capitalists. As competition and concentration among the capitalists increases, the weaker of them, along with small independent producers, will lose out to the stronger capitalists and become transformed into proletarians—wage-laborers. One point of clarification is needed here. In the everyday use of the word "proletarian," one thinks of people in absolute misery, poverty, and human degradation. This was not how Marx technically defined the word. To him, proletariat refers to wage-earners, whose only means of livelihood is to sell their labor-power. Some of them might make a pretty good wage bargain, if their skills were rare enough and in sufficient demand by the capitalists, but their relationship to the means of production puts them in the same class as all other wage-laborers regardless of the amount earned.

Was Marx right in predicting, on the one hand, a concentration of wealth and corporate capitalist power in fewer and fewer hands, and, on the other hand, a growth of the proletarian class, so that eventually almost everyone in society would have been thrown into one of these two polarized classes? Clearly, to the *consensus* theorists (the functionalists), he was wrong. In Chapter 7 we shall take up this problem again from the standpoint of the evidence offered by *conflict* theorists.

Mainline U.S. sociology, as it developed

during the twentieth century, admits to few if any explicit connections with Marx—although it has, in one sense, grappled with his ghost. As mentioned, to a certain extent the U.S. functionalists' harmonious view of the world and the stratification system may be seen as a deliberate reaction to Marx's vision of conflict and coercion.[11]

The sociological "founding fathers" from whom the functionalist theorists have borrowed most heavily are Emile Durkheim and Max Weber, who wrote at the turn of the century in France and Germany, respectively.

From Durkheim, the functionalists took the notion of modern society as a harmonious and organic entity. In a complex biological organism, each part may be quite different, but all are interdependent, and all are functionally necessary for the successful performance of the whole. So too with complex modern society, Durkheim held. As he put it: "What gives unity to organized societies, however, as to all organisms, is the spontaneous consensus of parts."[12] As actually translated into functionalism, Durkheim's view comes out more or less like this: even though everyone does their own thing, all those things together, fused by common shared values, form an interdependent whole in which the needs of the complex society are met.

Max Weber was in many respects a conflict theorist, quite unlike Durkheim. And in many respects, Weber has been the most influential of all the "founding fathers" on U.S. sociology. But the elements of his sociology that have been incorporated into the functionalist mainstream have not been his conflict views, but rather two principal ideas that have been used as analytic concepts for understanding modern society's complexity. First, they have adopted Weber's principled resistance to any monocausal explanation of society or stratification (he criticized Marx for overemphasizing the economic dimension). Second, Weber's conceptualization of three hierarchies of power

—economic classes, status groups based on social honor, and political parties—has been adapted and translated to a view that there are many criteria for stratification.[13] At the same time, though, Weber's notion of status groups has been reinterpreted, making *status and prestige* the most important of these dimensions of stratification. Unfortunately, something they did not borrow from either Weber or Marx was a broad, historically grounded vision of the bases and nature of stratification in capitalist-industrial societies. In contrast, the vision of social stratification that emerged among U.S. functionalist-consensus theorists was highly ahistorical, static, and descriptive. Thus, they undertake studies of the characteristics of socioeconomic status (SES) groups, but not the historical forces that created them. And when consensus tradition stratification researchers study change it is almost exclusively in terms of father-son or career occupational mobility. Generally ignored are the processes altering the shape and composition of the labor force and the class structure. We shall now trace the results.

THE U.S. FUNCTIONALIST APPROACH TO STRATIFICATION: EXPLORING THE TIP OF THE ICEBERG OF INEQUALITY

By the time sociology was established as an academic discipline in the U.S., in the early twentieth century, the social science pie had been pretty well cut up and par-

11. Some excellent sources on sociology's intellectual history are Neil J. Smelser and Stephen R. Warner, *Sociological Theory: Historical and Formal* (Morristown, N. J.: General Learning Press, 1976); and Randall Collins and Michael Makowsky, *The Discovery of Society* (New York: Random House, 1972).

12. Emile Durkheim, *The Division of Labor in Society* (Glencoe, Illinois: Free Press, 1964), p. 342.

13. Max Weber, "Class, Status, Party," in *From Max Weber: Essays in Sociology*, eds. H. H. Gerth and C. Wright Mills (New York: Oxford University Press, 1958).

celed out among economists (who claimed the economy), political scientists (who claimed the state and the exercise of power), and even psychologists (who claimed the individual and what went on inside her/his head), so that sociology was left to compete with anthropology for prime claim to the area of culture.[14] So even when studying problems intimately connected with the economic and political power systems of society, sociologists and anthropologists tended to explain them by cultural factors.

Accordingly, it is not surprising that early sociology paid scant attention to problems of inequality and stratification, and until the Depression of the 1930s, very little research or theory in this area was attempted. Moreover, when the classic statement of the functional theory of stratification, that of Davis and Moore, appeared in 1945, America was entering its greatest prolonged economic expansion of the twentieth century. Those years of the 1950s and early 1960s were good ones for academic sociologists, in the sense they were for other well-educated white male upper-middle-class occupational groups: their real income went up, jobs were not scarce, and the American Dream seemed a promise largely fulfilled. Sociologists had several other factors going for them: the proportion and absolute numbers of the nation's youth going to college were rising steadily (especially by the early 1960s when the post-World War II "baby boom" began to reach college age). College teaching was clearly a "growth industry," and even the occupational prestige of scientists (which most sociologists consider themselves) was rising slightly in the period from the end of World War II to the 1960s.[15] When stratification research became popular during this period, it was done almost exclusively in the functionalist tradition represented by Davis and Moore. And that tradition asserted that stratification was not only inevitable but integrative and necessary for the system. The most popular types

of research focused on *status* differences, rather than economic *class* differences (in Weberian terminology), and on *upward* social mobility.[16] Let us start with the U.S. functionalists' theoretical views.

Theoretical Underpinnings of Functional Stratification Theory

1. Davis and Moore—Stratification as Necessary, Inevitable, and Largely Just.[17] In their clear argument, Davis and Moore identify stratification with unequal rewards in society. Why does stratification (i.e., a system of unequal rewards) exist? According to them, it has to—it is a functional necessity for the survival of society; to continue, a society must place its members in all the different positions that its existence requires to be filled. To continue, a society must *fill* the various social positions that keep it going, and somehow get the people in the slots to perform competently, that is, do a good job at their position so that the societal need in question is actually met. Some of these positions are both especially crucial for societal functioning, and especially demanding on the individual. How can society guarantee that the best qualified fill these strategic slots?

---

14. Norbert Wiley, "Political Sociology," (Mimeo: University of Illinois, 1975).

15. R. W. Hodge, P. M. Siegel, and P. H. Rossi, "Occupational Prestige in the United States, 1925-63," *American Journal of Sociology* 70, 3 (Nov. 1964):286-302.

16. Randall Collins has suggested that many of these American stratification researchers were not necessarily committed to functionalist *theory*, but rather to the "traditional liberal" optimistic, pluralistic view of the U.S. as the land of opportunity and progress for all (personal communication, 1976). Thus, it may be more accurate to label them as loosely sharing the consensus approach (i.e., that the stratification system is basically just) than as strictly adhering to all tenets of functionalist stratification theory to be presented below.

17. Kingsley Davis and Wilbert E. Moore, "Some Principles of Stratification," *American Sociological Review* 10 (April 1945):242-249.

In other words, what motivates people to want to occupy important and difficult positions? Bigger *rewards*, such as high *income* and *prestige*. In this way, the positions with greatest functional importance to the survival of the society come to be rewarded with higher income and other incentives. A second determinant of high reward, in addition to the functional importance of the position, is the relative scarcity of qualified personnel. In short, Davis and Moore assert, "those positions convey the best reward, and hence have the highest rank, which (a) have the greatest importance for the society and (b) require the greatest training or talent."[18]

How do we know what is important for society and what is not? To this the functionalist answer is generally that the *value system* (the values shared by all in society) determines what is socially important (Davis and Moore admit that functional importance is difficult to establish).

Davis and Moore's arguments would seem to explain the difference in rewards accorded to, say, the top executive of a large corporation versus a person who shines shoes, but it gets a little awkward explaining the relative rewards of a man who is, say, an advertising agency vice-president who handles a large deodorant account versus a man who is, say, a nurse. Is it for the society or for some (still unidentified) subgroup that the talents of the advertising executive are important and scarce enough to justify his income and expense account?

Nonetheless, Davis and Moore stress that stratification arises from the functional needs of *societies,* not the special interests of some of its members:

Social inequality is thus an unconsciously evolved device by which societies insure that the most important positions are conscientiously filled by the most qualified persons.[19]

So stratification is not only *necessary* for your society's survival (and *inevitable*, since *all* societies face the problem of "placing and motivating individuals in the social structure"); it is also *good* for you, since your survival and welfare depend on that of your society. Thus you naturally would want the best qualified people to be on top.

Needless to say, the necessity, inevitability, beneficial effects, and implicitly meritocratic basis of stratification have been hotly contested by a long variety of critics since 1945. But despite the large extent of criticism, few asked the question suggested above—functionally important and scarce to *whom*, other than "society"?

2. Parsons—Stratification as an Expression of Common Values.[20] A question such as the above would have been very foreign to a U.S. sociology long dominated by the work of Talcott Parsons, the most eminent functionalist theorist from the 1940s through mid-1960s. He views social systems as stable, well-integrated structures, all of whose elements are functional, that is, contribute to system maintenance. Most importantly, social systems are based on *common, shared values.* These values are expressed in the stratification system, which shows us what the society finds most valuable and esteemed. In other words, a person's rank in the stratification system tells us how well that person measures up to the society's shared values. Stratification is inevitable because people differ in their abilities to measure up. And because stratification systems are based on common values, they are *integrative.*

Research Directions of Functionalist Stratification Theory

How do you study such a stratification system? The functionalist-consensus answer usually involves *status*, or relative prestige in a ranked social hierarchy. But functionalists

18. Ibid.
19. Ibid.
20. Talcott Parsons, "Equality and Inequality in Modern Society, or Social Stratification Revisited," *Sociological Inquiry* 40 (Spring 1970).

usually call status groups social classes. This was true of W. Lloyd Warner[21] who began the outpouring of functionalist empirical research on the topic with his late-1940s studies of "Yankee City" (Newburyport, Mass.) and other small American communities. And it remains true of Parsons in his latest restatement of his views on social stratification. ("We may suggest the usefulness of divorcing the concept of social class from its historic relation to both kinship and property as such; to define *class status*, for the unit of social structure, as position on the hierarchical dimension of the differentiation of the societal system; and to consider *social class* as an aggregate of such units, individual and/or collective, that in their own estimation and those of others in the society occupy positions of approximately equal status in this respect.")[22]

1. *Warner—Stratification in Small Towns.*[23] Warner, whose functionalist-oriented stratification research was actually begun before the Davis-Moore article appeared, was a social anthropologist. He studied stratification in Yankee City as though the town were a whole social universe, or society. What he termed social class he clearly saw as unifying and binding together the society; that is, the main function of stratification is to integrate group members into a cohesive whole. He and his associates studied stratification by letting the people themselves subjectively rank the statuses of individuals and groups. These rankings were combined with an index of more objective status characteristics such as income, occupation, housing, etc. There wasn't perfect agreement among the Yankee Cityites, because the poor saw fewer social classes or status categories than the middle and upper classes, who saw six. Nevertheless, Warner concluded that six separate and discrete social classes existed in Yankee City. These were identified as:

(1) *Upper-upper:* "old families" who were the aristocracy of birth and wealth.

(2) *Lower-upper:* "new families" lacking appropriate ancestry, but sharing similar occupations and life-styles with the top group.

(3) *Upper-middle:* "solid folk," but not society; business and professional people who "get things done."

The above three levels Warner ranks above the "Common Man." They comprise only thirteen percent of the population (10 percent being "upper-middle"), and there is a big gap between them and the three levels below.

(4) *Lower-middle:* top of the "Common Man" level; teachers, white collar, small tradespeople, etc. (28 percent of the population).

(5) *Upper-lower:* respectable, honest, working people, semi- and unskilled (34 percent).

(6) *Lower-lower:* "low-down, disrespectable, lazy and shiftless" people below the level of the "Common Man" (25 percent).

Warner claimed his results show that money alone did not guarantee high social position. Yet wealth differentiates his top two classes from the rest; age of wealth splits the top two. Do these findings convey an accurate picture of the kind of stratification system existing in the U.S. as a whole? Warner's work has been subjected to much criticism concerning his research methods. In addition, even many functionalist-consensus sociologists have argued that it is impossible to generalize from the internal

21. W. Lloyd Warner, with M. Meeker and K. Eells, *Social Class in America* (Chicago: Science Research Associates, 1949.)

22. Parsons, "Equality and Inequality," p. 24.

23. Warner, et al., *Social Class,* 1949.

stratification of a small community to the entire USA.

2. *Occupational Prestige—National and International Convergence on a Smooth, Stable Hierarchy.* Functionalists have, however, attempted to study the U.S. as a whole, the most notable effort being the NORC[24] studies of *occupational prestige.*[25] Sociologists often find empirically that occupation is the most important component of "socioeconomic status" (SES), which also usually includes measures of income and education. Combining functionalist sociologists' interest in status with the great observed importance of occupation in determining our place in the system, occupational prestige has proven a very popular research variable. The findings show that it has changed little in the U.S. in recent years (the Hodge et al. study remeasured occupations tested in the 1947 study by North and Hatt and found a correlation of .99). A few findings are presented in the following table:

Table 6.1

Prestige Ratings of Selected Occupations (highest possible score = 100; lowest = 20)*

Occupation	Score
U.S. Supreme Court Justice (highest-scored job)	94
Scientist	92
College professor	90
Banker	85
Owner of a factory employing about 100 people	80
Electrician	76
Bookkeeper	70
Manager of a small store in a city	67
Garage mechanic	62
Clerk in a store	56
Taxi driver	49
Soda fountain clerk	44
Garbage collector	39
Shoe shiner (lowest-scored job)	34

*Source: Selected from the 90-occupation table in R. W. Hodge, P. M. Siegel, and P. H. Rossi, "Occupational Prestige in the United States, 1925-63," *American Journal of Sociology* 70 (November 1964):286-302. Reprinted by permission of the publisher.

All in all, people mentioned *high income* as the most important criterion they used in rating a job "excellent." Moreover, Duncan found that there was a near-perfect correlation (.91) between a job's occupational prestige score and a measure combining the average income and educational attainment of its practitioners.[26]

Occupational prestige studies have been replicated widely around the world, and show remarkably similar results. But even though they seem to very reliably tell us about variations in prestige of selected occupational titles, occupational prestige studies do not convey information on the total extent of stratification in the U.S. (or elsewhere). One important difference between occupational prestige and Warner's "social class" measures should be noted. Whereas Warner claimed to find six (five in newer communities, such as "Jonesville"—Morris, Illinois) *distinct* social classes, separated from each other by greater or lesser differences, the occupational prestige scale shows a smooth and continuous distribution of scores. There are no sharp breaks to point to the existence of separate *strata* of occupations with clearly differentiated levels of prestige.

24. National Opinion Research Center, a well-known survey research organization (associated with the University of Chicago).
25. Hodge, Siegel, and Rossi, "Occupational Prestige," 1964.
26. O. D. Duncan, "A Socioeconomic Index for All Occupations," in *Occupation and Social Status,* ed. Albert J. Reiss (New York: Free Press, 1961). *See also* Joseph R. Gusfield and Michael Schwartz, "The Meaning of Occupational Prestige: Reconsideration of the NORC Scale," *American Sociological Review* 28, 2 (April 1963):265-271 for more evidence that people (especially lower-income people) rated the "prestige" of occupations on *factual* grounds such as income and security, rather than (or as well as) on evaluative grounds such as how much they esteemed the occupation. Yet, as Gusfield and Schwartz imply, too often functionalist users of occupational prestige scales conclude that what may be factual description of the system is equivalent to a favorable evaluation.

3. *Single and Multi-Variable Indexes of Socioeconomic Status.* But that is just the way most U.S. consensus-approach stratification theorists see the U.S. "class" system—as a smooth, even distribution of statuses ranging from low to high. Consequently, any divisions made into upper class—lower class, or low, medium, high, etc., are at the researcher's convenience. This is clearly the logic used by sociologists who combine measures of say, income, education, and occupation into a single index of socioeconomic status, and then arbitrarily divide the index into two, three, six, or whatever categories that are seen as reflecting the reality of American stratification. Such an approach harks back to Weber's insistence on the *multidimensional* nature of stratification, but it goes further since it implies that analytically distinct measures of status and class hierarchies can be added together and then converted into some sort of a composite index. Other sociologists use a *single*

criterion for their index of socioeconomic status, such as income, but also make arbitrary cutting points into, say, low, middle, and high strata. Of what use are these arbitrarily defined strata? Considerable, since American sociologists have learned that a multitude of life chances and privileges correlate with measures of SES. A shortened version of a table by Broom and Selznick[27] illustrates this point.

By this table Broom and Selznick wish to show that certain kinds of life-styles and life chances cluster around specific strata, that is, "that social rank has a pervasive impact on the ways people live, act, and think." Some of the findings seem quite commonsensical. For instance, dental care in the U.S. is very expensive and it may easily be

27. Leonard Broom and Philip Selznick, *Sociology: A Text with Adapted Readings,* 5th ed. (New York: Harper & Row, 1973), p. 183. Reprinted by permission of the publisher.

Table 6.2

Stratification Correlates: Life Chances and Privileges, United States*

Related Factors	Lower Strata	Middle Strata	Upper Strata
Lifetime births expected per 1000 wives, age 30-39	Husband's income under $3,000: 3,992 births	Husband's income $5,000-$6,000: 3,307 births	Husband's income $10,000 and up 3,069 births
Lifetime income	Less than 8 yrs. of school: $196,000	H.S. grads: $350,000	College grads: $586,000
Children enrolled in pre-primary school	Family income under $3,000: 24%	Family income $5,000-7,500: 32%	Family income $10,000 and up: 47%
Children attend college	Family income under $5,000: 9%	Family income $5,000-7,500: 17%	Family income $10,000 and up: 44%
Index of marital instability (% white males, 25-34, with broken marriage)	Low income: 23%	Middle income: 10%	High income: 6%
Dental visits per year per person	Income under $2,000: 0.8%	Income $4,000-$7,000: 1.4%	Income $7,000 and up: 2.3 %

*Source: Leonard Broom and Philip Selznick, *Sociology: A Text with Adapted Readings,* 5th ed. (New York: Harper & Row, 1973), p. 183. Reprinted by permission of the publisher.

expected that low income groups simply cannot afford several visits to a dentist per year. In this particular table, published in 1973, the authors' definition of income strata may strike some as surprising, since by that time, median U.S. family income was over the $10,000 figure they use to define their "upper strata" ("median income" means that one-half the families earned more and one-half earned less). But this merely points up the most noteworthy feature of this type of research: the breaking points of each variable used are arbitrary, and each researcher may have a different way of dividing Americans into "lower, middle, and upper" strata. One may also ask, why three strata—why not two or five or x strata? And in the table, we see that both income and education are used as bases for the measure of stratification (their complete table also includes one item where *occupation* is divided into lower, middle, and upper strata). That is because in this approach, income, occupation, and education all are viewed as components of socioeconomic *status*, which is what they are out to measure. This kind of conceptualization of status group is actually quite different than what Weber meant in his famous "Class, Status, Party" essay.[28] There, status groups share a common view of social honor and life-style, and are actually *groups*.

4. *Lack of Consistency between the Dimensions of Stratification—the Status Crystallization Approach.* Whereas in the preceding approach we saw attempts to make a single index of socioeconomic status— whether that measure was income, education, occupation, or a composite of some or all of these—the present approach takes off from the notion that in a complex society like ours, it is possible that some people have socioeconomic status characteristics that are not in smooth harmony. Thus, while some people might have "matching" characteristics (e.g., ninth-grade education, occupation—dishwasher, income under $5,000) others might not (e.g., ninth-grade educa-

tion, occupation—construction contractor, income over $40,000). Such "mismatched" status attributes are even more likely if we admit other bases of U.S. inequality, such as race, ethnicity, or sex. Here we find the status "anomaly" of the Ph.D. astrophysicist earning $25,000—who is black, or female. In other words, this approach takes the notion of the multidimensional nature of stratification seriously and investigates the extent to which a person's position on each relevant stratification hierarchy is in agreement with the others. When Lenski introduced this approach in a 1954 article, he called it "status crystallization,"[29] but subsequently it has been studied under the rubric of status consistency versus inconsistency. The original prediction was that people with inconsistent statuses would behave in different ways (e.g., politically) than people in similar positions all of whose status characteristics were in harmony. To date, much research has been done, but no firm conclusions have been reached as to how useful status inconsistency is as an explanatory concept. Moreover, one researcher[30] argues that the statistical techniques that have been used to test for status inconsistency effects did not in fact measure status inconsistency.

Up to this point, the four approaches we have presented have been noteworthy for their *unhistorical* character. There is no analytic discussion of how people got to their present socioeconomic status, how stratification changes over time, and whether and how some people get out of one socioeconomic status and into another. Rather, the approaches have been static descriptions,

28. Weber, "Class, Status, Party," in *From Max Weber*, eds. Gerth and Mills.
29. Gerhard Lenski, "Status Crystallization: A Non-Vertical Dimension of Social Status," *American Sociological Review* 19 (August 1954):405-413.
30. Keith Hope, "Models of Status Inconsistency and Social Mobility Effects," *American Sociological Review* 40, 3 (June 1975):322-343.

which nonetheless tend to give the impression to the reader of timelessness and eternity. (It would perhaps not be too wrong to label this *stratification* research, since stratification originally refers to a phenomenon in geology—how layers of rock are arranged on top of each other in a systematic way.)

Upward Social Mobility—Consensus-Influenced Research into the American Dream

However, one consensus-inspired approach to social stratification *has* been concerned with changes in the stratification system. One of the central assumptions of U.S. fundamentalist-consensus sociologists is that the stratification system is an *open* one. The way to the top is not blocked to the talented, the ambitious, and the hard-working, in their view. (When pressed, they will admit difficulties in the case of blacks and perhaps women, but then again, most of their studies concern white males.) In recent years, studies of social mobility—or how people move up or down in the stratification hierarchy—have been among the most popular and have received considerable attention. Critics of the consensus perspective often point out that the popularity of the topic of mobility is due to the conservative bias of functionalist sociology. In other words, it is claimed that consensus-oriented sociologists defend and legitimate the status quo by trying to prove through mobility studies that the U.S. system is essentially fair and just, that everyone has the opportunity of moving up the status ladder, and that the U.S. is, in fact, becoming one big (and perhaps even happy) middle class.[31] Whether such a criticism is warranted depends greatly on one's values. Nevertheless, the concentration of mobility studies is interesting in this regard. Mobility may be either (1) *horizontal* (e.g., movement from one occupation to another at roughly the same level, with no change in status) or (2) *vertical* (i.e., movement that

does lead to change in status). Moreover, vertical mobility may be either *upward* (a rise in status) or *downward* (Sorokin's classic 1927 work on mobility presents these concepts[32]). Yet the overwhelming majority of studies have concentrated on only one type of mobility—*upward* vertical movement—and have neglected the extent to which downward mobility exists.[33]

Be that as it may, some of the social scientists interested in mobility have attacked some important questions. For one thing, they have asked what *societal* characteristics tend to be associated with a more open stratification system and a higher degree of upward mobility.

Berelson and Steiner[34] have summarized some principal factors, the most important of which include:

(1) Social change, that is, the more rapidly society is undergoing change, the more one can be led to expect increased social mobility.

(2) Industrialization and urbanization, that is, when the bulk of job opportunities shift from rural/agricultural types to urban/industrial types it is clear that both vertical and horizontal mobility will be increased.

(3) Widespread education.

These factors seem to summarize what has been happening in the U.S. since the turn of the century. In fact, the U.S. has been changing very rapidly since it was

31. Not all sociologists in the functionalist-consensus approach share the conviction that there is a trend toward declining inequality, but belief in the essentially meritocratic nature of the system—that is, that rewards usually go to the best qualified—seems to be one of their implicit articles of faith.

32. Pitirim Sorokin, *Social and Cultural Mobility* (Glencoe, Ill.: Free Press, 1964) First pub. in 1927.

33. L. Reissman, *Inequality in American Society* (Glenview, Illinois: Scott, Foresman & Co., 1973), pp. 35-40.

34. B. Berelson and J. A. Steiner, *Human Behavior: An Inventory of Scientific Findings* (New York: Harcourt, Brace, and World, 1964).

born, perhaps more rapidly than any other society in the world. It remains the foremost industrial nation, a title acquired in the 1880s; it has become overwhelmingly urban (almost reversing the 95 percent rural/agricultural vs. 5 percent urban ratio that marked its early colonial days)[35] and it has one of the most widespread systems of universal education in the world. All this, combined with the growing size of the pie (Gross National Product), make it unsurprising that most U.S. sociologists have been optimistic about the prospects for the U.S. becoming one "big middle class" through social mobility.

An international comparison of mobility rates in the U.S., Australia, and Italy seems to confirm this idea. Broom and Jones found the U.S. showed the most upward mobility for sons of blue-collar fathers—thirty-six percent of U.S. sons moved up to white-collar jobs as compared with thirty-one percent in Australia and only twenty percent in Italy.[36] From these and comparable findings it has been concluded that the United States exhibits the most open stratification system with the best opportunities for moving up the social ladder.

Some of the most comprehensive studies on mobility in the U.S. have been done by Blau and Duncan, and Duncan.[37] They too investigated *intergenerational* vertical mobility between fathers and sons (the extent to which sons will end up in a differently ranked occupational group from that of the father). Blau and Duncan compared census data for 1932, 1942, 1952, and 1962, and found that the 1962 findings showed "more upward mobility—particularly into salaried professional and technical positions—and less downward mobility into lower blue-collar and farm occupations" than the three earlier sets of results.[38] Their study also showed that the correlation between fathers' and sons' occupational status is (only) .38, which they take as an indicator of much occupational mobility in the USA (since it implies that only one-seventh of the variance in son's occupational status is due to father's occupational status). What the father transmits to the son is not his occupational status; rather it is a probable amount of education. In other words, sons of fathers with high occupational and educational status themselves achieved high educational status. And the Blau-Duncan studies show that it is the son's *education* that *most* affects his occupational position. It is in this way that the heritage of social class is passed on intergenerationally. Still, many U.S. intergenerational mobility studies are quite optimistic. This picture of optimism is shadowed by a number of criticisms.

First of all, a high degree of mobility may be a mere reflection of *changes in the composition of the labor force*. This factor, although mentioned by Berelson and Steiner,

35. According to the U.S. Bureau of the Census, "Population of the United States, Trends and Prospects: 1950-1990," *Current Population Reports,* Series P23, No. 49, Table 5.7 (Washington, D. C.: U.S. Government Printing Office, 1974):153, U.S. farm workers comprise just over 5 percent of the male labor force.

36. These results are presented in Leonard Broom and F. L. Jones, "Father to Son Mobility: Australia in Comparative Perspective," *American Journal of Sociology* 74 (January 1969):333-342; and Broom and Selznick, *Sociology,* pp. 191-94. In the main table of the latter it can be seen that in both Australia and Italy the downward movement of sons of nonmanual (white collar) fathers into manual (blue collar) and farm occupations *exceeded* the *upward* mobility of sons of blue collar fathers into nonmanual jobs. But this is not even mentioned in the text. Perception of social reality is conditioned by one's theories.

37. Peter M. Blau and O. D. Duncan, *The American Occupational Structure* (New York: John Wiley & Sons, 1967); Peter M. Blau and O. D. Duncan, "Occupational Mobility in the United States," in *Structured Social Inequality,* ed. Celia Heller (New York: Macmillan, 1969); and O. D. Duncan, "The Trend of Occupational Mobility in the United States," in *The Logic of Social Hierarchies,* eds. E. O. Lauman, P. M. Siegel, and R. W. Hodge (Chicago: Markham, 1970), pp. 714-721.

38. Duncan, "The Trend of Occupational Mobility in the United States," p. 721.

has not been adequately measured in U.S. stratification studies. Yet a good amount of the mobility over the manual/nonmanual line (which is what many of the intergenerational mobility studies concentrate on) may be the result of (a) the large-scale evaporation of agricultural jobs, plus (b) the relatively constant proportion of blue-collar workers since the 1940s, plus (c) the large-scale expansion of white-collar jobs. In fact, these three points summarize what *has* happened to U.S. job availability over the last generation or two. Since white-collar jobs have higher occupational prestige than manual jobs, a son pushed into such a job by the general shift in the occupational distribution automatically will be classified as upwardly mobile. Thus, such mobility, while real, cannot be used as evidence that the U.S. stratification system is uniquely open and will respond to the efforts of hard-striving individuals. In sum, the relatively high social mobility of the U.S. seems to have been due more to *structural changes* in labor force composition than to democratic values and equality of opportunity.[39]

Second, the concentration on upward mobility tends to blind one to downward mobility that may equal or outweigh upward movements. S. M. Miller[40] gave special attention to downward mobility in a cross-national study comparing a large number of industrialized countries. Contrary to the Blau and Duncan findings, Miller came to a rather pessimistic conclusion: downward mobility was appreciably greater than upward mobility in industrialized societies as a whole. In fact, upward mobility exceeded downward in *less than a third* of the nations studied. This higher rate of downward mobility implies that the system is becoming more rigid and closed. For example, he found that in Great Britain there was considerably more downward movement from nonmanual to manual (42.1 percent) than upward mobility from manual to nonmanual (only 24.8 percent). For the USA he found there is still more upward (28.7 percent)

than downward (22.6) mobility across the manual/nonmanual line, but the difference is not great. Furthermore, what Miller found for the industrialized nations subsequently has been found in underdeveloped countries.[41] For example, Tumin with Feldman found the highest downward mobility rates ever reported in their study of Puerto Rico: fully fifty-eight percent of the sons of *middle-class* fathers were in manual jobs when interviewed, as were a surprising forty-two percent of the sons of *elite* fathers.

Third, since the Blau and Duncan studies point to both the importance of *son's education* for his occupational success and to the influence his father's social class has on the amount of education he attains, we should take a closer look at equality of educational opportunity in the U.S. This we shall do when we examine the picture of

39. In fact, empirical support for this statement emerged shortly after this paragraph was written in an article by Robert Hauser, John N. Koffel, Harry P. Travis, and Peter J. Dickinson, "Temporal Change in Occupational Mobility: Evidence for Men in the United States," *American Sociological Review* 40 (June 1975):279-297. In a massive reanalysis of intergenerational mobility data, they find that all the father-son upward mobility documented in the U.S. for roughly the last half-century may have been due *solely* to changes in the occupational structure. In their words: "once trends in the occupational structure are controlled, there are no trends in the occupational mobility of U.S. men." Although they do not put it in this manner, their findings show that the system has *not* gotten a whit more democratic or open—just more urbanized and industrialized, with "upward mobility" consequences for the whole structure of U.S. occupations. But in keeping with the ideological stance of U.S. intergenerational mobility researchers, Hauser et al. ignore the sociopolitical implications of their important findings.

40. S. M. Miller, "Comparative Social Mobility," *Current Sociology* 9, 1 (1960):1-89 (whole no.)

41. Neil J. Smelser and Seymour Martin Lipset, eds., *Social Structure and Mobility in Economic Development* (Chicago: Aldine, 1964), pp. 45-50.

42. Melvin Tumin with Arnold S. Feldman, *Social Class and Social Change in Puerto Rico* (Princeton: Princeton University Press, 1961).

inequality in America uncovered by researchers of the conflict perspective, the topic of Chapter 7.

Summary

How can we tie together the three main strands of this chapter: Marx, the conflict theorist par excellence; the diametrically opposed American functionalist-consensus theorists; and the consensus approach-tinged work of the U.S. social mobility researchers? Davis and Moore provide the clue in their famous 1945 article delineating functionalist stratification theory. They argue that the question of why different social positions get unequal rewards and prestige is a *different* question than how certain people get into these positions and how easy or difficult it is to move from one social stratum to another. To summarize the chapter in a nutshell, Marx and the functionalist theorists have dealt with the first question—from dramatically opposed viewpoints—whereas the social mobility researchers have dealt with the second, but in a way that puts them in the functionalist-consensus camp.

Let us consider Marx versus the functionalist stratification theorists. First, Marx's approach to stratification was built around the notion of opposing *social classes*: the differing classes emerge out of their differing relation to the means of production, with the big split coming between those who *control* the means of production and those who do not. In contrast, the functionalists virtually ignore relation to the means of production and see stratification emerging from their assumption that to survive all human societies must insure that their most functionally important slots are filled by the most competent people. Unequal rewards and prestige are necessary, they assert, to insure that these people are motivated to take the crucial positions and to do them well. But rather than concentrate on what are the most functionally important positions (and

why), the functionalists concentrate on the unequal prestige itself. This typically is conceptualized in terms of *socioeconomic status* (SES), involving measures such as income and occupational prestige that to Marx would be mere consequences, not definers, of class position. Second, to Marx, social class stratification is inevitable only under certain historical conditions; in contrast, the functionalists see stratification as always being inevitable and necessary since it rises inherently from "human nature" and/or universal "functional requisites of society." Third, their opposing premises about the nature of stratification led Marx and the functionalist theorists to different ways of studying it. Marx examined concrete historical situations in which specific classes rose, interacted, conflicted, and changed; that is, he stressed history and process. In contrast, functionalist stratification theory, as embodied explicitly in Davis-Moore and Parsons (and implicitly in Warner), is ahistorical and emphasizes static, equilibrium conditions. In sum, on the basis of the comparisons made to this point, the Marxian and functionalist approaches seem to remain close to 180 degrees apart. The extent to which this gap could or should be bridged is discussed again on pp. 94-95 in Chapter 7.

Comparing the functionalist theorists and the social mobility researchers, we find that the latter rarely explicitly invoke and/or test the main theoretical tenets (i.e., the inevitability, necessity, and consensual basis of stratification) of the former. But the two groups do tend to share two assumptions about the nature and openness of the American stratification system: that it is basically a meritocracy (i.e., one moves up the ladder mainly on ability), and that there are lots of ladders—with more going up than down. Thus, the social mobility researchers may be considered to be in the functionalist-consensus camp. Nevertheless, they offer the apparent promise of moving a few big steps toward the larger, historical-process framework of Marx (and to a great extent, of Weber too) since they deal with the transmission of social class membership from one generation to the next. So far, however, that promise has not been fulfilled. Instead, they have elaborated sophisticated statistical techniques for measuring, say, differences between father and son's occupation. Often these involve fluctuations around the white-collar/blue-collar line. They have paid so little attention to history that for years they failed to control for long-term shifts in the composition of the U.S. labor force, that is, changing proportions of white collar versus blue collar versus farm workers. Yet, these changes clearly seem to affect their father-son, blue-collar/white-collar mobility results. As it happens, these optimistic results about the growing proportion of sons being upwardly mobile and ending up in white-collar jobs don't hold up when labor force composition changes are taken into account. New findings indicate that there seems to have been no net upward mobility over and above that accounted for by job mix changes. This casts at least some doubt on the meritocratic and open society premises of both the mobility researchers and the functionalist theorists.

All things considered though, the *notion* of social mobility studies still might lead to an expansion of the focus of U.S. stratification research (even though it hasn't yet). This could happen if serious attempts were made to analyze both structurally and historically how the occupational structure of a society is tied to its class system and how both are transmitted and transmuted over generations.

For Further Reading

Davis, Kingsley, and Moore, Wilbert E. "Some Principles of Stratification." *American Sociological Review* 10 (April 1945):242-249.

  Agree or disagree with it, this best-known presentation of functionalist stratification theory should be read.

Heller, Celia S., ed. *Structured Social Inequality.* New York: Macmillan, 1969.

  A good collection of consensus and conflict writings on stratification; most of the authors cited in this chapter are included.

Marx, Karl. *Karl Marx and Frederick Engels: Selected Works.* New York: International Publishers, 1968.

  Contains the Manifesto, the Preface, and the 18th Brumaire. The best-known section of the Manifesto is Part I, containing Marx and Engel's analysis of the rise (and predicted fall) of capitalism. The Preface is a succinct summary of much of Marx's theory of social change. The 18th Brumaire is his richest historical analysis.

Thompson, E. P. *The Making of the English Working Class.* New York: Random House, 1964.

  A vivid, professionally acclaimed description of the painful creation of a class of "free" wage-laborers.

Weber, Max. "Class, Status, Party," in *From Max Weber: Essays in Sociology,* eds. H. H. Gerth and C. Wright Mills. New York: Oxford University Press, 1958.

  A vastly influential article for U.S. sociology.

7 | The Icebergs of Inequality: The United States in Comparative Perspective

WE started out with the question, "Who gets what, and why?" We have seen that the *functionalists'* response to the question of "why?" involves the functional *needs* of society, the requirement to *motivate* individuals to fill difficult and demanding positions, and *common values* as to what these positions are and why they should be rewarded more or less as they are.

The answer of the functionalists to the question "who gets what?" has led us to consider prestige classes, seemingly high rates of mobility, and the rising level of prosperity in the U.S. as indexed by gains in real income—especially from World War II to the mid-1960s, the period of functionalism's virtually unchallenged sway.

The response given by the *conflict* theorists to the question of "why?" depends on whether their conflict sociology stems from a basically Weberian or Marxian mold. "Why" for the Weberian-oriented depends mainly on class and political power, with class defined in terms of market position, that is, in terms of an emphasis on differential advantages in property, scarce occupational skills, and so forth, that are reflected in differential distribution of income. "Why" for the Marxian-oriented depends mainly on class position with respect to the means of production, and much less on differential distribution of the rewards of production.

Moreover, the answer to "who gets what?" emerging from contemporary conflict theory has more often been provided by Marxian-oriented social scientists. Compared to the picture provided by the functionalists, their America is "another country," in James Baldwin's phrase. Specifically, what nonfunctionalist studies of American socioeconomic life have done is to lift the fabric of the American Dream covering the submerged extent of inequality and peek underneath.

But who is right? Paradoxically, both sides are. Confirming the functionalist view, income *did* rise greatly in the twentieth century, especially 1939-1965[1], greatly reducing the proportion earning below some government-defined poverty line, and greatly increasing the standard of living of ordinary Americans. The overwhelming majority

1. For example, manufacturing production workers, one-fourth of nonagricultural wage-earners, experienced a fifty-three percent rise in real income between 1939-44, and a further seventeen percent rise from 1944-60. *See* Gabriel Kolko, *Wealth and Power in America* (New York: Praeger, 1962), p. 77. Other figures on the U.S. labor force show good-size gains in real income through the mid-1960s, slowdown in the rate of rising real income in the late 1960s, and declines for the early 1970s (e.g., the *Economic Report of the President for 1972* reports no increase in real income for a worker with three dependents from 1965-71, a period of record corporate profits).

came to own cars, refrigerators, TVs, toasters, and other outpourings of the greatest consumer society in history. Furthermore, occupation, education, and income *are* the most important determinants of differences in life-style and well-being for almost all Americans, and are correctly perceived as such. The general likelihood of becoming a white-collar worker—and of ending up materially much better off than one's father —*has* indeed risen for American men (as the occupational structure has come to contain fewer farm and unskilled labor jobs and more nonmanual ones). Increasingly, education is what determines occupation, and for the majority of Americans, occupation is the most important determinant of income. So it *is* significant that the average educational level has risen greatly over this century.

The figures from the submerged portion of the iceberg of inequality uncovered by nonfunctionalists may not be as familiar to you; they are sometimes hard to come by, and rarely written up in your newspaper, news magazines, or college sociology texts. Ironically, most come from reanalysis of *U.S. government* statistics, hardly a radical source. Here is what they show.

WHO GETS WHAT?

First, we shall ascend the ladder of inequality from (1) *education,* which is somewhat more equally distributed than (2) *income,* which in turn is somewhat more equally distributed than (3) *wealth.* Then we shall take a look at (4) *taxes,* which are *supposed* to be very *unequally* distributed, on what is on paper a "soak the rich" basis— but turn out to be nearly the same for all levels of the population. We shall hold off on breaking these things down by sex (the topic of Chapter 8), and give only a little space to the plight of Black people, which is covered in *Racial and Ethnic Relations,* another volume in this series.

1. *Educational Inequality.* Since the Blau-Duncan studies clearly show that education is one of the single most important factors for mobility,[2] it is very important to see just how unequally opportunities for educational advancement are distributed. In the previous chapter, Table 6.2, taken from Broom and Selznick, showed an unequal probability of going to college even among three broad income strata. Let us now look at the more refined breakdown available from U.S. Census Bureau data in Table 7.1.

Table 7.1

College Attendance in 1967 among High School Graduates, by Family Income*

Family Income (1965; U.S. median = $6,957)	Percent Who Attend College
under $3,000	19.8
$ 3,000-$3,999	32.3
$ 4,000-$5,999	36.9
$ 6,000-$7,499	41.1
$ 7,500-$9,999	51.0
$10,000-$14,999	61.3
$15,000 and over	86.7
Total, all incomes	46.9

*Source: "Factors Related to High School Graduation and College Attendance," *Current Population Reports,* Series P20, No. 186, Table 8 (July 11, 1969):6.

Without college, poor and working-class students have little chance for mobility to upper white-collar status, so the basic outlines of the class system tend to get passed along from generation to generation. In fact, a reanalysis of the Blau-Duncan data revealed a *growing gap* between the sons of high versus low educated fathers in reaching college. Between the 1920s and 1950s,

2. P. M. Blau and O. D. Duncan, *The American Occupational Structure* (New York: John Wiley and Sons, 1967); and P. M. Blau and O. D. Duncan, "Occupational Mobility in the United States," in *Structural Social Inequality,* ed. Celia Heller (New York: Macmillan, 1969), pp. 340-352.

the proportion of sons from the top stratum who went to college rose over thirty percentage points, while the corresponding percentage among sons of bottom stratum fathers rose less than six points.[3]

How many of the children of the poor who don't make it to college really "deserve" to be there, on the basis of intelligence and merit? This is a crucial question for a system that stresses equal opportunity for equal ability. Bowles reports that a large study of U.S. high school students found the following probabilities of college entry among upper versus lower strata students from the *highest* scholastic ability quartile: highest SES quartile = 87 percent; lowest SES quartile = 48 percent. In other words, less than half the brightest students from the poorest families were likely to go on to higher education, as compared with almost nine out of ten students of the same ability level, but from the top socioeconomic stratum.[4] Still, the U.S. offers the most educational opportunity to working-class students of any of the industrial capitalist countries, as Parkin's Western European data make clear. (See Table 7.2.)[5]

Table 7.2

Percentage of University Students from Working-Class Families (ca. 1960)

Country	Percent Working-Class Origin Students
Great Britain	25
Norway	25
Sweden	16
Denmark	10
France	8
W. Germany	5

In the East European socialist industrial countries, even though children of professional, managerial, and Communist Party families—the elite—are overrepresented among university students, there are more working-class (and peasant) origin students

than in the capitalist industrial nations, Parkin documents. For example, fifty-three percent of top professionals (M.D.'s, scientists, etc.) in Hungary (1963) came from worker or peasant families.[6]

2. *Income Inequality.* The functionalist view stresses the rise in the average level of real income (e.g., from 1947-1970, median family incomes more than *tripled*, rising from a little over $3,000 to almost $10,000, when both figures are measured in 1970 dollars). What is rarely mentioned is income *distribution* during that period. Here we find a very different story: the relative *share* of the pie received by each family stayed almost exactly the same the whole time the Gross National Product (GNP) was getting bigger. Income distribution in 1970 is just about as *unequal* as in 1947, as U.S. census figures recently cited by a number of liberal and radical social scientists reveal. (See Table 7.3.)

What do these figures mean? If income were distributed equally, each fifth would get twenty percent. Instead, the richest twenty percent of families have well over *twice* the combined income of the poorest forty percent. Among unrelated individuals, the situation is even more unequal: the top fifth get more income (50.5 percent) than the bottom eighty percent put together (49.5 percent). Moreover, the very slight tendency toward equalization may be illusive, since this table doesn't include capital gains income (i.e., increase in the value of assets such as corporate stock). Ackerman et al. present data adjusting the income of the

3. S. M. Miller and Pamela A. Roby, *The Future of Inequailty* (New York: Basic Books, 1970), p. 133.

4. Samuel Bowles, "Unequal Education and the Reproduction of the Hierarchical Division of Labor," in *The Capitalist System*, eds. R. C. Edwards, M. Reich, and T. E. Weisskopf (Englewood Cliffs, N.J.: Prentice-Hall, 1972), p. 225.

5. Frank Parkin, *Class, Inequality and Political Order* (New York: Praeger, 1971), p. 110. Reprinted by permission of the author.

6. Ibid., p. 155.

Table 7.3

Percentage Share of Aggregate Income Received in 1947 and 1970*

	Families 1947	Families 1970	Unrelated Individuals 1970
Lowest fifth	5.0	5.5	3.3
Second fifth	11.8	12.0	7.9
Middle fifth	17.0	17.4	13.8
Fourth fifth	23.1	23.5	24.5
Highest fifth	43.0	41.6	50.5
Total	99.9	100.0	100.0
Top 5 percent	17.2	14.4	20.5

*Source: U.S. Bureau of the Census, *Current Population Reports*, Series P-60, No. 80, "Income in 1970 of Families and Persons in the United States," Washington, D. C.: U.S. Government Printing Office, 1971, Table 14, p. 28. Note that capital gains are *not* included.

top fifth of families for capital gains (since this is the group that receives almost 100 percent of it) and conclude that once "capital gains are included, the share of the top fifth has been constant over the past twenty years."[7] In monetary terms, the average income of the 10.4 million families of the top fifth was $23,100 in 1970—versus only $3,054 for the 10.4 million families of the bottom fifth.[8] It should also be noted that even though American families received the same *relative percentage* share of the rising national income, the *difference* in *absolute dollar* amounts between the top and bottom fifth of families *increased* greatly during the period. Just between 1958 and 1968, the gap rose from $13,720 to $18,888.[9]

An interesting question is whether the American pie (with a Gross National Product of over one-and-a-quarter *trillion* dollars in 1973) is big enough to carve up equally without reducing *all* to hardship. Roby points out U.S. Department of Commerce statistics that in 1972, average (mean) per capita before tax income was $4,478: "For a family of four, this came to an income of $17,912, or almost *$18,000*." So if income were distributed equally, *no one* need have

been poor, and the incomes of the *"eighty to ninety percent* of American families, which now fall below the $17,912 mean, would be increased" (emphases in original).[10]

One last point on income. In the 1787 U.S. Constitution, black males were counted as three-fifths of a [white] person (in order to apportion Representatives); in 1974 black per capita income was not even quite three-fifths: it stood at fifty-nine percent of white.

Income distribution data on other nonsocialist countries makes it clear that industrial capitalist nations have a more equal distribution than developing nations,[11] and that the U.S. is one of the *relatively* more *egali-*

7. F. Ackerman, H. Birnbaum, J. Wetzler, and A. Zimbalist, "The Extent of Income Inequality in the United States," in *The Capitalist System*, eds. Edwards, Reich, and Weisskopf, p. 209. When we attempt to go back before 1947, the statistics on income distribution are not quite comparable, and controversy arises over some of the fine points. Still no one has convincingly shot down the *substance* of Gabriel Kolko's (*Wealth and Power in America*, New York: Praeger, 1962, p. 14) findings that between 1910 and 1959: (1) the share of the poorest tenth plummeted from 3.4 percent to 1.1 percent of national (before tax) personal income; and (2) meanwhile, the share of the richest tenth dropped from 33.9 to 28.9 percent—a *proportionately smaller* drop than among the poorest tenth.

8. Letitia Upton and Nancy Lyons, *Basic Facts: Distribution of Personal Income and Wealth in the United States* (Cambridge: Cambridge Institute, 1972), p. 1.

9. Douglas F. Dowd, *The Twisted Dream* (Cambridge, Mass.: Winthrop, 1974), p. 120. Measured in 1970 dollars, the income of the bottom fifth rose from $1,956 to $3,085, while that of the top fifth rose from $15,685 to $21,973—so that the size of the gap in their dollar incomes increased over $5,000 in ten years.

10. Pamela Roby, ed., *The Poverty Establishment* (Englewood Cliffs, N. J.: Prentice-Hall, 1974), p. 2.

11. *See* Thomas E. Weisskopf, "United States Foreign Private Investment: An Empirical Survey," in *The Capitalist System*, eds. Edwards, Reich, and Weisskopf, p. 445.

tarian countries—only three industrial capitalist nations (out of nine on the list) have less income inequality than the United States: Norway, Britain, and Australia. In both the rich and poor countries, there is little variation in the income share received by the bottom forty percent; what varies is how the income is divided among the upper three-fifths, with somewhat less held by the top fifth among the richer countries. The data presented by Parkin show a good deal less income inequality in European socialist countries than in rich *or* poor nonsocialist nations.[12] In Russia, income inequality was deliberately fostered under Stalin. But in 1962, new reforms were made that seem to lower the differential in income to fifteen to one between the extremes in Soviet industry, that is, top managers earn around fifteen times more than a worker making the minimum wage.[13] In the U.S., by comparison, "American industrial executives receive from twenty to two hundred times the income indicated by the minimum wage law, and from 12 to 125 times the median income."[14] Still, the standard of *material* well-being is higher in the rich Western countries.

3. *Wealth Inequality.* Wealth refers to marketable assets. Included under total wealth are two main types of assets: (a) income producing, or investment assets (e.g., corporate stock, bonds, mortgages, bank accounts, trucks, factories, apartment buildings); and (b) nonincome producing, or inert assets (e.g., the family car, household possessions, home). The first point to note is that *investment assets* are the far more important type for economic power. Secondly, of investment assets, probably the most important category, given the U.S. corporate economy, is corporate stock. How are these distributed among the American population?

   —*the top one-half of one percent (1/2%) own one-third of investment assets*[15]
   —*the top one percent (1%) own sixty-one to eighty percent of corporate stock*[16]

   —*ownership of total wealth is less concentrated than ownership of corporate stock, as we see in Table 7.4*

To put the U.S. situation in perspective, I've included the available data on England —where wealth inequality is even greater. (See Table 7.4.)

Finally, what happened to "people's capitalism"? This is the concept of the U.S. promoted by the National Advertising Council and other business-oriented exponents. It is true that a very large *number* of Americans own corporate stock: 25,270,000 (about 12 percent) in 1975.[17] But it is equally true that most of these millions don't own very *much* stock since the lion's share is owned by a very small percent of very rich Americans.

4. *Tax Inequality.* Most Americans believe taxes to be "progressive," that is, taking a bigger *percentage* of income out of

12. Parkin, *Class, Inequality and Political Order.*

13. Gerhard E. Lenski, *Power and Privilege* (New York: McGraw-Hill, 1966), p. 312.

14. Ibid.

15. Summary by Ferdinand Lundberg, *The Rich and the Super Rich* (New York: Lyle Stuart, 1968) of the three principal empirical studies: Dorothy Projector and Gertrude Weiss, *Survey of Financial Characteristics of Consumers* (Washington, D. C.: Federal Reserve System, 1966); Robert J. Lampman, *The Share of Top Wealth-Holders in National Wealth, 1922-1956.* A Study by the National Bureau of Economic Research (Princeton: Princeton University Press, 1962); and Kolko, *Wealth and Power in America.*

16. The low figure, 61 percent, is that of Projector and Weiss for the year 1962; most figures are closer to 80 percent: Lampman found 76 percent in 1953, up from 61.5 percent in 1922; Robert Heilbroner in *The Future as History* (New York: Harper & Bros., 1959), p. 125, cites a U.S. Senate Committee estimate of over 80 percent; Charles H. Anderson, in *The Political Economy of Social Class* (Englewood Cliffs, N. J.: Prentice-Hall, 1974), p. 202, reports almost 80 percent, based on U.S. Treasury data.

17. New York Stock Exchange, "Census of Shareholders," reported in U.S. Bureau of the Census, *Statistical Abstract of the United States,* 1976 (Washington D. C., 1976), Table 807. This compares with 32,500,000 stock owners (about 17 percent) in 1972.

Table 7.4

Percentage Share of Wealth*

| | United States | | Great Britain |
	Total Wealth	Corporate Stock	Total Wealth
Poorest fifth	†	†	—
Second through fourth fifth	23	3	—
Richest fifth	77	97	—
Total	100	100	
Top 5 percent	53	86	75
Top 1 percent	33	62	42

*Source: Projector and Weiss, *Survey of Financial Characteristics* for United States data; Ralph Miliband, *The State in Capitalist Society* (New York: Basic Books, 1969) for British data.
† means less than 1/2 of 1 percent.

the pockets of the rich than the poor. On paper, the *federal* individual income tax laws are written to be very progressive, even though the maximum tax bite in the top bracket has been cut four times since 1964—plunging from a theoretical top of ninety-one percent down to a theoretical ceiling of fifty percent.[18] But most of the wealthy don't pay anywhere near this much, since they reap prime benefit from two major types of tax breaks: (1) the *capital gains* provision that taxes long-term profits at a maximum rate of twenty-five percent; and (2) a phenomenally complex batch of *deduction loopholes* that keep their tax accountants gainfully employed. As a result, the federal income tax, as actually *collected*, is only modestly progressive for those in the upper brackets.[19] But less than forty percent of all taxes are federal individual income taxes.

And when we turn to these other taxes, the picture gets worse: most of them are actually "regressive," that is, they take a bigger percentage of income out of the pockets of the *poor*. For example, most state and local taxes are *sales and property* taxes, and all together they amount to almost as much as federal income tax.[20] Most studies show that

these taxes are strongly regressive, and take the smallest percentage of income from the richest.[21]

Social Security is another tax whose percentage does not go up with income, and moreover, it currently is only deducted from the first $16,100 of annual wages; for many poor wage-earners with dependents, this takes a bigger chunk out of their paycheck than federal income tax withholding.

The net result? When we add together the mildly progressive federal income tax with the mostly regressive state and local taxes, we find that things just about balance out.

18. Dowd, *The Twisted Dream*, p. 285.
19. Joseph Pechman and Benjamin A. Okner, "Individual Income Tax Erosion, by Income Classes," Brookings Institute Reprint no. 230 (May, 1972); and Richard Goode, *The Individual Income Tax* (Washington, D. C.: Brookings Institute, 1966); and, for a popularized but readable survey of the same area, Philip M. Stern, *The Rape of the Taxpayer* (New York: Random House, 1973).
20. Ackerman, Birnbaum, Wetzler, and Zimbalist, "The Extent of Income Inequality in the United States," in *The Capitalist System*, eds. Edwards, Reich, and Weisskopf, p. 210.
21. *See*, e.g., Thomas Bodenheimer, "The Poverty of the State," *Monthly Review* 24 (1972):7-18.

Herman P. Miller, long-time head of the Census Bureau's population division, has estimated the total tax burden of federal, state, and local levies for people in different income categories, that is, what percentage of their income is gobbled up by taxes.[22] (See Table 7.5.)

Table 7.5

Total Tax Rate Combining Federal, State and Local Taxation

Income Class	Total Taxes: Percent of Income
$ 2,000-$4,000	35
$ 4,000-$6,000	31
$ 6,000-$8,000	30
$ 8,000-$10,000	29
$15,000-$25,000*	30

Source: Cited in James O'Connor, *The Fiscal Crisis of the State* (New York: St. Martin's Press, 1973); see also Miller, *Rich Man, Poor Man.*
*Income groups over $1 million averaged only 23.7-24.6 percent, according to U.S. Office of Tax Analysis figures cited by G. William Domhoff, *Who Rules America* (Englewood Cliffs, N. J.: Prentice-Hall, 1967), p. 163.

The general and accepted conclusion is stated by Dowd: "The best that can be said of the tax system . . . is that it is proportional to income and not, as most believe, progressive."[23]

Furthermore, although this area is more controversial, there are some studies presenting data that taxpayers of modest income pay out more than they receive in social welfare benefits. Kolko offers figures from 1949 through 1955 showing that tax payments by those earning less than $4,000 were greater than the federal government's total social welfare expenditures (including education, public health, public housing, public assistance, etc.)—which of course did not go exclusively to those earning under $4,000.[24] There have been more recent studies which seem to imply the opposite, but their findings have been contested by Wachtel and Sawers.[25] So the evidence is still inconclusive as to whether below-middle in-

come taxpayers as a group are more than paying their own way for government social welfare benefits.

But there is no doubt that over time the burden of U.S. federal taxation has shifted *from corporations to individuals:* in the 1920s corporations paid over fifty percent of all federal income taxes; in 1973, individual taxpayers paid seventy-five percent and corporations only twenty-five percent.[26] (Corporation income taxes accounted for only 20.6 percent of combined federal, state, and local tax revenue in fiscal 1966-67.)[27] Moreover, one source claims that "sixty-one percent of all individual federal income tax is paid by people with annual incomes of less than $15,000."[28]

All of the above gives us a great many statistics (perhaps too many for easy reading!) about the inequality of "who gets what." But the matter of "why" is more controversial. Conflict theory-oriented social scientists stress that America is *not* a virtually all middle-class society, as the functionalist sociologists tend to paint it; nor is it correct to speak of the "over-privileged two-thirds" as does David Riesman, a consensus-approach sociologist.[29] Some of the more radical, Marxian-oriented social scientists hark back to Marx's prediction that

22. Herman P. Miller, *Rich Man, Poor Man,* (New York: Crowell, 1971).
23. Dowd, *The Twisted Dream,* p. 285.
24. Kolko, *Wealth and Power in America,* p. 39.
25. Howard M. Wachtel and Larry Sawers, "Government Spending and the Distribution of Income," in *The Poverty Establishment,* ed. P. A. Roby (Englewood Cliffs, N. J.: Prentice-Hall, 1974) pp. 63-104.
26. Ray Howard, "Inflation," *Midwest Magazine, Chicago Sun-Times* (June 9, 1974):11.
27. Ackerman, Birnbaum, Wetzler, and Zimbalist, "The Extent of Income Inequality in the United States," in *The Capitalist System,* eds. Edwards, Reich, and Weisskopf, p. 210.
28. David Horowitz, "The Foundations: Charity Begins at Home," in *The Poverty Establishment,* ed. Roby, p. 57.
29. Cited in Kolko, *Wealth and Power,* p. 71.

capitalism would progressively increase the proportion of the population forced to work for wage labor (the proletariat), while progressively increasing the concentration of property-owning capitalists. What's the story?

ONE BIG MIDDLE CLASS?

First, we shall look at the standard of living and occupational class membership of average Americans, and second, we shall examine the wage labor proportion of the labor force over time.

Data on the standard of living are provided by the Bureau of Labor Statistics (BLS), which has worked out what it considers "lower," "intermediate," and "upper" budgets for a hypothetical urban family of four (husband, wife, and two children, ages 8 and 13). These budgets correspond to poverty, working-class, and middle-class lifestyles.[30] In 1970, the budgets were $6,960, $10,664, and $15,551, respectively (they are adjusted every year for inflation, of course).[31] Also during 1970, other government figures show thirty-two percent of all families fell below $6,960, and an additional twenty-two percent had incomes below $10,664; in short, the majority—fifty-four percent—of American families had incomes below the "intermediate" standard.[32] What is this standard? According to the BLS, it:

> provides one suit every two to four years for the father, a new winter coat every five years for the mother, and a new refrigerator and stove every seventeen years. A used car every four years. A movie once in six weeks. Nothing set aside [i.e., savings] for periods of joblessness, for illness, or for college education for the family's children. "Minimum" [i.e., the "lower" budget] pares everything down to food, clothing, and housing, and leaves nothing for other items.[33]

Meanwhile, 1970 census figures show that just under one-fourth of white American families (and 11 percent of black) earned

over $15,000 per year—so a full three-fourths of American families fell below the middle-class "upper" budget level.

Whatever happened to our middle-class majority, let alone two-thirds? Levison argues that the notion of a white-collar, middle-class majority is based on figures measuring the *total* labor force of both sexes. This gives a misleading impression, since so many white-collar jobs are clerical and sales positions held by women (and low paid women, at that, as we shall see in Chapter 8). In fact, in 1970, women constituted about two-thirds of clerical and sales workers.

Looking only at the *male* (nonagricultural) labor force, Levison shows, *we do not have a white-collar majority.* He presents 1969 Census Bureau figures documenting that only 42.4 percent of men worked in white-collar "middle-class" occupations (the Census's Professional and Technical, Managerial and Proprietor, and Clerical and Sales categories); the remainder, 57.5 percent, labored in the "working-class" job categories (Craftsmen and Foremen, Operatives, and Laborers and Service). In 1970, the average working-class *family*—that is, including the income of wife and children—earned about $9,500, "much closer to poverty than to affluence."[34] Wives' earnings have a great deal to do with even the modest standard of living the average working-class family enjoys. If we look at how much *one* working-class wage-earner brings in for a fifty-two-week full-time job, the figures are revealing: in 1970, the average full-time factory worker (with three de-

---

30. Andrew Levison, *The Working-Class Majority* (New York: Penguin, 1975).

31. The BLS budgets for 1975 were $9,838, $15,479, and $22,476 for "lower," "intermediate," and "upper" categories, respectively. Reported in the *San Diego Union* (April 17, 1976).

32. Anderson, *The Political Economy of Social Class*, p. 182.

33. Dowd, *The Twisted Dream*, p. 125-126.

34. Levison, *The Working Class Majority*, p. 33.

pendents) took home $6,032 for a full year's labor—nearly $1,000 under the BLS's "lower" budget.[35]

To survive at *any* budget level most Americans today rely on a paycheck—money made by selling one's labor. That would make one a member of the proletariat, by Marx's definition. Has this group remained constant or grown over history (as Marx hypothesized)? Michael Reich has tackled this question. He presents an analysis of trends in U.S. labor force structure. Selected years from his table are presented in Table 7.6.

From 1780-1930, 150 years, self-employed entrepreneurs dropped from eighty to twenty percent. In less than 190 years, the percentage of nonmanagerial wage-earners rose from twenty to over eighty percent. By 1969, there were nearly as many salaried managers and officials as entrepreneurs. Actually, not all of the managers are noncapitalists, and not all the entrepreneurs can be considered members of the capitalist class. But all in all, the table provides striking support for Marx's contention.

Who, then, are the capitalists? As Anderson notes, the small group that owns most of U. S. productive and investment wealth *cannot be distinguished occupationally* from the top U.S. Census occupational categories (Professional, and Managerial and Proprietor).[36] Rather than

being idle "coupon clippers," or "jet set" types, the great majority of males in this class work at full-time occupations, often related to the control of the assets they own (e.g., as industrial or financial executives). Using government statistics, Navarro defines a "corporate class" of corporate owners and managers, constituting 1.3 percent of the labor force, and earning an estimated median income of $80,000-$100,000 in 1970. In contrast, the highest-earning U.S. group shown by the standard *occupational* categories are M.D.'s, who had a median *reported* (which may not be the whole story) net income of $40,000 in 1970.[37] Before looking at the extent to which the large corporations, and this small "corporate class," dominate the U.S. economy, let us examine another aspect of "proletarianization"—unemployment.

UNEMPLOYMENT: HOW PREVALENT?

Once one becomes a wage-laborer, and has no other substantial income-producing

35. Anderson, *The Political Economy*, p. 183.
36. Ibid., pp. 102-103.
37. Vicente Navarro, "Social Policy Issues: An Explanation of the Composition, Nature, and Functions of the Present Health Sector of the United States," *Bulletin of the New York Academy of Medicine*, Series 2, 51, 1 (January 1975):199-234.

Table 7.6

The Proletarianization of the U.S. Labor Force, 1780-1969

Year	Percent Wage and Salaried Employees (excluding managers and officials)	Percent Self-Employed Entrepreneurs (business, professional, farm)	Percent Salaried Managers and Officials
1780 (estimate)*	20.0	80.0	—
1880	62.0	36.9	1.1
1930	76.8	20.3	2.9
1969	83.6	9.2	7.2

Source: Michael Reich, "The Evolution of the United States Labor Force," in *The Capitalist System*, eds. Edwards, Reich, and Weisskopf, p. 175. Reprinted by permission of the author.
*Excludes slaves, one-fifth of the population.

assets other than one's own labor, one becomes faced with the problem of whether or not (and at what price) one's labor is *wanted*. In short, one's economic welfare becomes dependent on the ups and downs of the labor market.[38] What are the ups and downs of the labor market for the average American? The answer to that question depends on how you measure *unemployment*, and that has been a raging statistical battlefield in recent years.

The Labor Department puts out the "official" figures—the ones you read in the paper. Once a month, a survey is taken, counting the people who happen to be unemployed (as officially defined; see below) during the week of the interview. If they had been unemployed earlier in the month, that isn't counted in these figures. The *annual* unemployment rate is simply the average of the twelve monthly surveys, *not* a total of all people who were *unemployed at some point during the year*. But such a total is available (although unpublicized), because the Census Bureau compiles it each year. And asking "how many people were out of work at some point during the last year?" produces a much more disturbing picture than the official annual unemployment rate, Levison shows. In 1969, when the overall unemployment rate was at 3.5 percent, a much higher proportion of the working class was jobless at some point. For example, 18 percent of the operatives and 24.4 percent of the construction workers were unemployed at some time in 1969. In 1970, unemployment rose, although the official rate never got above 6 percent in any monthly survey. Yet, the proportion of operatives and construction workers who were unemployed at some time during 1970 rose to 23 and over 30 percent, respectively. (The comparable figures for white-collar workers in 1970 are much lower, ranging from 5 percent for managers and administrators to 11.5 percent for clerical workers.) "The conclusion is obvious: Unemployment is tremen-dously widespread in working-class America."[39]

A number of social scientists have faulted the official definition of unemployment itself, rather than the way of measuring it by averaging the monthly surveys, charging that it underestimates the number of people who are actually without full-time work.[40] This is because the official definition does not count people who want full-time work but are working only part-time, or labor force dropouts who have given up actively looking for a job. When the Labor Department itself estimated what the figure would be if these two groups were added, the result proved nearly *double* the official rate.[41] And even this doubled rate is still an undercount, others argue. Gross and Moses propose adding still other groups who would prefer to work, such as those in manpower training programs, and a proportion of students, housewives, and nonworking fifty-five to sixty-four-years-olds; this would bring the 1971 rate up to a total of 24.6.[42] Sweezy also calculates a similar rate, 25.6 percent for December 1970, if all those working in military-related employment were added to

38. Michael Reich ("The Evolution of the United States Labor Force," in *The Capitalist System*, eds. Edwards, Reich, and Weisskopf, pp. 176-177) cites the U.S. government Projector-Weiss data to show how few Americans have a choice other than working (or welfare, if they qualify): in 1962, 45 percent of households owned under $500 in income-producing assets, and an additional 40 percent owned between $500 and $10,000—yielding a maximum of $800 per year, that is, for $10,000 at an eight percent return. (Recall that Projector and Weiss, *Survey of Financial Characteristics*, found one-third of all income-producing assets in the hands of the top 1/2 of 1 percent of U.S. households.)

39. The material in this paragraph is from Levison, *The Working Class Majority*, pp. 81-82.

40. Bertram Gross and Stanley Moses, "Measuring the Real Work Force: 25 Million Unemployed," *Social Policy* (Sept.-Oct. 1972):5-10.

41. Anderson, *The Political Economy*, p. 149.

42. Gross and Moses, "Measuring the Real Work Force."

just the "officially" unemployed.[43] And others argue for consideration of the problem of the working poor.[44] In short, no matter how it is measured the American economy has not provided full employment in recent years.

CONCENTRATED CORPORATE MIGHT, CONCENTRATED CONTROL?

We have been looking at individuals, now let us look at corporations, specifically the large corporations that dominate the economy in which individuals must find employment. First, we shall look at the biggest domestic corporations; second, we shall examine the gargantuan multinational corporations; and third, we shall see if the first two are connected with—and perhaps controlled by—the small group of top wealthholders.

1. *The Corporate Economy.* At the start of the Civil War, there were few corporations and little concentration in the U.S. economy.[45] In 1929, less than seventy years later, the situation had changed almost beyond recognition. Not only was corporate concentration a fact of life, but one that dominated the economy. In that year, the *100* biggest manufacturing corporations controlled *forty-four percent* of net capital assets (e.g., land, building, equipment) of *all* manufacturers. How had this happened? Not only had some firms grown stronger, more efficient and larger, it seems, leaving many small-scale firms unable to compete, they had also taken to gobbling up smaller firms in *mergers*. There had been two spectacular waves of mergers by 1929, an early one that peaked in 1898 (and led to much trust-busting legislation, which hasn't changed the overall picture very much), and a second one that crested in 1929.[46] In each of those two peak merger years, more than 1000 firms were merged out of existence. The pattern had been set. Mergers continued thereafter, and big business got bigger and more concentrated. The third, and

greatest, wave of mergers in U.S. history peaked in 1968-1969, when well over 2,000 corporations a year were swallowed up.[47] There was no question that the very biggest corporations were responsible for much of the mergers: in 1968, the all-time peak year, the *top 200* industrial corporations accounted for *three-fifths* of all assets obtained through mergers that year.[48]

A dramatic picture of just how concentrated the U.S. industrial economy has become is provided by Mueller in his testimony before the U.S. Senate Subcommittee on Antitrust and Monopoly. Mueller was Director of the Federal Trade Commission's Bureau of Economics, and his data have been criticized as *underestimates* because he failed to make adjustments to consolidate companies under common ownership.[49] Some of Mueller's "conservative" figures are shown in figure 7.1.

Just how concentrated U.S. industry is, is revealed by the fact that in 1962 there were close to 200,000 manufacturing corporations (out of about 5,000,000 separate businesses

43. Paul M. Sweezy, "Economic Stagnation and Stagnation of Economics," *Monthly Review* 22, 9 (1971).

44. Roby, ed., *The Poverty Establishment*, p. 13, notes that 25 percent of all persons aged 14-64 whose incomes were below the poverty line were employed full time, year round in 1971.

45. Gardner Means, *Economic Concentration*, from Hearings before the Subcommittee on Antitrust and Monopoly of the Committee on the Judiciary, U.S. Senate, 88th Congress, 2nd Session, pursuant to Senate Res. 262, Part I: Overall and Conglomerate Aspects (Washington, D. C.: U.S. Government Printing Office, 1964); and Dowd, *The Twisted Dream*, p. 68.

46. Means, *Economic Concentration*.

47. Dowd, *The Twisted Dream*, p. 66, using data from *Fortune*.

48. Ibid., p. 67.

49. Willard F. Mueller, *Economic Concentration*, U.S. Congress, Senate, Committee on the Judiciary (Subcommittee on Antitrust and Monopoly), 88th Cong., 2d sess., July 1964, pp. 111-129; and Maurice Zeitlin, ed., *American Society, Inc.* (Chicago: Markham, 1970), p. 18.

Figure 7.1 **Concentration of U.S. Manufacturing Corporations Assets and Profits in 1962**

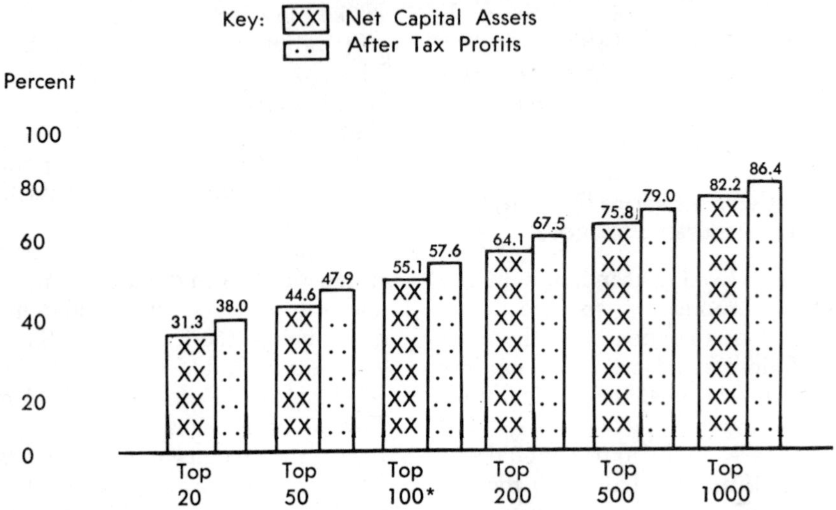

Key: | XX | Net Capital Assets
| .. | After Tax Profits

Source: Willard F. Mueller, 1964, based on Bureau of Economics, Federal Trade Commission Data.
*Means, another well-known economist who testified before the same Senate Antitrust and Monopoly Subcommittee, did make some adjustments for corporations under common ownership, and his estimate of 1962 net capital assets for the 100 biggest manufacturing corporations is 58 percent (vs. 55.1 percent for Mueller). Means notes that this 58 percent is up from 44 percent in 1929. See Means, *Economic Concentration*, p. 152.

in the U.S.).[50] So the top 1000, which control over eighty percent of assets and income, represent little more than one-half of one percent of manufacturing corporations. In short, the picture of concentration of wealth we saw in top U.S. wealth-holding *households* is repeated and emerges even more strongly in top U.S. *manufacturing* enterprises.[51]

Let us round off our view of the industrial economy with some 1972 data on the 1000 biggest corporations. (See Table 7.7.) It's clear from the information in Table 7.7 that what's left over for the remaining U.S. industrial corporations after we take these giants into account is, relatively speaking, chicken feed.[52]

2. *The Multinational Corporations (MNCs).* In recent years, these have become increasingly important, both for world production and as an ever more powerful factor in the world political economy.

With respect to world production, a few hundred of these mammoth MNCs already control about fifteen percent of the total: about $1/2 *trillion* out of a global sum of approximately $3 trillion in 1972. Furthermore, the MNCs are expanding at a rate of about ten percent a year.[53] Clearly, they are

50. *See* Edwards, Reich and Weisskopf, eds., *The Capitalist System*, p. 145.

51. *Banks* are very concentrated, too, with the top 50 of the U.S.'s 13,511 banks holding 48.3 percent of total bank assets; and *insurance companies* are the most concentrated of all; the top 18 of the country's 1790 hold 68.1 percent of all life insurance assets, according to Thomas R. Dye, E. R. Declercq, and J. W. Pickering, "Concentration, Specialization, and Interlocking among Institutional Elites," *Social Science Quarterly* 54, 1 (June 1973):8-28.

52. Edwards, Reich, and Weisskopf, eds., *The Capitalist System*, p. 145, cite Robert Heilbroner, the liberal economist, who goes even farther—he estimates that the top 150 corporations are so large and powerful that their removal "would effectively destroy the American economy." *See* Robert Heilbroner, *The Limits of American Capitalism* (New York: Harper & Row, 1965), p. 13.

53. Dowd, *The Twisted Dream*, pp. 73, 221.

Table 7.7
Share of Total Market Accounted for by
Top 1,000 Industrial (Manufacturing plus Mining) Corporations, 1972

	Biggest 500	Second Biggest 500
Total industrial sales	65%	6.5%
Total industrial profits	75	6
Total industrial employment	75	9
Total assets (in dollars)	$486 Billion	$46 Billion
Proportion of U.S. GNP (Gross National Product)	almost 50%	*

Source: Adapted from Dowd, *The Twisted Dream*, pp. 70-71.
*Figure not given.

a growing force as actors on the stage of world political economy.[54]

Who are they? Not all the MNCs are American based, but American-based companies are the largest of the multinationals. And who are these American-based MNCs? None other than the same firms that dominate the U.S. economy; that is, *the biggest American corporations are also the biggest MNCs.*[55]

How did the big U.S. firms get into the MNC business? Quite simply. Over time, in their search for markets and raw materials, their horizons expanded and they began to establish operations overseas. Since these foreign efforts produced appreciatively *higher rates of profit* than domestic operations (averaging 13-14 percent versus a 7-8 percent overall rate during 1950-1969),[56] and since profits attract business like magnets attract iron, the foreign involvements expanded enormously.

Actually, MNC *profits are highest* in the *underdeveloped countries.* And although the proportion of foreign investment in poor countries dropped to under thirty percent by 1969 (as MNCs devoted increasing resources to operations in *developed* countries), these underdeveloped nations still provided about *half* of overseas profits for the MNCs. Furthermore, the *profits gap* (between the income U.S. MNCs get out of poor vs. developed foreign nations) has been *widening* from 1959-1969.[57]

From whence stem these high MNC profits from underdeveloped countries? Overwhelmingly, the main U.S. MNC activity in Third World countries involves exploitation of *raw materials*—especially petroleum and minerals.[58] (The reason for this, of course, is that the U.S. *uses* such a disproportionate share of the world's resources.)[59]

54. Richard Barnett and Ronald Muller, *Global Reach: The Power of Multinational Corporations* (New York: Simon and Schuster, 1974).
55. Dowd, *The Twisted Dream*, p. 223. He notes too that about half the top 500 U.S. corporations now have substantial manufacturing interests abroad.
56. Weisskopf, "United States Foreign Private Investment," in *The Capitalist System*, eds. Edwards, Reich and Weisskopf, p. 428.
57. Ibid., p. 432.
58. Ibid., pp. 430-431; and Dowd, *The Twisted Dream*, p. 231.
59. This is shown graphically in data assembled from the 1969 United Nations' *Statistical Yearbook* by Ackerman, et al., 1972:208. A summary of their table shows:
In 1968, North America, with less than 9 percent of world population, had the following percentage of total world *energy* consumption:

natural and imported gases	68%
liquid fuel	39
total energy	38

Also in 1968, the U.S., with about 6 percent of world population, had the following percentage of total world consumption of these *resources:*

rubber	42%
tin	35

Much of these are imported.

Has this been beneficial or harmful to the underdeveloped Third World countries? Although the issue is controversial, the brunt of the evidence indicates that this MNC activity is generally *negative*. For example, U.S.-controlled enterprises in Latin America each year deliver over 1 billion dollars in earnings, most of it in repatriated profits.[60] The net result is that American foreign activity "takes three dollars out of the Third World for every one dollar invested."[61]

However, the bulk (about 70 percent) of U.S. MNC foreign investment has now shifted to *developed* capitalist countries, where over half of it is in manufacturing.[62] In fact, the importance of manufacturing for U.S. MNC activity is growing all around the globe—with some negative consequences for U.S. manufacturing employment.

Negative consequences of MNCs for the United States? Consider this example: only one-sixth of the $200 billion in U.S. products delivered to foreign markets in a recent year came from U.S. exports—the remainder was made and sold overseas by American-owned subsidiaries employing foreigners.[63] That's a lot of jobs to lose to "runaway shops."

Let's take another example of negative consequences: it's not only jobs the MNCs shuffle around—currencies move also. MNC currency transfers (or speculation) are widely perceived as a root cause of the 1971 international monetary crisis that led to the U.S. dollar devaluations.[64] This sort of thing exacerbates U.S. balance of payment woes, and since the MNCs are able to avoid a good part of their U.S. taxes under the intricate present rules, that doesn't help either.

Two more facts about American-based MNCs must be considered. First, they constitute a system even more concentrated than the U.S. domestic corporate economy: fewer than 50 multinational corporations account for the bulk of U.S. foreign assets—and U.S. foreign earnings.[65]

Second, and more important, the *economic power of the largest MNCs is now greater than that of many countries, exceeding most of the underdeveloped, and the smaller of the capitalist-industrial, nations.* Dowd notes the Library of Congress rankings of the world's 100 largest entities (measured by GNP for countries and gross sales for companies). In 1960, 59 countries and 41 companies (almost all MNCs) made the list. In 1970, companies predominated over countries, 51 to 49. In this list, General Motors comes in 24, just ahead of Yugoslavia, Pakistan, South Africa, AT&T, EXXON, Denmark, and Ford (in positions 25-31, respectively).[66]

60. *Statistical Abstract of the United States,* 1972 (New York: Grosset & Dunlap, 1972), p. 754. In developed countries, profits have been repatriated at only one-third the rate for the Third World, according to Anderson, *The Political Economy of Social Class,* p. 278. Considerable data concerning the often adverse impact of MNCs on underdeveloped countries are given in Ronald Muller, "The Multinational Corporation and the Underdevelopment of the Third World," in *The Political Economy of Development and Underdevelopment,* ed. C. K. Wilbur (New York: Random House, 1973), pp. 124-151.

61. Anderson, *The Political Economy of Social Class,* p. 278; he also provides much of the documentation for this paragraph.

62. Dowd, *The Twisted Dream,* p. 231.

63. Anderson, *The Political Economy of Social Class,* p. 276, citing Richard J. Barber, *The American Corporation* (New York: E. P. Dutton & Co., 1970), p. 8.

64. Dowd, *The Twisted Dream,* pp. 226-227 gives references.

65. Anderson, *The Political Economy of Social Class,* p. 277, discusses assets. Earnings are treated in Weisskopf, "United States Foreign Private Investment: An Empirical Survey," in *The Capitalist System,* eds. Edwards, Reich and Weisskopf, p. 432; and Howard J. Sherman, *Profits in the United States: An Introduction to a Study of Economic Concentration and Business Cycles* (Ithaca, N. Y.: Cornell University Press, 1968), p. 137.

66. Dowd, *The Twisted Dream,* p. 232. On a slightly different kind of list compiled by Weisskopf from various U.N. and economic statistical compendiums (Weisskopf, "United States Foreign

3. *Who Runs the Show?* We have already seen that wealth and stock ownership are very concentrated in the United States. Moreover, the one percent or so of top wealth-holders may be considered a "capitalist class," in that the majority of their income is derived not from their salaries, but from their *property*—capital gains, stock dividends, and interest.[67]

Do these top wealth-holders have any stake in running the concentrated corporate economy whose shares they own most of? Kolko poses the problem as follows: "(1) do a small group of very wealthy men have the power to guide industry, and thereby much of the total economy, towards ends that they decide upon as compatible with their own interests? (2) do they own and control the major corporations?"[68]

Although the matter is highly controversial, considerable research indicates that the answer seems to be yes. In a comparative analysis of the top 100 corporations' boards in 1957 versus 1937, Kolko discovered the same family names in board after board and a very strong family pattern in almost one-third of the seventy-two corporations for which data were available for both time periods. The conclusion was that "about 300 men"—the same number as in 1937—held most of the stock owned by board of director members in a sample of seventy-two of the top one hunderd corporations.[69]

If that's not enough, we should note that the majority (53 percent) of board members in the very biggest corporations are members of a narrowly defined "upper class,"[70] who as a group own the bulk of U.S. corporate stock. The second largest group represented on these corporate boards are hired managers, who although not themselves upper class tend to own enough stock in the corporation for it to constitute their major source of wealth.[71]

Thus, management tends to be tied into the same objectives as top shareholders, because what increases company earnings also enriches them personally. This becomes even clearer when we realize that research findings show that the most important factors affecting their compensation are their company's dollar profits and rate of return on equity.[72]

Therefore, it is hardly surprising that Larner also found that there was no real difference in the rates of profits earned by management-controlled versus family-controlled top-500 corporations. All this goes counter to the argument first advanced by Berle and Means that in the biggest corporations "ownership has become separated

67. Roby, *The Poverty Establishment*, pp. 10-11, uses Internal Revenue Service figures to show that 56.9 percent of the adjusted gross income of those receiving over $100,000 in 1970 came from these "capitalist" sources; C. Wright Mills, in *The Power Elite* (New York: Oxford University Press, 1956) pp. 149-150, cites figures for 1949, when $100,000 a year represented a much greater degree of wealth, showing that those receiving $100,000-$999,000 (13,702 people) earned 67 percent from property; those reporting $1 million or more (120 people) earned 94 percent from property.

68. Kolko, *Wealth and Power in America*, p. 69.

69. Kolko, *Wealth and Power in America*, p. 62. Interestingly enough, though, the percentage of stock *formally* held by these family board members had *declined* in a number of cases—at least in part due to the increasing practices of parceling out stock among more family members for tax purposes and turning over paper control to investment firms; both practice obscure ownership concentration.

70. Domhoff, *Who Rues America?*, p. 51.

71. For example, the amount of stock owned by twenty-five GM executives amounted to only an insignificant fraction of the corporation's stock, but it averaged $1/2 million per man in 1957. Ibid., p. 65, based on U.S. Securities and Exchange Commission data.

72. Robert J. Larner, "The Effect of Management-Control on the Profits of Large Corporations," in *American Society, Inc.*, ed. Zeitlin, pp. 251-262.

Private Investment," in *The Capitalist System*, eds. Edwards, Reich and Weisskopf, pp. 434-435), the companies come out as even more powerful: GM ranks 12 out of the top 50 (just behind Spain), and Ford and EXXON emerge as 19 and 20 (just behind Switzerland).

from control," and that the managers who control the giants are less profit-oriented than family firm owners.[73] Concerning the "separation of ownership from control" it is true that there are sometimes hundreds of thousands of shareholders, and the aggregate percentage of company stock owned by the top 200's board members is "only" around ten percent.[74] Lundberg, however, asserts that in most situations *five* percent of a company's stock brings effective control.[75] And the demonstrated convergence of behavior of management- versus owner-controlled firms implies that even in those companies where a small number of individual stockholders do not own enough stock to exert decisive control, *their interests are being served.* But once again, the evidence indicates that a very small group of individuals *do* own enough shares to guide corporate affairs *if* they so chose: Gordon's study of the top 200 corporations established that the total amount of the stock owned by each firm's top twenty shareholders averaged around twenty-nine percent.[76] Half of the top owners were individuals—about 4000 people in all—while the other half were institutions (and guess who was serving on their boards).[77]

Nevertheless, consensus theorists strongly criticized C. Wright Mills for his argument that a tiny group controls and dominates the top corporations and the corporate economy. For example, Talcott Parsons wrote that because of high confiscatory taxes on the wealthy, and the need for expert management, Mills's view is misguided.[78] We've already seen about taxes, and now the evidence indicates that "expert management" and the top shareholders tend to be bound together by common interests in the company's profits and growth. In short, it seems that top shareholders' objectives generally *are* served, whether or not they play a daily role in management.

When all the studies and supporting evidence are considered jointly, it appears that they make a substantial case to complete the equation as follows: *top wealth-holders = top corporate shareholders = frequently top corporate controllers* (personally on boards or as represented by typically like-minded management/directors).[79]

But to put into perspective what some have considered to be an American "ruling class," we should note that Djilas charges that a comparable group has emerged in the European socialist countries.[80] He asserts that those members of the Communist Party elite who administratively *control* the collectively owned means of production are in many respects comparable to the propertied capitalist class in the West,

73. Adolf Berle and Gardiner Means, *The Modern Corporation and Private Property* (New York: Macmillan, 1933).

74. Kolko, *Wealth and Power.*

75. Lundberg, *The Rich and the Super Rich.*

76. R. A. Gordon, *Business Leadership in the Large Corporation* (Washington, D. C.: Brookings Institute, 1945).

77. The proportion of stock controlled by "institutional investors"—such as pension funds—has been growing rapidly in recent years. In fact, Drucker has called the spectacular rise in pension fund holdings an "unseen revolution" in itself; one which is bringing about "pension fund socialism." He shows that already some 30 percent of stocks are held by pension funds and predicts they soon will control over half. But we should be cautious in interpreting this trend as "socialism." The pensions may one day be paid to "ordinary wage-earners" but the managers of the funds can hardly be classed in that group. *See* Peter F. Drucker, *The Unseen Revolution: How Pension Fund Socialism Came to the United States* (New York: Harper & Row, 1976).

78. Mills, *The Power Elite;* Talcott Parsons, *Structure and Process in Modern Societies* (New York: The Free Press, 1960), pp. 199-225.

79. Note that this equation is based on concentration of wealth and power, *not* on some alleged Machiavellian conspiracy whereby a small group of men deliberately scheme to run the economy and/or country to their liking. I am *not* implying that such a conspiracy, or ruling clique, exists. (But one may indeed wonder: with such a concentration of wealth and power, who needs a deliberate conspiracy?)

80. M. Djilas, *The New Class* (London: Thoames and Hudson, 1957).

and that their control of the means and surplus-value of production brings them economic power and special privileges. Parkin notes one big and important difference: the socialist "new class" cannot pass on their Party political post (often the basis of their control) and economic power to their children via inheritance, as the capitalists can bequeath their stocks.[81] However, they and the professional elite with whom they share a privileged position usually *can* assure that their children get the best *education*—which tends to be even more important for advancement in socialist lands than in capitalist.

Returning to modern U.S. capitalism we are left with the question: Are expansion and exploitation inherent? Here the liberal and radical wings of the conflict-oriented diverge, with the former criticizing militarism and foreign intervention, plus exploitation of Third World countries, U.S. blacks, ethnic minorities, and women—but viewing these as regrettable deviations from American ideals rather than anything built into our society. The latter criticize these same phenomena, but view them from a different perspective: as *intrinsic* to capitalism as a *system*. Unfortunately, there is no space here to present the radical justification and documentation of these assertions, or the specifics of expansion and exploitation seen as intrinsic to advanced U.S. monopoly capitalism.[82]

CONSENSUS VS. CONFLICT:

CAN THEY BE COMBINED?

Lenski presents a wide-ranging, holistic attempt to reconcile and synthesize the functionalist and conflict perspectives on stratification which we have been discussing.[83] His evidence is drawn from the whole of world history and his represents the best and most sophisticated attempt to merge these two disparate views. The attempt, however, is not very successful. There are two main problems. One is empirical: the theory he has erected on a synthesized foundation of consensus and conflict basic assumptions has been shown to be flawed in at least one significant element. This is his view that the political system is an independent, causal variable that, even after economic factors are controlled for, substantially affects the distribution of material goods and services (his main dependent variable). Several recent empirical studies[84] have come up with results that contradict this; in fact, their findings are much more in line with straight conflict theory predictions. The political system is intimately implicated in the economic system, and vice versa; neither is an independent variable, but of the two the evidence indicates that it is probably the economic, and not the political, system which comes closest to being so. The second problem with Lenski's proposed synthesis is theoretical. He traces inequality solely to the *distributive* system, that is, unequal distribution of goods and services.

81. Parkin, *Class Inequality and Political Order,* p. 153.

82. But to get an idea of the nature and impressive strength of the radical case, which I favor, Dowd, *The Twisted Dream,* and Edwards, Reich, and Weisskopf, eds., *The Capitalist System,* make fine introductory reading. For those interested, Paul A. Baran and Paul M. Sweezy, *Monopoly Capital* (New York: Monthly Review Press, 1966); James O'Connor, *The Fiscal Crisis of the State* (New York: St. Martin's Press, 1973); and Anderson, *The Political Economy of Social Class,* apply explicitly Marxian analysis to more specific topics.

83. Lenski, *Power and Privilege; See also* S. Ossowski, *Class Structure in the Social Consciousness* (New York: The Free Press, 1963); Pierre van den Berghe, "Dialectic and Functionalism: Toward a Theoretical Synthesis," *American Sociological Review* 28 (1963):695-705; and Celia S. Heller, ed., *Structured Social Inequality* (New York: Macmillan, 1969).

84. *See,* for example, Ain Haas, "The Origin of Inequality Among North American Indians," unpublished paper (Madison: Univ. of Wisconsin, 1973); and R. W. Jackman, "Political Democracy and Social Equality: A Comparative Analysis," *American Sociological Review* 39, 1 (Feb. 1974): 29-45.

But to many conflict theorists, beginning with Marx himself, the *roots* of inequality are not in the way goods are distributed but in the way they are *produced.* Accordingly, Lenski's synthesis falls short because it does not manage to include one of the key elements of conflict theory—the Marxian perspective that traces conflict between classes back to the relations of production, *not* the relations of distribution (I am grateful to Gösta Andersen, who formulated this and the next point). So the question of whether a synthesis theory is possible has not yet been fully resolved. To a certain extent, the consensus and conflict schools are looking at two different aspects of reality (two sides of a coin according to Dahrendorf),[85] and it is true that each ignores problems the other finds central. To that extent, a synthesized, expanded theory that looked at both realities *should* be possible. But then we are left with the problem of *which aspect of reality is the most important and decisive for inequality.* And it is precisely here that the divergence between the two approaches is greatest. Consequently, it seems doubtful whether a real synthesis may be achieved. The best test of which approach is most "right" must be the future developments of society.

For Further Reading

Baran, Paul A., and Sweezy, Paul M. *Monopoly Capital.* New York: Monthly Review Press, 1966.

An influential Marxian analysis that emphasizes the problem of "surplus absorption" (corporations' difficulties in finding reinvestment outlets for their growing profits). Difficult reading without some economics background.

Barnet, Richard, and Muller, Ronald. *Global Reach: The Power of the Multinational Corporations.* New York: Simon & Schuster, 1974.

They consider MNC's a different breed of cat than ordinary corporate giants, but agree or not, you'll find a wealth of information on them.

Braverman, Harry. *Labor and Monopoly Capital: The Degradation of Work in the Twentieth Century.* New York: Monthly Review Press, 1974.

A compelling, insightful, and well-written analysis that offers theory that could account for Terkel's (see below) descriptive data.

Dowd, Douglas F. *The Twisted Dream.* Cambridge, Mass.: Winthrop, 1974.

U.S. capitalism's checkered history—from 1776 to the present—is surveyed in Dowd's broad, but well-written analysis.

Edwards, Richard C.; Reich, Michael; and Weisskopf, T. E., eds. *The Capitalist System.* Englewood Cliffs, N. J.: Prentice-Hall, 1972.

A readable and cogent introduction to the problems of U.S. capitalism as seen from a radical perspective.

Mills, C. Wright. *The Power Elite.* New York: Oxford University Press, 1956.

Widely attacked by the sociological establishment when first published, this controversial classic may find a more receptive audience today.

O'Connor, James. *The Fiscal Crisis of the State.* New York: St. Martin's Press, 1973.

His Marxian analysis of growing municipal and state deficits and crisis preceded by two years the spectacular fiscal crisis of New York City.

Parkin, Frank. *Class Inequality and Political Order.* New York: Praeger, 1971.

Gives extensive data on Eastern European socialist countries. However, he stresses the importance of occupation (vs. class) as much as do orthodox functionalists.

Roby, Pamela, ed. *The Poverty Establishment.* Englewood Cliffs, N. J.: Prentice-Hall, 1974.

A good reader on the political economy of U.S. poverty.

Terkel, Studs. *Working.* New York: Random House, 1972. (Also available from New York: Avon, 1975.)

No theory, but a compelling collection of interviews of what Americans do all day and how they feel about it. Most people don't much like what they're doing—and with good reason, the reader may conclude from these vignettes.

85. R. Dahrendorf, *Class and Class Conflict in Industrial Society* (Stanford: Stanford Univ. Press, 1959).

8 From Patriarchy to Liberation? Today's Woman–United States and Worldwide

Rae Lesser Blumberg
with Julie Fein

WITH respect to the general system of inequality, we have seen that industrial societies—both capitalist and socialist—register a somewhat lower average level than the agrarian societies from which they sprang, along with an enormously higher material standard of living. We also have seen that in recent decades there has not been any visible trend toward a further *relative* decline in material inequality in the most advanced industrial society, the U.S. In fact, the shares of the top and bottom fifths in wealth and income have stayed virtually constant, and the bulk of the wealth and control over the corporate economy have remained concentrated in the hands of a minority not appreciably larger in percentage terms than the "governing class" Lenski describes for traditional agrarian society. In short, we have failed to confirm the consensus sociology view that inequality is low and has been steadily decreasing in America.[1]

With respect to sexual inequality, it turns out that here too industrial societies—both capitalist and socialist—register a somewhat lower average level than agrarian ones. But here too we are faced with conflicting views as to whether the reduction in inequality is: (a) as great as implied by that women's cigarette slogan, "You've come a long way baby!" (b) continuing to decline steadily; and (c) a worldwide phenomenon. Not surprisingly, consensus theorists (to the extent they have turned their attention to women in recent years) would answer "yes" to all three points, while those in the conflict approach would tend to take the opposite view (again, to the extent they have turned their attention to women in recent years).

We shall address (a) and (b) with respect to the United States, contrasting the consensus and conflict-type approaches. Then we shall explore the situation of women elsewhere. In much of this, we shall present the divergent evidence with a "first the good news, and then the bad news" format. Where relevant, the paradigm on sexual inequality introduced in Chapter 3 will be invoked, in an attempt to interpret the ups and downs of woman's fate in the contemporary world.

WOMEN IN THE UNITED STATES

First, the Good News

The *extent* of the American woman's progress toward equality is what is stressed by those holding the optimistic view. Implicitly or explicitly they suggest that she is practically there. What sort of evidence of prog-

1. On the other hand, in this book there has been no systematic attempt to "prove" the conflict view, despite my obvious leanings vis-à-vis say, Marx vs. Parsons.

ress do they cite? The "good news" includes such items as: (1) More and more American women are *working*—apparently because they want to work.[2] (2) With respect to the socioeconomic status (SES) variables, (a) three-fifths of women already are found in white-collar *occupations,* and the proportion of white-collar women keeps rising; (b) the *occupational prestige* rankings of women have risen too, and in fact are as high as those of men;[3] (c) over the 1950s and 1960s, the real *income* (corrected for inflation) of working women increased substantially; and (d) similarly, more and more women are taking advantage of higher *education,* which should translate to better, and better paid, jobs in the future.[4] (3) Women have more *freedom* in virtually every area of life: more women smoke in public, go in for sports, get credit cards in their own name, have premarital sex, control their fertility, get divorced, etc. Women who work have more household power,[5] ergo more women have a bigger say in their own homes. And so on. (4) Women are gaining more *power.* For example, there has been a large rise in the percentage of women elected to public office in recent years.

Now, the Bad News

"Yes, but . . ." characterizes the more critical conflict-oriented view that each of the above silver linings shields from sight a much darker cloud.

One of the problems people of this perspective see with most "silver lining" facts and figures is that they compare the position of women at a given time with the (lower) position of women at some previous time. Fine. That can tell us if women, as a group in isolation, are experiencing better or worse life chances. But these sorts of figures do not tell us about the *status* of women, because status implies a *comparison*—not only *within* groups (e.g., women), but also *between* groups (e.g., men and women) who differ in their po-

sition with respect to some dimension of inequality (e.g., income). Accordingly, much of the evidence of female status emphasized by the "yes, but . . ." crowd compares the *relative* position of men versus women, and how that has been changing over time. When we look at things this way, the news does not look as good.

(1) *More women are working all right.* In fact, more women are working than the figures we normally see published in newspapers, magazines, and sociology texts would lead us to believe. This is because of different ways of expressing the percentage of women in the labor force. For example, U.S. Department of Labor statistics for 1970 show that women in the labor force were:

38 percent of the *total* labor force

43 percent of the *female population 16 years and over* but fully—

50 percent of *females* in the prime labor force years, *ages 18-64.* (This last statistic is one you rarely see published.)[6]

2. Herbert Stein, "Women's Second Economic Revolution," *Ladies' Home Journal* (Oct. 1972).

3. Donald J. Treiman and Kermit Terrell, "Sex and the Process of Status Attainment: A Comparison of Working Women and Men," *American Sociological Review* 40, 2 (April 1975):174-200.

4. All assertions not followed by an author can be documented with U.S. Bureau of the Census publications including *Subject Reports: Earnings by Occupation and Education* (Washington, D.C.: Government Printing Office, Jan., 1973); and Abbott L. Ferriss, *Indicators of Trends in the Status of American Women* (New York: Russell Sage, 1971).

5. Robert O. Blood and Donald M. Wolfe, *Husbands and Wives: The Dynamics of Married Living* (New York: Free Press, 1960).

6. For the 38 and 43 percent figures *see* United States Department of Labor, Bureau of Labor Statistics, *Employment and Earnings, June 1971,* 17: 12, tables A-1, 2, 3, and A-18 (Washington, D. C.: Government Printing Office, 1971); for the 50 percent figure, *see* United States Department of Labor, Bureau of Labor Statistics, *Marital and Family Characteristics of Workers, March 1970,* Special Labor Force Reports, no. 130 (Washington, D. C.: Government Printing Office, 1971).

Many more are working for the same reason as most men—economic necessity.[7] But their desires or needs are not what makes it *possible* for them to enter the labor force. When one wants to become a wage-laborer, one has to find a buyer. In other words, the view stressed here is that it has been the *demand* for their labor, rather than a sudden upsurge in the *supply* of women wanting to enter the labor force that has been the most important factor in explaining U.S. women's rising labor force participation since the turn of the century. This argument is brilliantly expressed and documented by Valerie Kincaid Oppenheimer. (See footnote 10.)

She notes that in 1900, when only twenty percent of women aged eighteen to sixty-four were in the labor force, the great majority of them worked before marriage and children. As it happened, by 1900 patterns of sex segregation in jobs had emerged (which have remained almost constant since), and women were increasingly monopolizing precisely those sectors of the labor force destined to increase the *most* in subsequent decades: *clerical* and *service* jobs.

As a result, between 1900 and 1940, labor demand slowly grew to the point where married women were pulled in; single ones were no longer enough. But these were usually married women without school-age children. Then, during World War II, rising demand required pulling in still another group of women: married ones *with* school-age children. Though most worked in "women's" jobs, others briefly achieved popular acclaim ("Rosie the Riveter" became a folk heroine) and high (men's) wages working in normally male manufacturing jobs in defense-required production. After the war, the likes of Rosie the Riveter were rapidly laid off; for example, 600,000 of these women lost their jobs within a month after the war ended.[8] This occurred even though surveys just prior to the end of the war revealed that the overwhelming majority *wanted to continue* working.[9] But the economy still

needed Rosie's lower paid sisters in those clerical and service jobs.

So women's labor force participation continued to increase, especially after 1960. By then, the economy had grown to a state where labor needs could be met only by tapping the last major nonworking female group: mothers of preschool children.[10] During the 1950s, as few as 6 out of 100 women with preschool children worked, but by 1970, fully 30 out of 100 did.[11] In short, the reason women have been *able* to work has been economic *demand*. Attitudes adjusted to reality: Gallup polls show that in 1936, at the depths of the Depression, seventy-two percent *"disapproved"* of a married woman holding a job "when her husband is able to support her." Just after the end of World War II in 1945, eighty-six percent disapproved. But in 1969, when over three-fifths of women workers *were* married women, only forty percent disapproved.[12]

7. For data, *see* Natalie J. Sokoloff, "A Description and Analysis of the Economic Position of Women in American Society" (paper presented at the meetings of the American Sociological Association, Montreal, 1974).

8. J. E. Trey, *Women in the War Economy—World War II*, Warner Modular Publication, Reprint 44 (1973). Reprinted from the *Review of Radical Political Economics* 4, 3 (July, 1972).

9. Sheila Tobias and Lisa Anderson, *What Really Happened to Rosie the Riveter: Demobilization and the Female Labor Force 1944-47*, MSS Module 9 (1974):1-36; and Trey, *Women in the War Economy.*

10. For example, in just one decade, 1960-69, the "proportion of working married women, 20-24 (husband present) with preschool children" rose by eighty-two percent, from eighteen percent in 1960 to thirty-three percent in 1969. Valerie Kincaid Oppenheimer, "Demographic Influence on Female Employment and the Status of Women," *American Journal of Sociology* 78 (1973):946-961.

11. Renee Blakken, "Women Workers in America," *The Guardian* (March 29, April 5, April 12, and April 19, 1972).

12. Howard J. Ehrlich, *Selected Differences in the Life Chances of Men and Women in the United States* (Baltimore: Research Group One, Report No. 13.), pp. 16-17.

(2) *When we look at the "big three" SES variables: occupation, income, and education*, we see that the position of women *relative to men* has *not* improved; in fact, census data shows that it *declined* on each count between 1940-64.[13] More recent government figures show this decline is continuing.

Occupation. Let's start with *occupation*, and let's start at the top: the professional-technical category. Government statistics show that even though the number of women with these jobs increased, the *proportion* of all professional-technical workers who were women *decreased*. A drastic example concerns grade school principals: in 1928, fifty-five percent of them were women; in 1968, only twenty-two percent were women.[14] But the greatest number of women work in clerical jobs, and these have become increasingly "women's work"—that is, the proportion of men in clerical work has decreased steadily. And a strange thing has been happening to the relative earnings of male versus female clerical workers: the women keep falling farther and farther behind. In 1939, a female full-time clerical worker's paycheck was about twenty percent smaller than that of a male clerk. By 1969, her paycheck was over a third smaller. The "earnings gap" between men and women has long been largest among *sales* workers, and it too has been growing. By the end of the 1960s, a woman in sales earned only about $.43 for every $1.00 made by her male counterpart. This is the worst ratio found in any occupation.[15]

Income. Let us examine male versus female income differences in general. We find that comparing *all* men and women over the age of 14, *the income of women is only one-third of the income of men*.[16] This figure is much lower than the one you usually see, because it includes women working part-time, as well as welfare and social security recipients, etc. And women are much more likely than men to be confined to part-time work.

When we examine only men and women who work *full-time, year-round*, the gap is not as great: the income of women is almost three-fifths the income of men. Thus, in 1970, a *woman working full-time earned $.59 for every $1.00 earned by a man* (women's median = $5,403 vs. male median = $9,104). But in 1955, women had made $.64 for each $1.00 in male income, so the *gap* in the ratio of women's versus men's income has been *growing larger*.[17]

Education. Schooling is supposedly the great stairway to opportunity in America. But women (like blacks) do not get as much of a payoff for "investing" in education.[18] Consider this: *a woman college graduate working full-time earns the same income as a male high school dropout*.[19] At every educational level, women working full-time earn less than men with the same schooling, although here diligence does bring some reward. Census data for 1970 show that among those with only an eighth-grade education, women earn $.55 for each $1.00 earned by men. Among those who are college graduates, the situation is a little more favorable for women: they earn $.63

13. Cited in Dean D. Knudsen, "The Declining Status of Women: Popular Myths and the Failure of Functionalist Thought," *Social Forces* 48, 2 (1969):183-193.

14. Cynthia Fuchs Epstein, *Woman's Place* (Berkeley: University of California Press, 1970), p. 10.

15. See Ehrlich, *Selected Differences in the Life Chances of Men and Women in the United States*, p. 3.

16. Ehrlich, *Selected Differences*, p. 1, cites Census Bureau data showing that in 1970, women's income was thirty-four percent that of men, down from forty-six percent in 1947.

17. Ehrlich, *Selected Differences*, p. 2. In fact Census Bureau figures for 1975 show that the gap has widened still further: women are down to $.57 for each $1.00 earned by males.

18. Treiman and Terrell, "Sex and the Process of Status Attainment."

19. U.S. Bureau of the Census, *Subject Reports*, (January 1973):1, 242.

cents for every $1.00 earned by men. The story goes on and on. And it tells us the same thing: in general, women's *relative* educational position has *declined* on a variety of measures since the 1940s.[20]

So with respect to women's socioeconomic position, the good news seems swamped by all the bad news. This is so even if we add to the positive side of the ledger women's recently won legal *rights* with respect to equal employment (affirmative action laws). But in *practice* women still face massive discrimination as a group: the declining ratio of women's income relative to men makes this quite clear. And there is further proof that income discrimination against women is not *their* fault. For example, Suter and Miller set out to see if the fact that women lag behind men in most of the factors that affect income (e.g., occupational level, education, number of weeks and hours worked, career experience) explained why their wages were so much lower than those of men.[21] They did a complicated statistical analysis, and learned that even if these differences were removed, women's income would *still* be almost one-third less than men's. It would appear that most of this remaining income differential is due to just plain discrimination.

(3) *Concerning women's freedom in various areas of life,* let us focus mainly on what seems an offbeat topic—that is the proportion of women who become family or household heads. At one level, it is a measure of autonomy, for if a woman is heading her own household, it means she somehow has managed to survive minus a mate without having to give up her independence and move in with relatives or friends. Since about 1960, the proportion of female-headed households has risen rapidly.[22] In part, this is because more women have been able to find work, as we have seen, and because welfare officials have been accepting a larger percentage of women who apply.[23] At the same time, the pool of women without mates—divorced, widowed, separated, never-

married—has been growing proportionately larger. So far so good.

Now for the bad news: being the female head of a household very frequently means being condemned to poverty. Women's income is so much less than men's that their households are *bound* to be poorer on the average. And a woman household head doesn't have a working wife to help out—as do over forty percent of U.S. husbands. Yet, in the United States, the female-headed household has *not* been viewed as a problem of *women;* rather, it has been viewed primarily as a problem of black people.[24] Exploring it will permit us to highlight some of the interrelated problems of poverty, race, and sex in America.

Often, the reason the woman-headed family gets studied is because it is viewed as something abnormal. Not just unusual, but *pathological*—a breeding ground for an alleged "culture of poverty"[25] transmitted from

20. Knudsen, "The Declining Status of Women," p. 187; and Ferriss, *Indicators of Trends in the Status of American Women,* contain a number of good statistics showing this.

21. Larry E. Suter and Herman P. Miller, "Income Differences between Men and Career Women," *American Journal of Sociology* 78 (January 1973): 962-974.

22. United States Department of Labor, Employment Standards Administration, Women's Bureau, "Facts About Women Heads of Households and Heads of Families" (Washington, D.C., 1973); and Robert L. Stein, "The Economic Status of Families Headed by Women," *Monthly Labor Review* 93 (December 1970):1-8.

23. Richard A. Cloward and Frances F. Piven, "Migration, Politics and Welfare," *Saturday Review* (Nov. 16, 1968). Also appears as Warner Reprint #625 (1973).

24. *See* Rae Lesser Blumberg with Maria Pilar Garcia, "The Political Economy of the Mother-Child Family: A Cross-Societal View," in *Beyond the Nuclear Family Model,* ed. Luis Leñero-Otero (London: Sage, 1977), pp. 99-164 for references.

25. Oscar Lewis, *La Vida: A Puerto Rican Family in the Culture of Poverty* (New York: Random House, 1960) originated the concept, but not the "blame the victim" manner in which it has been reformulated by his successors.

one generation to the next that produces shiftless, welfare-prone dropouts, and crime. And it is black people who are accused of carrying this social disease of female-headed familism. Moynihan wrote the best-known statement on women-headed households as a growing social cancer among blacks; he even implied that this family "disorganiation" was becoming more important than discrimination as the thing holding blacks down.[26]

One statistic usually used to document that this is a racial problem is this: among urban households, thirty-five percent of those of blacks have female heads, vs. only twenty-two percent of the white units.[27] But if we consider female-headed units in terms of the greater relative poverty of women than men, we are led to re-examine the statistics in a somewhat different manner. Let us look only at households at or below the "poverty line," since all studies show that female-headed units become rarer and rarer as we check out the figures for each higher income category. Once again, we shall look at the data for urban households. In 1969, the poverty line stood at $3,700 for a family of four.[28] The U.S. Census table we shall use (see Table 8.1) gives income in $1000 intervals for low-income groups. Let us look at the *really* poor—those earning under $2000.

Even remembering that the data refer to households, not just families, and thus can include people living alone such as elderly widows, it is rather sobering to learn that *almost two-thirds of all U.S. households earning under $2,000 are headed by women.* And when we look at the figures for each race separately, the results are really startling: *there is absolutely no consistent difference between blacks and whites.* In other words, the huge *racial difference* shown by the total urban figures on female-headed households utterly vanishes among the urban poor: sixty-five percent of black and sixty-five percent of white households with incomes under $2,000 are headed by females. When we look at all those making under $4,000, we *still* find that *more than half* these households are female-headed. Here, the racial difference is very slight, fifty-five percent among whites, and fifty-nine percent among blacks.[29] Then why is

26. Daniel Patrick Moynihan, *The Negro Family: The Case for National Action* (Washington, D. C.: Office of Policy Planning and Research of the Department of Labor, 1965).
27. U.S. Bureau of the Census, *United States Summary*, PC(1), D1, 1970, *Detailed Characteristics*, Table 258, 1-959-61.
28. Stein, "The Economic Status of Families Headed by Women," p. 3.
29. Repeating our examination of the under $2,000 and under $4,000 categories for *rural* households, we find the same pattern—no difference between the proportions of white and black households that are headed by women. For a theoretically guided analysis, *see* Blumberg with Garcia, "The Political Economy of the Mother-Child Family." This article presents a series of structural conditions associated with higher rates of mother-child families. Meanwhile, however, it has recently been brought to my attention that when we consider *families*, vs. *households*, there do appear to be some racial differences—although there remains a clear and strong inverse relationship such as income decreases, frequency of female-headed (family) units increases. These racial differences appear to lessen as other structural factors, e.g., poverty areas, central cities, etc., are controlled for. As a result, the above data on households must be treated with caution. The issue will be decided only by further detailed analysis of recent family data.

Table 8.1

**Percentage of Urban Households
Headed by Women, 1969**

	Total	Under $2,000	Under $4,000
Black	35	65	59
White*	22	65	55

*Includes a minute fraction of Orientals and Native Americans.
Source: U.S. Bureau of the Census, *United States Summary*, PC(1), D1, 1970, *Detailed Characteristics*, based on Table 258, 1-959-61.

the racial gap on female-headed households so large for the total urban figures—thirty-five versus twenty-two percent? Much of this can be explained by the facts that not only are female-headed units found most frequently among the poor, but also that blacks are *so much* poorer than whites: in 1970, black families earned only $.64 for every $1.00 earned by white families, and their respective median incomes were $6,516 versus $10,236. Let's see what happens when we simultaneously look at the incomes of white and black men versus white and black women (see Table 8.2).

Table 8.2

Income by Sex and Race for Year-Round, Full-Time Workers, 1970

	Median	Percent White Male's Income
White men	$9,223	(100%)
Black men	6,368	69
White women	5,412	59
Black women	4,447	48

Source: U.S. Bureau of the Census, *Current Population Reports*, Series P-60, No. 80, "Income in 1970 of Families and Persons in the United States," 1971, Table 52, pp. 113-14. (Family incomes listed above from same source, Table 9, p. 23.)

Black women are doubly victimized. But the table makes clear that *sex is a greater penalty than race when it comes to earnings.*[30] And this table shows only the fully employed. Women have consistently higher unemployment rates than males, and, as noted, women are much more likely than men to work less than full-time. Failing that, they do have better access to welfare than men, but that *guarantees* a standard of absolute penury.

In short, the confluence of a number of trends points toward a fairly gloomy future for the growing proportion of women who are becoming heads of households. They have to combat a low and declining ratio of income relative to men, and the further perils of high rates of unemployment. So long as sex discrimination remains at such high levels, the often unchosen "freedom" of household headship comes at a very stiff price.

There is one other topic that should be mentioned under the heading of women's freedoms. This is *housework,* and the point is that women have not yet been freed of that burden. In fact, it is their gift to the maintenance of the economy, as well as their families. The time women spend on housework has *not* decreased over time, despite those "automated, labor-saving devices." Instead, the standard of cleanliness seems to have risen. This means that working women with families work two jobs, not one. In addition, thirty million American women are "unemployed" housewives. These women are doing for nothing work and services that the Chase Manhattan Bank calculated to be worth at least $257.53 a week in mid-1960s prices, for a work week of an incredible 99.6 hours![31] But being "just a housewife" is not considered "real" work. This, according to Benston, is because: "In a society in which money determines value, [these] women are a group who work outside the money economy."[32] Being outside the money economy means no Social Security and no pensions for one's own efforts. No wonder all the census data show that the largest group of people living in poverty are women over sixty-five.

(4) *What about women's power?* Electing a few female officials and Congresswomen and appointing an occasional woman to a White House post hasn't dented the *virtually all-male* representation in the halls of political power, even though the per-

30. *See also* Jessie Bernard, *The Impact of Sexism and Racism on Employment Status and Earnings, with Addendum,* MSS Modular Publications, Module 25 (New York, 1974):1-19.
31. Ann C. Scott, "The Value of Housework" *Ms.* (July 1972):56-59.
32. Margaret Benston, "The Political Economy of Women's Liberation," *Monthly Review* 21 (1969):13-27.

centage of women in such posts has risen spectacularly. But that percentage rise is misleading since it involves such a small *number* of women. If you have two apples and someone gives you two more, your apples have *doubled*—for a whopping *100 percent* increase. Now try to start a supermarket with four apples. The same thing holds true when we start to examine the figures on the "dramatic" increases among the very few females serving as board members of the top 500 corporations. Check them out: are they large shareholders or otherwise powerful individuals—or public relations tokens? Although to my knowledge, no systematic study has yet been undertaken, I'd give pretty generous odds that the new women do *not* have an independent base of power in corporate shares, or executive position in a top corporation—as is the case with the largest group of male board members. If we define economic power in terms of access to control of the means and surplus-value of production, we're left with little to talk about concerning U.S. women. All those "wealthy widows" and other females who (for tax purposes) allegedly "have most of the wealth" in this country are conspicuously sparse in the controlling positions of our concentrated corporate economy. So much for the U.S. Obviously the picture is mixed. Now, what's happening elsewhere?

WOMEN IN THE U.S.S.R.

First, the Good News

William Mandel's description of the position of women in the Soviet Union is so glowing that even though it's difficult to sort out fact from propaganda, it would seem almost picky to give equal space to a "Yes, but . . ." approach. His statistics *are* impressive:[33] by any indicator, the Soviet Union *does* lead the entire world with respect to women's participation in the labor force and—more importantly—women's

status in the labor force. It far surpasses the other Eastern European socialist countries in both respects, and the countries of the capitalist West are in a totally different league by comparison.

We learn that the Soviet Union is the only country where women are *equal in numbers* with men in *professional* employment: women are fifty-two percent of all employed college-educated persons. Numerically, they have *more women doctors* (females are almost three-fourths of the physicians there vs. 7 percent in the U.S.) and *more women engineers* (about three-tenths are female vs. 1 percent in the U.S.) *than the rest of the world put together*. And numerically, there are two-and-a-half times more women engineers than M.D.'s. The list just goes on and on. It becomes almost an afterthought to add that women are half the labor force in the Soviet Union, and that eighty-eight percent of women are either gainfully employed or students.

With respect to freedoms in personal life, both divorce and abortion are virtually free and easily available. Paid maternity leave is automatic. And we are told that "70 to 80 percent of pre-school-age children of urban workers and white-collar people" are found in childcare facilities. Retirement is at age fifty-five for women (vs. 60 for men), and all retirees receive pensions that average seventy percent of their highest salary. Utopia? Well, Mandel freely admits that men don't help much around the house, so women have a double burden—which is why a large percentage of females don't have a second child. If the husband wants the baby, and she doesn't, she has an abortion anyway, Soviet studies have found.

Even in the area of *power* Mandel paints

33. Much of the information and statistics in this section about women in the U.S.S.R. (unless otherwise specified) have been drawn from William Mandel, *Soviet Women* (Garden City, N. Y.: Anchor Books, 1975), especially pp. 107, 109, 128-30, 234, 296-99, and 321-22.

a fairly rosy picture, heavily emphasizing "you've come a long way, baby!" types of statistics. We learn how much women's Communist Party participation has *risen* (while the low rate of female membership— even today only about 22 percent—is glossed over). Similarly, he stresses the proportion of females elected as local council members (almost half vs. 3 percent in the U.S.) and to the national congress (about three-tenths in each of the Supreme Soviet's two houses, vs. highs of 3 and 1 percent for the U.S. House and Senate). That women are almost totally absent from the real centralized power—the Central Committee of the Communist Party and the ruling Politburo—is mentioned only in passing. Yet, from his figures, we can calculate that women are less than four percent of the Central Committee (an all-time high), and that only one woman has ever served in the Politburo. The implications of this definitely *unglow*ing power picture will be explored below.

Now, the Bad News

Some of it is provided by Mandel himself: Soviet women industrial workers earn only about three-fourths the pay of men, because they tend to be concentrated in less-skilled jobs and in low-paying "light" (vs. "heavy") industry. Sound familiar? But Mandel counters this by noting that a survey of Soviet working-class families found that in over half, the wife's earnings equalled or exceeded those of the husband.

A less triumphant view of the Soviet Union's achievements concerning women, paradoxically, can be gotten from social scientists writing from a more radical, conflict-oriented perspective than Sovietologist Mandel. For example, let us examine the picture drawn by Goldberg from the same sorts of statistical materials Mandel uses.[34] As background to why such a high proportion of Soviet women work, we learn that on the one hand, the U.S.S.R. long has stressed economic expansion and develop-

ment, and that on the other, World War II killed so many millions of Soviet men that at war's end, the sex ratio stood at only seventy-four males per one hundred females. All this, of course, creates economic demand for women's labor, even in "nontraditional" tasks. And in Chapter 3, we noted Goldberg's statistics that up to seventy-three percent of the heaviest, nonmechanized agrarian labor is done by women.

But to get a *good* job in the Soviet Union, you need education—more so even than in the West. And Mandel stresses the equality of women in this regard—they are currently almost half the students in higher education. Goldberg relates the enrollment figures for higher education to the country's demographic history, and comes up with quite a different story for the recent past.

Until 1957, university admission depended only on entrance exam scores, and women (partly because of the war deaths) were over half the students. But by the late 1950s, the sex ratio had returned to normal for the college-aged population. And in 1958, representatives from the overwhelmingly male ranks of Young Communist (Komsomol) and trade union leaders were added to the admissions committees, and applicants began to be chosen not only by test scores but also on the basis of recommendations from their Komsomol or trade union as well.

By 1964, women were down to only forty-three percent of the students in higher education, versus fifty-two percent in 1955. By 1964, Moscow State University was admitting only thirty-five percent women to its science faculties, even though they were forty-seven percent of the applicants.[35] As it happened, things picked up for women in the late 1960s, and their proportion in the college population began edging back up

34. Marilyn Power Goldberg, "Women in the Soviet Economy," *The Review of Radical Political Economics* 4, 3 (July 1972), pp. 60-74.

35. Goldberg, "Women in the Soviet Economy"; and N. T. Dodge, *Women in the Soviet Economy* (Baltimore: Johns Hopkins Press, 1966).

toward the fifty percent mark. Those were years of strong economic growth and expansion for the U.S.S.R. But the way women students were reduced proportionately as the demographic pyramid normalized could point to future trouble for Soviet women should the pace of economic expansion, and the demand for college-educated workers, slack off.

Goldberg also cites figures on how much more likely the relatively low proportion of males in medicine are to get to the top jobs, and notes that the *majority* of Soviet women work in the low-paid, less skilled blue-collar jobs, while female professionals tend to be concentrated in the lower ranks of their field.

What about housework, childcare, shopping (and waiting in long lines)—women's second job? It long has been a tenet of socialist equality that communal childcare, laundry, and eating facilities would be required to liberate woman from her traditional burden, and free her for productive labor—and equality. But all those things are *expensive*. And when women do them in their homes they are *free*, since then no one need be paid wages. Accordingly, even though the Soviet day-care program is the most ambitious anywhere, it too falls short, and investment to collectivize or streamline "women's work" long has been relatively low. Moreover, Goldberg notes that there has been no attempt to change men's attitudes about helping out with the children and domestic chores. On their days off, men in East European socialist countries do spend more time helping out at home than men in industrial capitalist nations, a twelve-country survey has shown, but even in the "winning" country, Bulgaria, it amounted to no more than five hours (the loser was England, with 2 hours, 45 minutes).[36] To top it off, Soviet women have fewer labor-saving appliances, and lack the convenience of a one-stop supermarket at which to buy most food and household supplies.

In recent years, investment in these areas has risen—but the birth rate has dropped so much that this well could be the underlying motivation of the economic planners: make things easy enough for urban women so that they'll have that second child. (Population growth is a top level economic consideration, whereas women's complaints about housework do not register in GNP, so long as they are reproducing, this seems to imply.)

But the root problem is women's lack of power at the top. Their representation among those who actually *control* the means of production (they are "owned" by "the people") is close to nonexistent and they are as rare in top government posts as in the U.S. And in as centralized an economy as that of the U.S.S.R., it is perhaps even more important to have representation at the very top. Otherwise, we must assume, with Goldberg, "that the goal of equality for women will continue to be subordinate to a policy of economic growth within a context of continuing male privilege."

DEVELOPMENT AND WOMEN OF THE THIRD WORLD

If any group of countries has been attempting to achieve a "policy of economic growth" it is the Third World. Has this occurred "within a context of continuing male privilege"? There appears to be no negative case. But the "good news" side of the present section stresses that development, modernization, urbanization, and other synonyms for Westernization are bringing freedom and more equal status to the downtrodden women of the Third World.[37] Are they?

If we focus on civil rights, there is no question that the answer is yes. After World

36. *Wisconsin State Journal*, "Englishmen are the Laziest Husbands," Part 6, Sec. 3 (April 12, 1974).

37. Elizabeth Johnstone, "Women in Economic Life: Rights and Opportunities," *The Annals of the American Academy of Political and Social Science* 375 (1968):26-33 is one exponent of this upbeat view.

War II, women gained the vote in country after country of the Third World. Today, there are only a handful of holdouts on the globe. As of mid-1975, women were denied the vote only in Liechtenstein, seven Arab countries (Bahrain, Kuwait, Oman, Qatar, Saudi Arabia, the United Arab Emirates, and Yemen), and six states within Nigeria.[38] But these new political rights for the remainder of the Third World's women came to them by government decree in most cases, rather than as the result of a women's movement.

To put the remainder of women's situation in perspective, we have to see where they were before "development"—and where it is taking them.

A number of (female) social scientists agree that in those countries where women were active in subsistence farming and/or as own-account traders, there has been a general *deterioration* of their economic position and economic autonomy.[39] Sometimes their situation has eroded to the point of desperation; in other areas, they have "merely" slipped into being dependents of their husbands, stripped of their traditional economic independence. Prior to Boserup's book, development planners seemed unaware of all this. But now, the international development agencies have begun to look into the problem.[40] The two regions where this situation has been most studied and documented are the "female farming—female marketing" countries of West Africa, plus those areas of Southeast Asia where women also are active in trade and work in irrigated rice agriculture.

A typical scenario, especially in horticultural West Africa, might go like this: Women had grown most of the food by traditional methods, and often were active in trading the little surplus they produced. Gradually, cash crops were introduced, as well as more modern methods of cultivation. The outsiders (usually Europeans) who introduced the new crops and/or taught the rural people about the new methods were not ac-

customed to a situation where women were the farmers. So they concentrated their efforts on the *men*. Sometimes it worked, and the men picked up on the innovations (usually involving *export crops*, not food crops grown for local consumption). In such cases, the men often encroached on the land the women had used for traditional food crops. This caused other problems for their governments: recently, a number of countries who whose people were mostly rural *farmers* were forced to the "development" irony of having to spend scarce foreign exchange to *import food* to feed their growing urban populations. At other times, the innovations did not catch on among the men, especially where they had never devoted much effort to farming. For example: "It was reported that as recently as 1974 the government of Liberia brought in Taiwanese experts to improve rice growing in that country, and paid local men three days wages to learn the improved techniques. Of course, it is the women who farm. Extension services in Ethiopia typically consisted of men, so men who never farmed taught farming to men who were not farmers."[41] In those cases, too, produc-

38. Stanley Meisler, "Status Reported Low around World: 9 Countries Still Deny Women the Vote," *Los Angeles Times* Part I (June 26, 1975):1.

39. *See*, for example, Ester Boserup, *The Role of Women in Economic Development* (New York: St. Martin's, 1970); Marianne Schmink, "Development and the Economics of Sex Roles," University of Texas, 1974; Irene Tinker, "The Adverse Impact of Development on Women," in *Women and World Development*, eds. Irene Tinker and Michele Bo Bramsen, prepared under the auspices of the American Association for the Advancement of Science (Washington, D. C.: Overseas Development Council, 1976), pp. 22-34; Judith Van Allen, "African Women—Modernizing into Dependence," in *Women in the World: A Comparative Study*, eds. Lynne Iglitzin and Ruth Ross (Santa Barbara: ABC Clio, 1976), pp. 25-54.

40. *See*, for example, United Nations, *Participation of Women in Community Development* (New York: U.N. Publication no. E/CN. 6/5/4/ Rev. 1, 1972.)

41. Tinker, "The Adverse Impact of Development on Women," p. 5.

tivity remained lower than what it might have been had the women been brought into development.

It was economic development-related facts like these that ultimately brought the international development "Establishment" to pay some attention to the problems of women's participation in integrated rural development. But meanwhile, the women often had suffered at least as much as their country's targeted development objectives.[42] Their output, and their tiny income from the sale of surplus, remained stagnant or even declined—while prices for what they had to buy invariably rose. Moreover, migration of males out of the rural areas often left women with an even heavier work load.

Where women had been active in market trading on more than just a sporadic basis, development had other effects on their lives. The women's traditional trading generally involved local markets, small volume, and low profit margins. As mass-produced goods (mostly imported) began to enter the economy, other distribution networks—dominated by local and foreign males—typically arose, often undercutting the women's fragile market position. There are exceptions: in Ghana a small group of women have managed to sell the new merchandise—and prosper.[43] Mass-produced goods also frequently signaled the end of traditional handicrafts as a source of income for rural women—a hand-decorated gourd doesn't compete with an inexpensive plastic bowl from Taiwan.[44]

The areas where women's position in farming and trade has been adversely affected by development are those where it traditionally had brought them considerable economic autonomy and sometimes power. In terms of subsistence base, these areas usually are based on hoe horticulture or irrigated paddy rice agriculture.

What about the women in the dry agrarian regions, where we previously have located the general nadir of female status? Here, the picture is very mixed. Where

women had little or no political or property rights, their lot has been eased by gradual reforms, although they remain at great political, legal, and economic disadvantage. Such a situation generally prevails in the predominantly Moslem countries of the Middle East, North Africa, and Southwest Asia. In these countries, women's economic participation was relatively low in the traditional rural milieu, and it has remained low in the modernizing urban milieu. Nevertheless, a few women of middle- or upper-income origin have experienced relatively great opportunities for professional advancement. Education *is* spreading among girls in these lands (even though most of the illiterates remain female, and girls' enrollment is usually a tiny fraction of boys'). And so is the Western-type health and social services system. Given traditional sex segregation, those who deal with females in the schools, the clinics, etc., must themselves be female.

In the agrarian-based Latin American countries, a rather different situation prevails. The traditional economy and culture were different, and women were never as secluded and oppressed there. Nevertheless, rural and urban women had low rates of economic participation, and were subject to considerable legal, political, and economic inequality. One very unique thing about Latin America is the sex composition of the migrants streaming out of the rural areas— most are women.[45] They leave because there is no economic opportunity for them, and

42. *See* Boserup, *The Role of Women in Economic Development*, for details.
43. Esther Ocloo, "The Ghanaian Market Woman" (paper presented at the 14th World Conference of the Society for International Development, Abidjan, Ivory Coast, 1974).
44. Once again, Boserup, *The Role of Women in Economic Development*, is an excellent source for details.
45. *See*, e.g., Julia J. Henderson, "Impact of the World Social Situation on Women," *The Annals of the American Academy of Political and Social Science* 375 (1968):26-33; and Tinker, "The Adverse Impact of Development on Women."

go to the cities where there is still a big market for female domestic servants,[46] and, to some extent, other service workers. In general then, the economic participation of Latin American women is higher in the urban areas than the villages.[47] But the rates are lower than in more industrial countries, in part because there is so much more problem with unemployment. Male unemployment often spells female nonemployment.

Venezuela provides a unique case, because its oil boom has involved a relatively small proportion of the labor force in a prosperous, capitalist-oriented, rapidly growing modern economy, while un- and underemployment still cause grave problems for the remainder of the population (who are not needed as workers in the highly capitalized modern sector). Overall, women are only about twenty percent of the labor force.[48] But they are a very atypically distributed twenty percent: Venezuela has extremely high proportions of women in professional and career public administration jobs, and—for a developing nonsocialist country—perhaps uniquely high proportions of women among the university students studying for such occupations.[49]

It seems that the early years of the oil boom corresponded to the regime of the dictator Pérez-Jiménez (1948-1958). His immigration policies brought close to a million people—mostly Southern Europeans—to the small country.[50] When he was overthrown, the immigration and employment laws were changed to stop the flood of foreigners and require the oil companies and other modern sector enterprises to hire greater numbers of native Venezuelans. Venezuelan men, especially well-educated ones, were the immediate beneficiaries. But the oil boom continued (except for 1958-61), while the government share of oil revenues grew. The need for educated professionals and bureaucrats of many kinds became more pressing. Only one untapped group of educated people remained legally available for the new slots: Venezuelan women. They were pulled in. So at the upper levels of Venezuela's labor force, 18.8 percent of women versus only 6.3 percent of men held professional or technical jobs in 1970.[51] (In the U.S. for that year, the corresponding figures were roughly 14 percent for each sex.) And educationally, Venezuelan women began graduating in high proportions (though small numbers) in fields where U.S. women receive a minute fraction of the diplomas. Figures from most of the nation's universities in 1969 showed that over 4/5 of the pharmacists, 2/3 of the dentists, 1/2 of the architects, and 4/10 of the economists receiving degrees were women. Law and business administration/accounting degree recipients were about 36 percent female.[52] To contrast this with the U.S., let us note two examples: in 1964-65 women received only 0.8 percent of the dentistry degrees and 3.4 percent of the law degrees.[53] Of course, the Venezuelan women who have benefitted have been a small group, drawn largely from the middle and upper strata—and it remains to be seen if their extraordinary career pat-

46. Margo L. Smith, "Domestic Service as a Channel of Upward Mobility for the Lower Class Woman: The Lima Case," in *Female and Male in Latin America: Essays*, ed. Ann Pescatello (Pittsburgh: Univ. of Pittsburgh Press, 1973), pp. 191-207.

47. Boserup, *The Role of Women in Economic Development*, p. 186.

48. *Encuesta del Hogar* (Caracas, Venezuela: Ministerio de Fomento, April, 1970).

49. Rae Lesser Blumberg, "Women and Work around the World: A Cross-Cultural Examination of Sex Division of Labor and Sex Status," in *Beyond Sex Roles*, ed. Alice Sargent (St. Paul: West Publishing, 1976), pp. 412-433.

50. Mary Monica Kritz, "Immigration and Social Structure: The Venezuelan Case" (University of Wisconsin, Ph.D. Dissertation, 1973).

51. *Encuesta del Hogar.*

52. Rebeca Urbaneja de Itriago and Barbara L. Millar, *La Participación de La Mujer en el Desarrollo* (Caracas, Venezuela: Promoción Popular, 1971), pp. 42-43.

53. Epstein, *Woman's Place*, p. 60.

tern survives the depletion of oil reserves predicted for within a couple of decades.

In short, women have done best in developing countries where there has been a demand for labor that they could best fill. Most Third World countries are plagued by enormous surplus labor problems, and women usually *lose* ground to men under conditions of high unemployment. Finally, women also have declined in income and productivity relative to men in precisely those Third World countries where they were most economically active in the traditional village economy.

THE ISRAELI KIBBUTZ: RETREAT FROM SEXUAL EQUALITY

One final case will be presented in this chapter: what happened to women in the Israeli kibbutzim (plural of kibbutz). One of the goals upon which the kibbutz movement of collective agricultural settlements was founded was that of sexual equality, and it has been in this area that the kibbutz most visibly has fallen short of its founding principles. In most respects, the kibbutzim have been amazing success stories. The first ideologically full-blown kibbutz was founded in 1921, and a half-century later 233 of these collective settlements, with about 100,000 people, flourished economically while living up to most tenets of their socialist ideals.[54]

What happened to the women? The pioneer kibbutz women began as equals, toiling side by side in the fields with the men, but within a single generation ended up working in the nurseries, kitchens, laundries, and sewing rooms from which they ostensibly had been liberated. Accordingly, this retreat from sexual equality usually has been interpreted to mean: "there is something biological and/or psychological in women that pulls them back to their traditional domestic role." In other words, Woman's Fate boils down to Laundry is Destiny.

But what happened to the kibbutz women

also can be interpreted in terms of the paradigm presented in Chapter 3.[55] First, however, we have to know who were the kibbutz founders, and what were their guiding principles.

Who were the founders? Eastern European Jews who were dedicated and idealistic socialists. They were mostly men: only twenty to thirty-five percent of the pioneering era kibbutz population was female—and the proportion of women who were actual guiding lights of the fledgling movement seems to have been even lower.[56] (Incidentally, women were even less represented among the leadership of the U.S.S.R. Bolsheviks, who were then building their own, much less democratic, socialist revolutionary society.) Both women and men tended to be young, revolutionary—and childless. Even so, and with every hand working to put the land into shape for agriculture, they barely survived the hardships that were typical in the early years of the pioneer kibbutz.

54. *See* Dov Weintraub, M. Lissak, and Y. Azmon, *Moshava, Kibbutz, and Moshav* (Ithaca, N.Y.: Cornell University Press, 1969), pp. 68-121 for details of the emergence of the fully collectivized kibbutzim after 1921; and *Statistical Data on the Kibbutz Population as of Sept. 30, 1970* (Tel Aviv: Central Control Commission of Agricultural Workers' Cooperative [Hebrew] 1970), gives a full demographic picture of contemporary kibbutzim.

55. The complete paradigm is found in Rae Lesser Blumberg, "Structural Factors Affecting Women's Status: A Cross-Societal Paradigm" (paper read at the meetings of the International Sociological Association, Toronto, 1974); fuller versions of my kibbutz argument are found in Blumberg, "From Liberation to Laundry: A Structural Interpretation of the Retreat from Sexual Equality in the Israeli Kibbutz" (paper read at the meetings of the American Political Science Association, Chicago, 1974); and Blumberg, "Kibbutz Women: From the Fields of Revolution to the Laundries of Discontent," in *Women in the World: A Comparative Study*, eds. Lynne Iglitzin and Ruth Ross (Santa Barbara: ABC Clio, 1976), pp. 319-344.

56. Yonina Talmon, *Family and Community in Kibbutz* (Cambridge, Mass.: Harvard University Press, 1972), p. 19.

What were the founding principles? Foremost, the founders *chose* their mode of production: *agrarian socialism.* In other words, their techno-economic base was to be agrarian, and their relations of production, socialist.

Historically, an *agrarian* base has been least favorable for females, and where fields are spread out (as they are in the kibbutz), daily participation in agrarian fieldwork once women have children is most problematic.

Kibbutz *socialism* proved not to be a fully consistent system in its implications for female equality, as we shall see. Some of the basic ideas and practices of the socialist kibbutzim included:

(1) They were to be a revolutionary vanguard, committed to growth and the building of socialism, not romantic retreatists playing peasants.

(2) They were to be dedicated to the principle of self-labor (i.e., avoid the hiring of wage-labor).

(3) They were to absorb *immigrants,* both for growth and self-labor; and to promote economic productivity and equality for *women,* both for self-labor and as a basic element of socialist doctrine.

(4) In order to free women for social production, their usual domestic and childcare tasks were to be *collectivized:* children would be raised in unique communal children's houses, and all meals, washing, mending, etc., would be done communally as well. Unfortunately, there was no insistence that these collectivized services were to be more or less equally performed by both sexes. And at the start, life was so hard, there really was little if any "service sector"—cooking tended to be the common pot, and laundry tended to be catch as catch can.[57]

(5) Services were not to be considered productive labor for ideological reasons; and from the start, they actually were disesteemed and thought to be low prestige work.

(6) They were to be committed to the labor theory of value: that of the three factors of production—land, capital, and labor—only labor added to the value of a product. This was actually put into practice with a bookkeeping system based on "income per labor day" that *ignored* the costs of land and capital, and considered only how much labor was involved in each production activity.[58] By this yardstick, that which was least labor-intensive looked best in the books.

(7) Within the constraints of their ideology, they were to be economically rational and committed to maximizing production—and return.

One additional ideological tenet should be mentioned, though it stems not from socialism, but rather from the Freudian-tinged European intellectual culture from which they emerged: breastfeeding and frequent contact between parents (especially mother) and child were to be encouraged even though the children were to be raised in the children's houses. In practice, this meant women had to hike in from their work at least once a day—a long, hot trip if their work was in the distant fields (see [*b*] on page 114).

When we add four more points of information, we shall be ready to examine the erosion of sexual equality in the kibbutz in terms of the paradigm: (a) *agrarian* field crops and large animal husbandry are *less labor-intensive* than the gardening and small animal activities of *horticultural* production, that is, agrarian production looks better in

---

57. Even so, there are pioneer-era memoirs and archival data indicating that women got stuck with a disproportionate share of even this tiny service burden. This point is best documented in Lionel Tiger and Joseph Shepher, *Women in the Kibbutz* (New York: Harcourt Brace Jovanovich, 1975). Paradoxically, the authors espouse "biology is destiny" views while presenting source material that seems to offer firmer support to my own, diametrically opposed, explanation of why kibbutz women fared as they did.

58. Haim Barkai, "The Kibbutz: An Experiment in Microsocialism," Research Report No. 34 (Jerusalem: Hebrew University of Jerusalem, 1971), p. 18.

the kibbutz's ledgers; (b) an aerial view of a typical kibbutz shows the agrarian field-crops out at the farthest perimeter; vegetable and fruit (horticultural) crops, chickens, etc., fairly close in, and the nurseries, dining hall, and other service facilities located at the center; (c) as early as 1936 (which was *after* children began to arrive), the women expressed fears of being squeezed out of production, and urged greater concentration on horticultural activities, in which they felt themselves to be at no sexual disadvantage;[59] and (d) all during the pioneering 1920s and Depression 1930s, *immigrants* kept arriving to swell the kibbutz population (despite Depression hardship and what Barkai terms "disguised unemployment"[60]); like the first pioneers, the immigrants were *young, childless, and predominantly male.*

It could be speculated that if there had been no immigrants, the kibbutz might have heeded the women's pleas to de-emphasize the importance of the "glamor sector," the agrarian field crops, in favor of a more balanced mix giving greater weight to the women's preferred horticultural activities. After all, without immigrants—and with hired labor ideologically repugnant—the wishes of so large a fraction of the only available labor force might not have been easily ignored. But there *were* immigrants—and they had no reason to find fieldwork inconvenient, since *they* were not trudging in every day to nurse or check up on a small child. Given the availability of a willing, unencumbered labor force for the kibbutz's "glamor sector" field crops, there was no reason to emphasize the more labor-intensive, apparently less profitable, horticultural activities.[61]

So gradually, in a slow process of attrition, pioneer women were *replaced* in the fields—and as they left, their places were filled by *men.*[62] Where did they go? Well, the arrival of children meant more of an investment in nutrition, laundry, mending, cleaning—not just in childcare. And since it would be con-

sidered a shame and inefficient to "waste" an able-bodied man in these activities (for by this time the kibbutzim had passed from their first phase of revolutionary fervor into one in which economic efficiency and development were stressed), the tasks inevitably fell to the women.[63] Dorit Padan-Eisenstark (in personal communication with me) stressed that, to many women, this was a choice between the frying pan and the fire: doing inconvenient and disliked agrarian fieldwork, or doing convenient but disesteemed as well as disliked "domestic drudgery" services. Since about half the service jobs involved the relatively higher prestige "childhood education" sector of nurseries, childcare and elementary education, many of the younger mothers chose such posts when they were available. The remaining women grumbled, and came to view themselves—and be viewed—as occupationally inferior.[64] By the 1950s, less than ten percent of the women in a typical kibbutz were in agricultural production of *any*

59. Harry Viteles, *Book Two: The Evolution of the Kibbutz Movement* of *A History of the Cooperative Movement in Israel: A Source Book in Seven Volumes* (London: Vallentine-Mitchell, 1967), pp. 323-4, gives the proceedings of the 1936 conference airing these views.

60. Barkai, "The Kibbutz," p. 23.

61. I do not yet have exact data on the relative profitability of kibbutz agrarian vs. horticultural crops on the external market, although Barkai (in personal communications with the author) doubts a consistent advantage to the former. This would suppose that both were grown on the same scale, with the same degree of modern, mechanized techniques—which may not have been the case, since it was the field crops that seem to have been given most of the early investment priorities.

62. Melford Spiro, *Kibbutz: Venture in Utopia* (New York: Schocken Books, 1963), p. 225.

63. Spiro, *Kibbutz: Venture in Utopia*, p. 225; and Talmon, *Family and Community in Kibbutz*, p. 19.

64. Menachem Rosner, "Women in the Kibbutz: Changing Status and Concepts," *Asian and African Studies* 3 (1967):35-68.

sort.[65] The remaining ninety percent were in domestic and childcare services—which had become so labor-intensive that they sopped up more than half the labor force (women had finally become half the population by then). Concomitantly, women participated less than men in the town hall democracy of the weekly members's meeting and rotating kibbutz offices. Much more important, as they left production, they lost whatever voice they might have had on the *economic committees.*

These committees may be considered the main locus of power in the kibbutz, since these are the committees that *control* the means of production that everyone owns—and make the crucial decisions on how surplus is to be reinvested. Many basic decisions are made here, and come to the members' meeting only for debate and ratification. As women's representation on these committees dropped down to negligible levels (today, they are equally or over-represented only on the committees dealing with domestic and childcare services),[66] so did their voice in controlling the allocation of the kibbutz factors of production—including their *own* labor. This, of course, is just what socialist theory predicts.

But—comes the revolution. The industrial revolution, that is. It hit the kibbutzim full blast in the early 1960s, and proved more profitable than even agrarian field crops. Industrial production, however, requires a larger work group than the average agricultural production branch. Immigration to Israel continued, but the post-State immigrants did not want to come to the kibbutzim.[67] Hiring labor was still viewed with intense disfavor, although it was resorted to more to staff industrial production than in any other area. Still, even under the impetus of manufacturing, by the late 1960s hired labor had risen to only 8.5-9.2 percent of total kibbutz employment, versus 8 percent in 1954—and only a small minority of kibbutzim have been responsible for this increase.[68] Squeezing additional labor out of

the kibbutz's highly mechanized agriculture would have been impossible. That left only one source of ideologically acceptable extra hands: the unmechanized, labor-intensive services—by this time equated with "women's work." Investment at last came to the service sector—after a generation of complaints by the women. The laundries were made automatic, and partial self-service was adopted in the dining halls. Labor was freed. (And the first males in living memory entered the laundries—as technicians for those new machines.)[69]

So even though less than ten percent of the agricultural labor force remains female, women already are thirty percent of the total manufacturing work force.[70] And given manufacturing labor demand, that percentage may well increase. Does this mean a new shuffle of the deck for the women of the kibbutz? It's too soon to tell, since manufacturing *could* develop the much-feared split between specialist managers and "mere" workers currently being debated by kibbutzniks. In that case, guess which sex would be relegated disproportionately to the ranks of "mere" workers?

But the two biggest strikes against kib-

---

65. Spiro, *Kibbutz: Venture in Utopia,* pp. 221, 225; Viteles, *Book Two: The Evolution of the Kibbutz Movement,* pp. 333, 336.

66. I. A. Rabin, "The Sexes: Ideology and Reality in the Israeli Kibbutz," in *Sex Roles in Changing Society,* eds. G. H. Seward & R. C. Williamson (New York: Random House, 1970).

67. Sol Stern, "The Kibbutz: Not by Ideology Alone," *New York Times Magazine* (May 6, 1973).

68. All material in this paragraph not otherwise footnoted is from Barkai, "The Kibbutz: An Experiment in Microsocialism," pp. 20, 25, 43; and Uri Leviatan, "The Industrial Process in the Israeli Kibbutzim: Problems and Their Solutions" (paper presented at the International Conference on Trends in Industrial and Labor Relations, Tel Aviv, 1972), p. 7. Both treat kibbutz industrialization.

69. E. Leshem, interview with author, Jerusalem (June, 1972).

70. Leviatan, "The Industrial Process in the Israeli Kibbutzim," p. 3.

butz women, in terms of my paradigm, were (1) the agrarian techno-economic base (in conjunction with the custom of breastfeeding and checking up on small children during the day), and (2) the demographic situation (i.e., the flow of immigrants) that eliminated the demand for women in agricultural production. And both of these are changing: first, the kibbutzim are becoming industrial, and second, immigration is down to a trickle. (In addition, two high-casualty wars since 1967 in which the kibbutzim suffered the highest relative manpower losses[71] have created a deficit of young males in their demographic pyramid and presumably increased the need for female labor.) This bodes well for women, as does the existence today of a worldwide women's movement. This was absent in the years when women's equality was eroding away—and socialists still preached that separate women's caucuses were diversionary since socialism would solve the problem of sexual inequality along with that of class inequality. However, it didn't work out that way, and today such caucuses have undergone a resurgence and are found even among socialist groups in the West. There is an emergent women's movement in Israel as well,[72] which could foreshadow dramatic changes in the fate of the women of the kibbutz. Time will tell.

SUMMARY

To conclude in terms of the paradigm, the case of the Israeli kibbutz makes it appear that in order to come within shooting distance of equality: (1) Women must be substantially engaged in productive labor. (2) They must be strategically indispensable: there must be demand and low substitutability for their labor, and this seems greatly enhanced by organizing on their own behalf. (3) A favorable ideology of sexual equality is an advantage, but not indispensable. (4) Taking the brunt of domestic chores and childcare out of the home is im-

portant, but so is the requirement that the new labor force to which these activities be transferred not be overwhelmingly female. (5) Since new social planning at the highest levels would be required to implement the above—especially (4)—it seems very important that women not be substantially underrepresented among the top-level controllers of the political economy. It has been precisely here that women have remained frozen out in all the "socialist" nations to date. And their low political clout in such centralized societies seems to be the reason for their relatively low degree of power to reallocate the domestic chores burden—for their labor is important and their status fully equal under the law. (6) Our final point is more problematic so let us phrase it as a question: Do women need to control their *own* piece of the action—that is, are they unlikely to make it under a system where ownership of the main resources is collective? Here, the evidence is not fully in—although in my sixty-one-society sample, the societies where women enjoyed the *highest* freedom in life options were those in which women controlled their own (large) chunk of the group's assets, rather than in those where everything was ostensibly "community" controlled. Because of male predominance in the political sources of power, women may be at a disadvantage in such situations. Empirically, the only one of the main sources of power (political, force, economic) in which women are known to have ever achieved an equal *or better* position is the economic sector: control over means of production and allocation of surplus. But that may not necessarily be a "rule of nature" for *future* societies.

71. Stern, "The Kibbutz: Not by Ideology Alone."
72. Rivka Bar-Joseph and Dorit Padan-Eisenstark, "Role System Under Stress: Sex Roles in War" (paper read at the meetings of the International Sociological Association, Toronto, 1974).

In sum, for both socioeconomic and sexual equality, things have been more equal under different circumstances in the past—and could conceivably become more egalitarian in the future. There seems to be no *inherent* reason for reifying the social system and the era in which we live and proclaiming that these arrangements are unalterable laws that will govern human societies for all times.

For Further Reading

Benston, Margaret. "The Political Economy of Women's Liberation." *Monthly Review* 21 (1969):13-27.

A good Marxian analysis of the problem of women's housework as nonproductive labor.

Boserup, Ester. *The Role of Women in Economic Development.* New York: St. Martins, 1970.

The most comprehensive treatment of how development often undercuts rather than enhances women's labor and economic autonomy. Boserup is a famed Danish economist.

Goldberg, Marilyn Power. "Women in the Soviet Economy." *The Review of Radical Political Economics* 4:3 (July 1972).

A hard-headed examination by a U.S. radical of women's position in the U.S.S.R. economy.

Oppenheimer, Valerie Kincaid. "Demographic Influence on Female Employment and the Status of Women." *American Journal of Sociology* 78 (1973):946-961.

Her excellent article appeared in a fine special issue on women of the *American Journal of Sociology* (edited by Joan Huber) that is also available in paperback.

Tobias, Sheila, and Anderson, Lisa. "What Really Happened to Rosie the Riveter: Demobilization and the Female Labor Force 1944-47." *MSS Module* 9, 1974.

Rosie the Riveter didn't want to quit, so she was "let go."

Appendix

WHAT is *mode of production?* As a concept, it encompasses what may be considered a society's most basic institutions—the way its technology, economic organization, and stratification systems are organized. In most definitions, it is conceptualized as consisting of two major components: the social relations of production, and the forces of production.[1]

First, the *social relations of production* refer to *who* (e.g., the whole group communally, a small hereditary aristocracy, etc.) *controls* the means of production, and who allocates any surplus the group may produce. Basically, the means of production boil down to three major factors that are utilized in some combination to produce anything and everything humans have wrought to date—from food to fuel-injection engines and fashion magazines. These three factors, or means of production, are land, capital, and labor. The "land" factor includes natural resources, and the "capital" factor includes all the know-how and hardware (i.e., the technology, equipment, buildings —which Marxians often call "dead labor" since it was produced by human mental and physical labor to begin with). The "labor" factor is the human element: both physical and mental contributions to production. With the means of production at their disposal—their level of technology, numbers and abilities of their population, endowment of natural resources—humans take care of their basic needs, and in many groups produce something extra as well. This something extra, which is over and above what is needed to sustain the basic standard of living, is referred to as "surplus."

Second, the *forces of production* is one overarching name for the other main component of the mode of production, which tells us what gets produced and with what configuration of the means of production. The leading element of the forces of production I refer to as the *"techno-economic base."* The techno-economic base involves the nature and level of the technology used by the group to produce their subsistence (i.e., ultimately, how they manage to feed themselves). This techno-economic base has implications for many things, including the *division of labor* and the *organization of work,* two other aspects that may be conceived of as part of the forces of production. One aspect of the division of labor that concerns us in this book is the *sexual* division of tasks in a society's main productive activities. Do women confine themselves to childbearing, childrearing, and housetending, or are they *producers* who help "bring home the bacon" for their families?

1. *See* Richard C. Edwards, Michael Reich, and Thomas E. Weisskopf, eds., *The Capitalist System* (Englewood Cliffs, N. J.: Prentice-Hall, 1972), p. 50, for a concise discussion.

The answer has important consequences for many dimensions of women's lives, including prospects for equality (see Chapter 3).

The techno-economic base is often referred to as the "mode of subsistence" in preindustrial societies—the ones examined in Chapters 1-4 of this book. This mode of subsistence, or basic food-getting technique, is very important in a number of evolutionary theories of societal development, which see societal complexity growing in direct proportion to the development of the society's productive base. In this book, we ride up an "evolutionary elevator" of preindustrial techno-economic bases that include, in ascending order, hunting-gathering, shifting hoe cultivation (horticulture), permanent field plow agriculture (usually combined with animal husbandry), and intensive irrigated agriculture. (For evolutionary treatments of societal development anchored to somewhat more elaborate typologies of techno-economic bases, see Goldschmidt; Lenski; and Lomax et al.)[2]

In general, there is a tendency for certain types of social relations of production to be found with certain types of techno-economic bases. Thus, the overwhelming majority of hunting-gathering societies have egalitarian, communal relations of production, while a great many plow agriculture societies have feudal, highly stratified relations of production. But this tendency is not invariant. About two percent of hunting-gathering groups have become class societies, where a small hereditary stratum of nobles have productive, power, and privilege advantages over the common people. And among agrarian societies, a minority have managed to maintain—or deliberately adopt, as in the case of the Israeli kibbutz —an egalitarian, communal system of control over the means and surplus-value of production.

Despite these exceptions, there is a general tendency to consider the techno-economic base as of greater evolutionary importance. Specifically, both Marxian and non-Marxian evolutionary theories in which the mode of production or mode of subsistence is central view the forces of production—especially their technological component—as more important for social change than the social relations of production.

But there is an important difference. The social relations of production are seen in Marxian theories as coming into *conflict* with further advances in the forces of production, thus generating major social change. In contrast, in many non-Marxian evolutionary theories, the social relations are viewed merely as *lagging behind* the advances in the techno-economic sphere. In short, though both types of materialist evolutionary theories stress the ultimate importance of advances in the forces of production, their theories of the dynamics of social change are very different.[3]

Moreover, the Marxian evolutionary approaches tend to place much more weight on the importance of the social relations of production in shaping other institutional areas of society, such as the political, legal, religious, and ideological systems. So ironically, in the final analysis, it is the non-Marxian evolutionary theories based on mode of subsistence that tend to steer closer to the straight techno-economic determinism of which Marx is so often accused.

2. Walter Goldschmidt, *Man's Way: A Preface to the Understanding of Human Society* (New York: Holt, 1959); Gerhard Lenski, *Human Societies* (New York: McGraw-Hill, 1970); and Alan Lomax, et al., *Folk Song Style and Culture* (Washington, D. C.: American Association for the Advancement of Science, 1968).

3. References to the components of mode of production are scattered through the book; Marx's conceptualization is discussed in chapter 6.

Glossary

Agrarian Societies—Societies whose techno-economic base involves plow cultivation on permanent fields. Some of the world's most rigidly stratified societies have been agrarian.

Bourgeoisie—A term used by Karl Marx to refer to the class which, under the capitalist mode of production, controls capital by the ownership of property or the means of production of a society.

Capitalism—An economic system in which the greater proportion of economic life, particularly the ownership and investment in production goods, is privately controlled and carried on through the process of economic competition and with the incentive of profit. See also *Laissez-Faire Capitalism*.

Conflict Theory—An approach to social science based on the view that real interests between classes and groups are frequently in conflict. There are both Marxian and non-Marxian conflict theorists; the latter are usually influenced by Weber.

Consensus Model—A synonym for the "functionalist" approach within sociology which implies the harmonious integration of society. See *Functionalism*.

Division of Labor—A scheme for subdividing the basic tasks or activities of a society into components with the allocation of these to individuals or groups. In the sexual division of labor, this allocation is based on sex. See Appendix.

Ethnographic Atlas (EA)—Murdock's impressive collection of data encompassing dozens of variables for each of some twelve hundred pre-industrial societies. Empirical results based on the EA are cited throughout the book.

Forces of Production—The technology, equipment, and know-how involved in a society's production. In this book, it is subdivided into two main components: techno-economic base and the nature and division of labor. See Appendix.

Functionalism—A theoretical approach in sociology which emphasizes social systems as stable, well-integrated structures, all of whose elements contribute to the maintenance of that system. See also *Consensus Model*.

Horticultural Societies—Societies with a techno-economic base involving hoe (or digging stick) cultivation on plots that are rarely used for more than a few years at a time.

Hunting and Gathering Societies—The techno-economic base of the simplest human bands, involving gathering plants and hunting game and fish. Most hunting and gathering societies are quite egalitarian.

Industrial Societies—Societies in which industry has supplanted agriculture as the main techno-economic base, and production is dominated by nonanimate sources of energy. Both capitalist and socialist social relations of production are found among today's industrial societies.

Laissez-Faire Capitalism—An economic philosophy emphasizing the nonintervention by the state in the market or in the economic activity of individuals or groups.

Life Options—Used in this book to refer to an individual's degree of control over basic life situations occurring in all human groups, for example, relative freedom to: initiate marriage or divorce; control one's sexuality and fertility pre-, extra-, and maritally; enjoy freedom of movement; seize educational opportunity; and exercise household authority.

Matrilineality—The reckoning of descent exclusively through females.

Matrilocality—Postmarital residence in which the married couple live near or with the wife's female kin.

Means of Production—Also called "factors of production." Generally, these are subsumable under the categories of labor, capital, and land (including resources). In Marxian usage all the other factors rest on human labor. See Appendix.

Mode of Production—How a society's production is realized and organized. The two broad principal components of mode of production are thus forces of production and social relations of production. See Appendix.

Polygyny—A cultural pattern prescribing the marriage of one man simultaneously with two or more women.

Power—According to Weber, "the probability of persons or groups carrying out their will even when opposed by others."

Proletariat—A term used by Karl Marx to refer to the class, under the capitalist mode of production, whose livelihood stems from the sale of its labor and not from the profit derived from some capital.

Primates—A biological categorization of mammals; the primate family tree includes monkeys, apes, and humans in ascending evolutionary order.

Sexual Dimorphism—Differences in the size, musculature, strength, etc., of the male and female of a species.

Social Class—A social group distinguished by its differential relationship to the means and fruits of production, i.e., by its differential access to strategic resources and its differential power per capita.

Social Mobility—The movement or change in rank of individuals or groups within a stratification system. Movement may be vertical (downward or upward) or horizontal.

Social Relations of Production—Who controls the means of production, and who controls the flow of benefits from production. See Appendix.

Social Stratification—The process whereby groups or individuals in a society are located in a hierarchical arrangement on the basis of their differential access to both the means and fruits of production.

Socialism—A system in which the major means of production are communally rather than privately owned.

Status—In Weber's terms, it represents social honor; it may also be considered a symbolic expression of the class structure, one's overall rank in it, or one's position relative to a specific criterion such as income, education or prestige.

Surplus—Production over and above what is needed to keep the producers alive and productive.

Techno-Economic Base—Refers to the economic activities engaged in by people to feed themselves, and to the level and efficiency of the tools and techniques they bring to these economic pursuits. See Appendix.

Index